THE NEW CATHOLICS

THE NEW CATHOLICS

Contemporary Converts
Tell Their Stories

Edited by DAN O'NEILL

With a Foreword by Walker Percy

CROSSROAD • NEW YORK

1987

The Crossroad Publishing Company
370 Lexington Avenue, New York, N.Y. 10017

Printed in the United States of America

Library of Congress Cataloging in Publication Data

The New Catholics.

1. Converts, Catholic — United States — Biography.
I. O'Neill, Daniel W.
BX4668.A1N48 1987   248.2′4   87-12445
ISBN 0-8245-0842-4

To true seekers everywhere

Contents

Acknowledgments

The editor wishes to express deep gratitude to Bernard Cardinal Law, Dale Vree, and Sheldon Vanauken for their inspiration, guidance, and support in preparing this manuscript for publication.

The following persons also deserve special recognition for their encouragement and assistance: Michael Leach, Mary Lucia McKnight, Melba Jean O'Neill, Cherry Boone O'Neill, and Ed Durst.

Introduction

The November 7, 1986, issue of *Christianity Today*, the flagship magazine of America's evangelical Protestants, carried a bold feature headline on its cover: "AMERICA'S CATHOLICS: WHO THEY ARE; WHAT THEY BELIEVE; WHERE THEY ARE GOING; WHY SOME STAY; WHY OTHERS LEAVE." As a Catholic convert from evangelical Protestant ranks, I found this focus on American Catholicism as interesting for what was not said as for what was. There might have been a final subtitle: "WHY NON-CATHOLICS JOIN." It would have been a newsworthy complement to the other articles, for there is indeed a new breeze blowing into the Catholic Church—a new breed of convert entering its ancient Church doors.

Who are they? They are converts to the "Roman Obedience" who have become "Churched," as Sheldon Vanauken is fond of saying. In their search for authentic Christian roots they have found the apostolic Church of two millennia to be the faith community founded by Christ—the same Church that gifted us with, among other treasures, the Scriptures.

Even as renewed pockets of anti-Catholicism have reportedly emerged around the country, a movement is afoot that finds the likes of Malcolm Muggeridge, Walker Percy, Thomas Howard, Sheldon Vanauken, and multitudes of lesser-knowns swimming upstream against a current of disaffected Catholics, many of whom have become alienated. The new Catholics are drawn to the Church of the ages, to orthodox Catholicism, to the magisterium and the pope. On the whole they seem to be socially liberal yet theologically conservative in outlook, therefore escaping generalizations that would peg them with Right or Left labels overall.

There is a new Oxford movement in America today that, like its nineteenth-century namesake, is witnessing many who are discovering—and entering—liturgical churches, including the Roman Catholic Church. The Oxford movement in England resulted in many notable conversions, including Anglican priest John Henry Newman, who rocked the religious establishment with his conversion to Roman Catholicism in 1845. Newman eventually became a cardinal and is acknowledged as one of the Church's greatest twentieth-century minds.

While some demographers may point out that the actual number of conversions to Catholicism are fewer today than in earlier years, it is important to note that the kind of converts appears to be quite different, with fewer obligatory conversions for such reasons as marriage. A significant number of Protestant evangelicals, for example, are among those moving toward Rome, and intellectuals who previously regarded Catholicism as a superstitious, religious dinosaur are changing their minds and taking the plunge.

At a time when Protestant fundamentalism is making inroads among Catholics, this new Oxford movement assures the faith pilgrim that one need not abandon the Catholic Church to find a meaningful relationship with Jesus Christ. The following chapters are personal stories by those who have found Catholicism to be their home — the ecclesial resting place at the end of their spiritual search.

The new Catholics who share their stories in this book include several best-selling authors, well-known university professors, a peace activist, a former Protestant missionary, an entertainer, a former Episcopal priest, a rock star turned Franciscan monk, an ex-Buddhist, a feminist, a political scientist, a one-time Marxist radical, and others. The contributors to this book come from a wide range of backgrounds, yet there are common denominators in their stories that exemplify this new Oxford movement we are witnessing today. And it is this broad spectrum of selected personalities that makes the manuscript representative of a much larger multitude who yearly opt for Rome.

Their narratives may challenge or assure you. Their journeys may surprise or inspire you. They have become "Churched" — they are the New Catholics.

Dan O'Neill

WALKER PERCY

Foreword

How to write about conversion if it is true that faith is an unmerited gift from God? How to describe, let alone explain it, if this is the case? When it comes to grace I get writer's block. How to write about other people's conversions when one hardly understands one's own? What one does, of course is write about the causes other than God's grace, the "proximate," the "material," the "psychological" causes.

One can write about conversion two ways. One way is to put the best possible face on it, recount a respectable intellectual odyssey. Such as: well, my tradition was scientific. I thought science explained the cosmos—until one day I read what Kierkegaard said about Hegelianism, the science of his day: that Hegel explained everything in the universe except what it is to be an individual, to be born, to live, and to die. And for me this "explanation" would be true enough, I suppose. But then there is this. When I was in college, I lived in the attic of a fraternity house with four other guys. God, religion, was the farthest thing from our minds and talk—from mine at least. Except for one of us, a fellow who got up every morning at the crack of dawn and went to Mass. He said nothing about it and seemed otherwise normal.

Does anyone suppose that one had nothing to do with the other? That is, thinking about Kierkegaard's dilemma and remembering my roommate's strange behavior—this among a thousand other things one notices or remembers, which, if they don't "cause" it, at least enter into it, at least make room for this most mysterious turning in one's life.

Here follows a motley crew of converts with whom I felt immediately at home, as motley (in the old, best sense of the word) as Chaucer's pilgrims.

Reading these seventeen very personal accounts, one finds oneself casting about for reasons for the variety, so many different kinds of people coming from so many different directions. One reason of course is the tumultuous pluralism of this huge country. Our materialism and consumerism are so commonplace that we are apt to forget the other term of the paradox: that we are the most religious of countries, more so than India, a vaster maelstrom of contending creeds and cults, not merely the hundreds of Protestant sects, the mainline Protestant churches, the Catholic Church, the varieties of Judaism, but also the new wave from the East, Far and Near, with more varieties of Buddhism, imported and homegrown, than are to be found in Tibet.

But there's another reason. It is not merely the catholicity of these Catholic-to-be pilgrims, coming as they do from every walk of life but also from every other sort of pilgrimage. These folk may be Rome-bound, but they've been most other places as well—Canterbury (C of E), Vienna (Freud), Albany (Seventh-Day Adventists), Down South fundamentalism, Up North New England parsonages, Harvard and Smith and Yale skepticism, "Jewish atheism" (as one writer described it), also "Orthodox Reformed Freudianism," Marxism-Leninism, Buddhism, rock music, the earthly love of men for and by women. Augustine always made more sense to me about this last than Freud, that is, the translation from the love of women (or men) to God. "Repression" and "sublimation" surely says more about Freud's dislike of women than his quarrel with God.

No, it is not merely the exotic provenances of these pilgrims that dazzle the reader, but the inkling that it is the very catholicity of the Thing, the old-new Jewish-Christian Thing, the one holy Catholic apostolic and Roman Thing that, come at from so many directions, looks so different at the beginning and finally so much the same. Sure enough, all roads seem to lead to and so forth. Here they certainly do. She is the object of the pilgrimage and there She is, blemishes and all. Or as one convert puts it here: what else do you expect anything this enormous and this old to be than, at times, something of a horror show?

Some themes recur. More than one pilgrim finds himself standing at a strange rectory door, wondering how he got there, never having said two words to a priest—and here I have to smile, remembering how it felt and also hoping that he, she, would not run into some exhausted, unhappy, and otherwise messed-up human. They didn't. In one case the housekeeper answered the door, matter-of-factly shook her feather duster toward the parlor: "In there." That helps. "Well, here I am," one fellow said abruptly to the bemused priest. "What do I have to do?"

An interesting Anglican current runs here. In no case is the tone polemical. Rather there is a lasting affection for the lovely Anglican things, for the Book of Common Prayer, for dear England herself—and a sadness at her cutting off the magisterium. One pictures this pilgrim as he turns away from the spires soaring above empty cathedrals in the gracious countryside and takes the road to downtown, bustling Saint Agnes's where, lovely or not, the Lord is housed.

Books and reading figure here as largely as one might expect, and the writers one would expect, from Aquinas to Merton. But guess who turns up most often? C. S. Lewis! — who, if he didn't make it all the way, certainly handed along a goodly crew.

Sometimes it is the very prosaicness of the reading that catches the eye. One woman — and she is my fellow traveler because I did the same thing — read Saint Augustine's *The City of God*, was duly impressed, and then read *Father Smith Instructs Jackson*, no masterpiece to be sure but maybe all the better for the humble prose.

I can still see the grayish paperback, probably picked up from that rack at the back of the church, with the good Father Smith on the cover and Jackson — *Jackson!* — an earnest young man with a 1920s Harold Lloyd sort of haircut, head cocked attentively, listening. There was some good news here.

And there is good news in these remarkable stories.

1

JOHN C. CORT

A Bizarre Conversion

John C. Cort is a 1935 honors graduate of Harvard College. He has also pursued studies at Brandeis University, Weston School of Theology (Cambridge, Massachusetts), and Ateneo University in the Philippines. He has worked as a reporter, editor, union organizer, Peace Corps and antipoverty official. Cort has been widely published, with over two hundred articles and book reviews in the Boston Globe, *the* Progressive, *the* Nation, Catholic Digest, National Catholic Reporter, Commonweal, *and the* New Oxford Review. *He is currently publisher and coeditor of* Religious Socialism *and a free-lance writer whose history of Christian socialism will be published in 1988.*

Perhaps because his conversion came much earlier than the other New Catholics who share their faith journeys here, he has become something of a role model for many of them, and we asked him to lead off this book with his own unique and charming story.

L ove was the thing that got me started. My first intimation of the joy and anguish that lay ahead came one night in the summer of 1926. We were all over at the Hardies' cottage on Bluff Island for some kind of party. I was standing alone against the wall watching the dancing. More specifically, I was watching Flora Hardie dancing. She was a dark-haired girl from New Orleans and as I watched her in the flickering light of the kerosene lamps it occurred to me that she embodied all the qualities in the song that was playing at that very moment:

> *Isn't she cute? Isn't she sweet?*
> *She's gentle and mental-ly nearly complete.*
> *She's knockout, she's regal, her beauty's illegal,*
> *She's the girl friend.*

I concluded that I must be in love with Flora Hardie. Since I had never been in love before, this was an arresting thought. A powerful

force within me was moving me toward the decision to ask Flora
Hardie to dance.

Take her to dance, take her to tea,
It's stunning how cunning this lady can be.
One glimpse of this vision would cause a collision,
She's the girl friend.

On the other hand, there were countervailing forces and considerations that palsied my will, One, I was only twelve years old and
Flora was seventeen.

She is smart, she's refined
How can she be real?
She has heart, she has mind,
Shucks, the girl's ideal.

Two, she was a lot taller than I. Three, I did not know how to
dance. And so I stood pinned against the wall, paralyzed by indecision. The record came to an end. I never asked Flora Hardie to
dance, never saw her again after that summer, never even moped
very much. After all, it is difficult to sustain romantic melancholy at
age twelve.

Nevertheless, in some curious way—perhaps the juxtaposition of
the song and Flora's distant beauty—I conceived in my mind a
hopelessly idealized concept of the woman I wanted. The formula
was simple: perfection—a beautiful mind and a beautiful soul in a
beautiful body.

Years went by and it began to look as though I might be waiting
for a long time. Came the summer of 1932. My oldest brother,
David, the family intellectual, had sold his younger brothers on the
virtues of the British novelists of that era, notably Aldous Huxley,
Evelyn Waugh, and D. H. Lawrence. A more obscure but still
influential one was William Gerhardi, who wrote a book called *Eva's
Apples*. One day that summer I was sitting naked in the sun on the
rocks of Little Huckleberry Island reading this novel when I came
upon the following passage: "Thus I prefer Eva to earnest women
who can talk of Pessimism and Buddha but have no living and
spontaneous form themselves. When an object like Eva shows no
visible sign of containing a subject but appeals beyond all analysis, it
may be taken that the divine spirit has found in her a happy home.
She is God's art, perfect like a flower."

From the context it was obvious that the character who said this
was speaking for the author. And if the less intellectual woman was

good enough for Gerhardi, why should she not be good enough for me? Clearly, I had set my sights too high. I lowered them. As Thomas Aquinas said, love is an act of the will. I saw under my eyes a lovely girl with a sweet personality who also played the piano very nicely. The people she was visiting, friends of ours, asked me to escort her to a dance at the Thousand Island Yacht Club. There was a moon that night and a long ride across the silver river. I looked into her eyes and saw there, shining like onyx and carnelian, the divine spirit. I went home in a state of mild delirium.

While I was working up the courage to declare myself, she left the river and returned to Montclair. Something in her eyes as she stood on the train steps waving good-bye gave me hope and I wrote and told her that I loved her. She wrote back that she loved me too.

When we had returned to Long Island she asked me to her home for the weekend. There was another dance at some country club, and between dances we walked out and sat in the car and I kissed her for the first time. I cannot say that I was disillusioned, at least not in her as a perfectly lovable and desirable representative of the human race. She was beautiful in a red evening dress and I was crazy about her, but suddenly I was overcome by a strange sadness and I knew what Shaw meant when he wrote: "There are two tragedies in life: one is not to get your heart's desire and the other is to get it." Clearly there was a problem with the capacity of human love to satisfy the hunger of the heart for perfect joy.

That passed quickly, however. I returned to Harvard absorbed with the idea of getting married, although I was only eighteen and the girl sixteen. I regretted my choice of concentration in French history and literature and was thinking of changing to English so that I could prepare for a writing career and be ready to make some money as soon as I graduated.

In this condition I approached my first tutorial conference with Paul Doolin. He was then a man about forty whose dark suits and black ties, combined with black hair and moustache, gave him an austere, somber look that was shattered at intervals by sudden, violent laughter. He had been a fighter pilot in World War I and once asked me if I was related to the Marquis de la Cour, beside whose chateau he had made an emergency landing in the French countryside.

The tutorial conferences were held in Doolin's barren study in Dunster House. One of the first was on the *Chanson de Roland*, which he had told me to read. He said it was a great epic poem. It was about a nephew of Charlemagne who died at Roncevaux in the Pyrenees fighting the infidel Saracens. It left me cold.

I was in love. I was not only in love, but I was a romantic in love. I had accepted the gospel according to Wagner and Metro-Goldwyn-Mayer that the feeling of a man for a woman, and vice versa, is the most important thing in life. And here was a poem, supposed to be a great poem, that had no love interest at all. I complained to Doolin.

He took the poem apart and put it back together again. In the process I somehow felt that he was taking me apart as well and that somehow, somewhere, I must find the way to put myself back together again. What follows is an account of what led up to and away from that watershed conference with Paul Doolin in which he showed me that the love of God can be even more interesting than the love of woman.

I was the youngest of five brothers, sons of Ambrose and Lydia Painter Cort. Father was the son of the Reverend Cyrus Cort, a big man with a beard who looked like God and at one time was a frontier missionary of the Reformed Church in Iowa.

Father spent most of his professional life as a public school principal in Brooklyn, doubling as a night school teacher of Latin and English. Mother was a lovely woman who played the piano beautifully and was the daughter of a stove manufacturer in the city of Reading, Pennsylvania. Her family were Quakers. Since there were no Reformed churches in or about Woodmere, Long Island, where we lived, we all became Episcopalians and sang in the choir. I continued singing in choirs, spending three years in the Cathedral Choir School of Saint John the Divine in New York City. From there, on a full scholarship, I proceeded to Taft, a prep school in Connecticut where rich boys spent their idle hours dreaming up ways to torture each other.

One of these, the product of weird circumstances and normal adolescent fun, was the practice of calling me "Jesus." This provided much pleasure to some of my fellow students and what may, in the long run, have been salutary pain for me. I had no defense against it. After all, it was not exactly a dirty name. It was worse. Against a dirty name you could fight, but who could fight against "Jesus"? And yet it remained insulting. Such was the high esteem in which Jesus Christ was held in an American prep school in 1929. Such was the high esteem in which he was held by J. C. (for Jesus Christ) Cort. Despite all those years sitting in choir stalls, religion flowing over me like water over a stone, very little had penetrated.

My father was more of a deist than a believing Christian. David, our intellectual mentor, was a typical product of the post–World War I generation of hedonistic, atheistic writers who frequented the bars and garrets of Greenwich Village. Father and David disagreed with each other on every conceivable subject, but they agreed on this: the ancient teachings of Christianity were outmoded by the advance of science and enlightenment.

This, then, more or less, was the frame of mind and irreligious prejudice with which I approached my freshman year at Harvard.

I once told the wife of a Harvard professor that I had been converted to Catholicism while an undergraduate there, and her reaction was, "How positively bizarre!"

"The University of Chicago," a wit of the thirties pointed out, "is a Baptist institution where Jews go to become Catholics." This could never have been said about Harvard. At that time not a single course in the philosophy department dealt seriously with Thomism. The introductory course in philosophy jumped from Aristotle to Descartes, a period of nearly two thousand years during which, according to the department, there was no philosophy worth mentioning.

In addition, the elective system left it up to the student to select courses that would qualify him for the title of Educated Man, an admission that the faculty did not know what a proper education was. And so it happened, as Chicago's Robert Hutchins wrote, that chemistry majors could not speak to economics majors, and hardly anyone was speaking to God.

I was elated when I first came to Harvard, which seemed to be everything Taft was not. Within a day, however, I had lost my wallet and a sizable sum of money Father had given me to start me off. I was plunged into depression. And so I began my search for a truth that might give me something more durable than fifty-nine dollars in a wallet.

At Taft Mr. Reardon had persuaded me to like history and Wallace Fowlie had persuaded me to admire French literature. At the end of my freshman year, therefore, I elected to concentrate in French history and literature, and someone in the bowels of the university assigned Paul Doolin to be my tutor, the one who, under the system then in effect, was to guide me through that field.

Doolin was not a Catholic at the time, although he later became one. He was a Harvard rebel in revolt against the ideas that dominated the university and the Western world; the ideas of romanticism and materialism; the ideas of William James's pragmatist who, in James's words, "turns away . . . from fixed principles, closed systems and pretended absolutes and origins" and "turns toward concreteness and adequacy, toward facts, toward action and toward power."

Doolin was a Platonist, a medievalist, and a disciple of another Harvard professor, Irving Babbitt, cofounder of the humanist school with Paul Elmer More of Princeton. They did not want to close any systems or ignore any facts. They merely insisted on the reality and the primacy of another set of facts, the facts of the spirit.

What Doolin did that first day (described earlier in this chapter) was to begin to set me straight on the relative values of love, sacred and profane. He showed me that because a man like Roland died fighting for the love of God he was not therefore a lesser man than one who died for the love of a woman. Doolin's opinion was that, other things being equal, he was a greater man. He almost made me see it.

Almost. I was in love, and not with God. I rebelled against a course assignment I had been given to write a paper on the medieval history of Brittany. I could not see how that was going to help me make a living and marry my girl. I told Doolin I wanted to transfer to the English department to prepare myself for a writing job. He talked me out of it. He also talked the history professor into changing my assignment to a paper on the romances of Chrétien de Troyes, which were more to my liking.

Chrétien was a French poet of the twelfth century who worked mostly at "the court of love" run by an erotic old duchess named Marie de Champagne. One of the laws of this court was that true love was impossible between a man and a woman who had been joined in legal wedlock.

Chrétien's most famous romance was *Tristan and Iseult*. Young Tristan, a handsome knight, was sent across the sea by King Mark to bring back Iseult, the king's betrothed. On the voyage home they drink by mistake a love potion that Iseult was supposed to take just before she met King Mark. After that they cannot help themselves.

The appeal of this story to composers like Wagner was no accident. He gave it some visceral music that I used to listen to up at the river, swinging in the hammock and gazing out across the water, dreaming of my love. Nor is it strange that it has attracted modern poets like Edwin Arlington Robinson. The destruction of free will in the love potion, the opportunity for Tristan and Iseult to enjoy all the melancholy zest of their forbidden passion and still escape the pangs of conscience and remorse — these things naturally appeal to the modern mind and heart.

When I read these stories in their crude originals, without benefit of Wagner, Robinson, or Twentieth Century-Fox, they struck me as strangely unconvincing. They gave me pause. They made me think. They led me to reexamine some of my illusions about the nature of life and love.

Doolin also got me reading Plato. Plato and Socrates were not great admirers of democracy, as I. F. Stone has reminded us, and Plato's idea of the ideal government was rule by a philosopher-king. As a philosopher you might say he was a great poet. In any event he was the kind of poet I needed at the time. I was deeply moved by the *Apology* of Socrates before the court that condemned him, one of the great statements of religious faith and one of the great confrontations in the history of confrontation between faith and conformity:

> "Men of Athens, I honor and love you; but I shall obey God rather than you, and while I have life and strength I shall never cease from the practice and teaching of philosophy, exhorting anyone whom I meet and saying to him after my manner, 'O my friend, why do you who are a citizen of the great and mighty and wise city of Athens care so much about laying up the greatest amount of money and honor and reputation, and so little about wisdom and truth and the greatest improvement of the soul, which you never regard or heed at all? Are you not ashamed of this?' . . . Wherefore, O judges, be of good cheer and know this of a truth—that no evil can happen to a good man, either in life or after death . . . "

Plato takes us to Socrates' cell and in the dialogue with Crito, who is urging him to escape, shows us that the end does not justify the means. Anticipating the words of Christ, Socrates says that "we ought not to retaliate or render evil for evil to anyone, whatever evil we may have suffered from him." Crito leaves Socrates determined to "follow the intimations of the will of God."

The *Phaedo* is even more moving, as it brings together Socrates' closest friends in his cell on the day of his execution for one last discussion of the basic questions: can the soul exist independently of the body? Is it immortal? Is there a heaven for the good, a hell for the bad, and a purgatory for the indifferent?

At last, having answered all these questions in the affirmative (the existence of God seems to have been taken for granted by everyone), Socrates concludes that "when the foolishness of the body will be cleared away, we shall be pure and hold converse with other pure souls, and know of ourselves the clear light everywhere, and this is surely the light of truth." And so he lies down, drinks the poison, and dies.

What Plato did for me that sophomore year at Harvard was simply to take the old Christian words and the old Christian concepts, dust off the accumulations of a thousand dull sermons, the associations of a thousand pious platitudes, and all the bigotry, hypocrisy, and general dry rot of two thousand years, and leave them shining with the intellectual glamor of ancient Greece.

For it is surprising how fashionable the old Greeks have remained. Even those who sneer at everything that Plato, Homer, Sophocles stood for will generally not venture to attack head-on the highly moral and religious standards of that magnificent civilization, except perhaps to remind us from time to time, rightly, that the whole magnificent thing rested on a foundation of slave labor.

I readily admit that as a young man I was sensitive to the canons of intellectual fashion. Most young men are. God was old hat to the men and authors I admired. At that time neither Waugh nor Huxley had shown any interest in religion, and I was shocked to discover that there was a very respectable tradition on the other side of the debate between believers and unbelievers; that a powerful and persuasive body of philosophers, poets, and writers upheld the primacy of the spirit, and upheld it with as much passion, eloquence, and more sense than the moderns upheld the primacy of matter.

Whole phrases and even sentences of Plato sound as if they had been lifted from the New Testament. Socrates' ringing defiance, "Men of Athens, I shall obey God rather than you," calls to mind the defiance of Peter and the other Apostles before the Sanhedrin when they cried out, "We must obey God rather than men."

"Whence do wars and quarrels come among you?" wrote Saint James, whose knowledge of Plato must be considered doubtful. "Is it not from this, from your passions, which wage war in your members?" And four hundred years before him Socrates said in the *Phaedo*, "For whence come wars and fightings and factions? Whence but from the body and the lusts of the body?"

This conviction of the duality of human nature and of the existence of a higher world of ideas and ideals — God's world of absolute truth, absolute beauty, and absolute goodness — was what impressed me in Plato. No need to go along with his peculiar theory of reminiscence or the Gnostic implications of his dualism. It was the general picture he painted, with the skill of a great artist, that started an echo in the depths of my own soul and found a reflection in the muddy waters of my own experience.

Another man at Harvard who moved me was Alfred North Whitehead, the English philosopher and mathematician. I took one of his philosophy courses, which was well over my head. The only thing I can remember from the course is Whitehead insisting that every concept that passes through the human mind, even if it be the coldest mathematical formula, is received in the mind of the receiver with a certain emotional coloring, or sets up a certain emotional reaction.

I struggled through his books and understood very little, but I still believe Whitehead was the greatest teacher I can remember. He was a little old man with a cherubic face, a bald head, and a white fringe of hair that curled up in the back. He wore wing collars and almost always a blue ascot tie that set off his bright blue eyes. He had a wonderfully cheerful smile, and he smiled a good deal.

Whitehead would sit behind his desk on the high lecture platform in Emerson Hall, his pink, shiny face barely visible to his students, and almost every day he would go into a kind of public rapture of love for the truth.

Still another influence was C. H. McIlwain, the star of the government department. His fire did not burn as brightly as Whitehead's, but it burned nonetheless. He taught political theory. He was one of the few men at Harvard who knew and respected Thomas Aquinas. He was quick to point out that the chain of theories that produced our modern notions of democracy, popular sovereignty, civil rights, and representative government runs back through Cardinal Bellarmine, Suarez, and Saint Thomas, and to the New and Old Testaments.

It was his view that the political theory of the Catholic Church is bounded on one side by the words of Saint Paul, "Let every man be subject to the higher powers, for all authority is from God," and on the other side by the statement of Peter to the Sanhedrin, "We must obey God rather than men." That lesson in political geography has stayed with me ever since.

Louis Mercier in the French department was the very picture of a middle-class Frenchman who had all the virtues and none of the vices. He had a tremendous number of children, a strong faith in the Catholic Church, and a mission in life, which was to reconcile the humanism of Irving Babbitt with the teachings of Christianity. His influence on me was mostly that of example. He was a Catholic, the real thing—and there were few in evidence at Harvard—a man not only of intelligence and faith, but of works; a good man and a happy man. I looked at Professor Mercier and I thought to myself, if a man like that can be a Catholic, then there can't be very much the matter with Catholicism.

But mostly, next to Doolin, there was Babbitt. I never even saw the man. He died during the summer of 1933, just before I was scheduled to take his course. His erudition was overpowering. His field was French literature, but he was also at home in Greek, Latin, English, and German literature. He read Buddhist texts in Pali and in one of his books apologizes because he had to read Confucius in translation. His books ranged over the whole field of human thought, art, and history. I think I read all his books, although none were ever required reading. I can still remember the sense of excitement I felt as I sat in the Lowell House library reading Babbitt as he demolished popular fallacies. In the midst of the slaughter I could see some of my own favorite dogmas and prejudices going down, but I did not care. What was happening to me was a genuine conversion from one view of life to another.

Babbitt's favorite target was romanticism, which he described as a movement that had forerunners in the Renaissance and the Middle Ages (Chrétien de Troyes) and even back as far as the Taoists of ancient China, but did not gather speed and momentum until the eighteenth century. At first it was a rebellion against the rigid formalism of seventeenth- and eighteenth-century writers who almost killed imagination in the name of reason, morality, and good taste. But Rousseau and his disciples, he maintained, were not content to fight for the legitimate rights of the imagination. They launched a counteroffensive along a wide front that sought to wipe out the wisdom of the ages and set up canons of morality based on a new concept of human nature.

In short, according to this view, human nature did not fall, either through Adam's sin or by way of a basic weakness in its makeup (Niebuhr's "inclination to injustice"). It was naturally and completely good as long as it remained in the primitive state. Society and civilization ruined it. Too much law, too much reason, too much religion — especially formal, dogmatic religion. Our salvation was therefore to get back to simple, spontaneous, emotional living; to be more natural and uninhibited.

The following are some of Babbitt's favorite quotes from romantic writers, taken from his basic work, *Rousseau and Romanticism*:

Goethe in *Faust*: "Feeling is all." And again: "The devil is the spirit that always says 'no.'" (Babbitt acknowledged, however, that Goethe later reformed and turned against the romantic notions of his earlier career.)

Rousseau: "The only habit the child should be allowed to form is that of forming no habit." Also: "The man who reflects is a depraved animal." Also: "Let us lay it down as an incontrovertible rule that the first impulses of nature are always right."

Babbitt quotes another passage in which Rousseau speaks of his own "warmth of heart," his "melting feeling, the lively and sweet emotion that I experience at the sight of everything that is virtuous, generous, and lovely." Babbitt adds that Rousseau "abandoned his five children one after the other, but had, we are told, an unspeakable affection for his dog."

To show the political effect of this glorification of feeling Babbitt quotes a speech by Robespierre before the French assembly at the height of the Reign of Terror:

> "Yet virtue exists as you can testify, sensitive and pure souls; it exists, that tender, irresistible, imperious passion, torment and delight of magnanimous hearts, that profound horror of tyranny, that compassionate zeal for the oppressed, that sacred love for one's country, that still more sublime and sacred love for humanity. . . . It exists, that egoism of undegenerate men who find a celestial voluptuousness in the calm of a pure conscience and the ravishing spectacle of public happiness. You feel it at this moment burning in your souls. I feel it in mine. But how could our vile calumniators have any notion of it?"

And so, off with their heads.

Babbitt refused to admit that virtue was either a passion or a feeling—voluptuous, ravishing, burning, or otherwise. He defined his terms and the definitions he used were those that have been common to the great moralists of all ages, starting with Moses and proceeding to Buddha, Confucius, Plato, Aristotle, and Christ. He insisted on the distinction between soul and body; between the law of the spirit and the law of the flesh; between the law for thing and the law for man.

I realize that dualism has had a bad press of late—some of it deserved. Human nature is a unity, not a duality. Or let us say it is both, just as God is both a unity and a trinity. Since the time of the Gnostics, the Manicheans, the Jansenists, and the Puritans, we have had to struggle against false doctrine to the effect that the body is in some way evil or shameful. As Saint Augustine put it, "It is not the bad body that causes the good soul to sin, but the bad soul that causes the good body to sin."

But this is not the same as saying, with Rousseau, that the instincts of the body are always true and trustworthy, and more safely obeyed than the promptings of the mind and the spirit. Let me illustrate some of the confusion that Rousseau and the romantics sowed in the modern world, and also the human truth that shines through that confusion, by some quotes from Aldous Huxley's *Point Counter Point*. Up until the time I read *Rousseau and Romanticism* the Huxley book was easily the most influential book of my life, particularly if we exclude the indirect, subconscious influence of the Bible. Propelled by my brother David's enthusiasm, it had become a sort of

surrogate Bible for the Cort brothers, and by the time I was seventeen I had read it twice.

The only really admirable character in the book is Mark Rampion, an artist-writer whom Huxley is supposed to have modeled on
D. H. Lawrence. Rampion is contemptuous of Christ and Christianity and singles out for special contempt Saint Francis, whom he
calls "a disgusting little pervert . . . going about getting thrills of
excitement out of licking lepers." He was also contemptuous of dis-
embodied romantics like Shelley and in a passage that I greatly
admired and often quoted he comments on the *Ode to a Skylark*: "'I
wish to God the bird . . . [had] dropped a good large mess in his
eye. It would have served him damned well right for saying it wasn't
a bird. Blithe spirit indeed!'"

Rampion (Huxley-Lawrence) was more of an earthy romantic.
On one page he recommends "renunciation of mental self-consciousness and abandonment to instinct." A few pages later he says, "The
moment you allow speculative truth to take the place of felt instinc-
tive truth as a guide to living, you ruin everything." Having thus
identified himself with Rousseau and the romantics, he then contra-
dicts himself by saying something that identifies him with Babbitt
and the humanists. Namely: "A man's a creature on a tightrope,
walking delicately, equilibrated, with mind and consciousness and
spirit at one end of his balancing pole and all that's unconscious and
earthly and mysterious at the other." Clearly, if the tightrope walker
were to follow Rampion's earlier advice and abandon himself to
instinct, renouncing mental self-consciousness and speculative
truth, he would soon be nothing but a splatter on the pavement.

Babbitt classified most people as living on one or more of three
planes: naturalist, humanist, and religious. Rousseau was to him
a romantic naturalist. There were also the scientific naturalists.
For these he had more respect because they at least believed in
reason and discipline, if only in pursuit of physical phenomena. But
he could be rough with them when they tried, as he maintained
John Dewey had done, to set up science in the place of philosophy
and religion. His attack on them was on the ground that they were
not scientific when they denied the reality of moral and spiritual
facts.

On the positive side he was harder to follow. He seemed to feel
that Christianity was "symbolically . . . but not literally true." His
favorite characters were Aristotle and Buddha. He was not foolish
enough to back reason exclusively against feeling and imagination.
With Pascal he agreed that "the imagination disposes of everything."
What he wanted was "the ethical imagination," that is, an imagina-

tion at once sobered by respect for the universal and the ideal and yet intoxicated by the romantics' wonder for the new and the strange. This is a difficult formula, but Babbitt showed that it had been realized in the work of the classic authors, such as Homer, Pindar, Sophocles, Virgil, Dante, Shakespeare, and Milton.

The problem was this: could you fashion it into a formula to live by? To rephrase Gilbert, of Gilbert and Sullivan, if you took the books of ten classic authors and ten classic moralists, boiled them over a slow flame for ten years and removed the scum, would a happy little humanist be the residuum?

Babbitt himself did not seem to be sure. He distrusted the extremism of the religious mentality, but still he had to admit that "though religion can get along without humanism, humanism cannot get along without religion." At another point he emphasized "the nothingness and helplessness" of human nature and "its dependence on a higher power." He admired Christianity because he felt that its essential virtue was humility.

Babbitt's view of the good life and the good person did suffer from coolness and an accent on the negative. He quoted with approval, for example, a comment by Edmund Burke on Goethe's identification of evil with "the spirit that always says 'no.'" Burke said that that would throw out "ninety percent of the virtues."

This was a far cry from Christ, who summed up the whole law and the Prophets in two commandments, love of God and love of neighbor. Not "thou shalt not" but "thou shalt." Humility was not king, though it might be queen. The greatest of these was love.

Recently I went back to the original texts and read Rousseau at greater length and with more detachment than I had read him at Harvard. Somewhat to my surprise I found him to be an eccentric and highly inconsistent Christian who despised Voltaire and the Encyclopedists for their unbelief and once described himself as "the only man in France who believes in God." His writing is full of sensible and corny bromides, together with some foolish statements such as those Babbitt seized upon and some ringing prose that did much to prepare the ground for democratic government and socialism. I concluded that Babbitt had been a little unfair to Rousseau, but I remained persuaded that he had had a profoundly beneficial influence on me. His lucid distinctions and definitions were precisely what I needed at the time.

One night I was sitting in my room in Lowell House reading one of those books called *The Making of the Modern Mind*, or some such title. There must be a dozen of them, at least. It was written in a crisp, dogmatic tone and it gave you the feeling that everything was really pretty right and tight and simple as long as you stuck to reason. I put the book down and I said to myself, "I will be a rationalist. I will believe what is clearly evident to my reason and I will not believe what is not clearly evident."

The trouble was that Babbitt had made clearly evident to my reason that people cannot live successfully on that plane, but must either sink below reason to the level of their emotions or rise above it to the level of ethical insight and perception. The question was, how could I acquire ethical insight and perceptions? Babbitt said by a study of the great books. But could a man live by great books alone?

Mark Twain said that "a classic is something that everybody wants to have read, but nobody wants to read." There was the time I was reading Dante's *Divine Comedy* in the Lowell House library. I was sitting in an easy chair and began to doze off, so I transferred to a hard chair at one of the tables. That kept me going for another half hour, but then my head was down on my hands and I was gone. The head resting on the wrists cut off the circulation and the pain woke me up. I shook myself. If I was going to sleep I might as well go up to bed, but it was still afternoon. I got up and wandered into the fiction section, looking for something that would keep me awake. I picked up a modern novel, opened it at random, and found myself in the middle of an erotic passage. Suddenly I was sleepy no longer. I took the book up to my room and read it all night. When dawn came I went out and sat on a bench by the Charles, still reading and occasionally looking up to admire the gulls flying over the river in the early sunlight.

I don't remember a single thing in that book, nor the title nor the author. I would have stayed there and finished it, but Wallace Fowlie came along on his way to early Mass at the Anglo-Catholic monastery a little way up the river. He invited me to go along. It was a beautiful chapel, done in the best of taste. The service was simple and moving. I came out feeling refreshed, cleaner than when I went in, and persuaded of the difficulty of absorbing ethical insight from the great books, the comparative facility of going to church, and the even greater facility of getting absorbed in an erotic book.

Another example and one that is wet, or at least damp, with my own heart's blood: not far into sophomore year my girl forgot me in favor of a young man who bore an uncanny resemblance to Joel McCrea, the movie actor. Being forgotten in favor of somebody who looks like Joel McCrea is a painful experience. Moved by this pain and the promptings of Doolin, I began to read Plato with more than usual seriousness.

I sat at my desk, a volume of Plato open before me and I said to myself, "This is working. I feel better already. I am really beginning to rise from *phenomena* (appearances) to *noumena* (realities). I am going up the ladder of love from the less beautiful to the more beautiful. I am getting out of the world of shadows on the wall of the cave; out into the light of the sun and the real world of Ideas. I am progressing from the Many to the One."

The next summer I went back to our cottage on the river and told myself that if I saw her again or I did not see her again, it was all the same. I was cured of my fever. And I went to bed one night on the small porch upstairs overlooking the river. I fell asleep, but was awakened by the sound of a motorboat approaching our dock, apparently bringing some of our neighbors home from a party.

I stared out into the dark to see who this might be. As the boat came closer and was illuminated by its own running lights I recognized it. There was the sound of voices saying good-bye and then, quite clearly, there was the sound of a girl's voice and I knew that it was hers. I didn't even see her. I didn't even hear what she said. All I heard was the sound of her voice, but that was enough. Plato, Babbitt, Doolin, Dante, Sophocles, Shakespeare, Homer, Virgil, Buddha, Aristotle — all the classical poets, philosophers, and heavy-duty thinkers in the world might as well never have lived or written a word.

None of them could save me. The only thing that could save me was another swig of the love potion. I fell for Sally, a tall, beautiful blonde. She was no more interested than the girl from Montclair, but she was easier to forget and in forgetting her I forgot both of them.

The truth was that I was even more helpless than Babbitt had given me credit for. And Plato was wrong when he identified knowledge and virtue; when he said that it was enough to know what was right in order to do it. Aristotle was correct when he commented simply on this statement: the facts are otherwise.

What do we have so far? We have a competitive, energetic, self-centered young man who was born with the capacity to enjoy a wide variety of experience. Although he seems fairly well adjusted, he has not entirely recovered from the humiliation suffered in prep school when a funny twist of fate subjected him to the indignity of being called "Jesus" by his schoolmates. This leaves him with a flaw, but perhaps an advantage. If death is the final humiliation, which none can escape but few really anticipate, then dividends in "ethical insight and perception" may be gained by those who have experienced some form of minideath by way of an intense humiliation of this kind. Possible.

His situation therefore might make him receptive to religion, but he is also aware of the contempt into which religious faith has fallen among most of the contemporary intelligentsia. By another twist of fate his path falls across that of a man, Doolin, who introduces him to other men, from Plato to Babbitt, who persuade him that religious faith is by no means intellectually contemptible.

Somewhere about this point he opens the Bible and reads all four Gospels. There are inconsistencies, but nothing that cannot be accepted as the understandable disagreement of honest witnesses or the understandable failure of honest memories. There are many consistencies and agreements, notably, that a poor Jew named Jesus lived in Palestine and that this man had extraordinary powers of speaking and healing.

These powers attracted a sizable following, especially among the poor. He claimed to have a special and unique relationship to God, and this claim, together with His denunciations of corruption in high places, brought down upon Him the wrath of the Jewish and Roman power structures. He was therefore crucified. And the central and most basic point of agreement among the witnesses: several days after His crucifixion He rose from the dead in a form that seems to have been alternately tangible and intangible.

The internal evidence has credibility. The evangelists write like conscientious reporters. The detail is realistic and much of it is unflattering to the founders of the Christian community, such as the denials of Peter and passages highlighting the mental and spiritual obtuseness of the Apostles. The zeal and missionary success of the early Christians, revealed in the Epistles and Acts of the Apostles, give further evidence of the strength of their conviction that Christ rose from the dead and remains alive.

While he is thinking about all this, our Harvard undergraduate is going to Christ Church on the Cambridge Common and singing in the choir, for pay, for the nice middle- and upper-middle-class Christians among whom he was born and raised. He begins to listen a little more attentively to the sermons of the rector and various visiting preachers of the liberal Episcopal persuasion. He gets the impression that these preachers do not take very seriously the teachings of the creed that all of us recite together during the service. The folks in the pews, in effect, are encouraged to pick and choose those teachings that suit their fancy. The young man thinks that this does not make much sense, that a proper church ought to have some teaching authority that commands respect and is recognized as having the right and power to teach *with* authority, and is not afraid to use that authority. Perhaps he is even too conscious of that kind of need. And while he is thinking along these lines he is taking a course entitled the Intellectual History of the Middle Ages.

Although there was no course offered by the philosophy department in the thought of Thomas Aquinas, or any medieval philosopher, the history department was not quite so prejudiced. There was this course taught by Charles Taylor, master of Adams House, a tall, lean, hawk-nosed man who looked like a medieval knight himself.

Taylor introduced us first to Augustine, and Augustine introduced us to his own concerns about predestination and free will, based largely on his reading of Saint Paul's Epistle to the Romans. We discussed these subjects in class and I proceeded to contract an intellectual headache that lasted for about a week. It revolved around the question: if God knew from the beginning of time (recognizing that with God there is no time) that Johnny Jones was going to shoot his dear old mother on the night of November 21, 1933, how could it be maintained that Johnny was free not to shoot his dear old mother? Or: if certain people are predestined by God to be saved and others to be damned, must we not, as Calvin did, deny free will? And doesn't that make God basically unfair and irrational?

Of course, if we read Saint Paul carefully it becomes evident that my headache sprang from a misunderstanding of what concerned him, for he was not so much dealing with the salvation or damnation of individual Jews, but rather with their predestination as a people fated, in the main, to reject Christ as the Messiah.

At any rate I was worried about some legitimate questions. In this mood I went to Widener Library and consulted the *Catholic Encyclopedia*. Just why or how I came to do this I do not recall. I read two articles by J. Pohle, Jesuit professor of dogmatic theology at Breslau University. One was on grace and the other on predestination. I have a very vivid memory of the experience, including just where I was sitting, facing west at one of the tables in the big reading room near the windows that looked out toward Memorial Church. When I came to Pohle's statement that the Church teaches that all are given sufficient grace to be saved and that "grace is condemned to unfruitfulness only in the event of the free resistance of the will," I stopped reading the article on grace. That was enough for me. My sense of fairness was satisfied.

In the article on predestination Pohle distinguished between the Calvinist view and the Catholic view by way of two Latin phrases that I found peculiarly clarifying as well as reassuring. He wrote that Calvin believed in *praedestinatio ante praevisa merita* (predestination before foreseen merits), a teaching that effectively negates free will, whereas the Catholic Church holds to *praedestinatio post praevisa merita* (after foreseen merits). Pohle quoted Saint Ambrose: "He did not predestine before he foreknew, but for those whose merits he foresaw he predestined the reward."

As I read I conceived a pleasantly anthropomorphic image of God as a man sitting in a balloon suspended over the River of Life. Because, however, He is not a man, or woman, but God and because with God there is no time, no past or future, but everything is present, He sees and knows simultaneously everything that has happened, is happening, or will happen on the river. He knows the speed and direction of all currents, the location of all rocks. He knows the size and capabilities of all boats that proceed down the rapids of the river and, most important, He knows precisely how the free will, intellect, nerves, and muscles of the men and women who guide those boats will react to the rocks and whirlpools of the river as well to the assistance (grace) that He Himself gives them. Then, knowing all that, He predestines how they will come out, whether they are wrecked along the way, get stuck on a sandbar, or arrive safely at the mouth of the river and float serenely into the Sea of Paradise.

My headache was gone. I walked out of Widener Library into the Yard, not with a sense of being born again but with a profound sense of gratitude to the Catholic Church for having produced a book like the *Catholic Encyclopedia* and a writer like J. Pohle and two Latin phrases that could preserve my faith in the fact of my own freedom on the one hand and the basic intelligence and decency of God on the other.

Out of that gratitude I went to Saint Paul's Church and asked to see a priest. A pleasant young man, Father Greene, proceeded to instruct me in the Catholic faith. I informed my family. My father was so upset that he wrote an angry letter to the dean of Harvard complaining about Doolin and told me that if I insisted on being received into the Church he would insist on withdrawing me from Harvard. This rather appealed to my sense of melodrama, but I felt I should at least inform Father Greene. He in turn asked the pastor, a Monsignor Hickey, for guidance and Monsignor Hickey advised me to wait until after graduation. Being then much more receptive to the counsel of monsignori than I have since become, I agreed and did not officially become a Catholic until after graduation in June of 1935, when I was received at the altar of a church on Pineapple Street in Brooklyn Heights. My witnesses were the housekeeper and the sexton, who put down his broom for a few minutes to stand beside me.

As I write now, more than fifty years later, I thank God for that "sufficient grace" that led me to Paul Doolin and Plato and Irving Babbitt and Father Pohle and, yes, perhaps also to the pangs of unrequited love and the humiliation of being called "Jesus."

I have been happy in the Roman Catholic, Christian faith — very happy. My only regret is that some of my fellow Catholics — lay and cleric — seem to be losing their faith in the magisterium of the Church and in those ancient truths of the gospel that the magisterium upholds. I keep telling them, "I've been where you are heading and, believe me, you wouldn't like it."

Granted the Church should be more democratic and more respectful of the rights of dissent *in dubiis*, in the doubtful things, but please God, let us cling to our unity *in essentiis*, in the essential things that Jesus promised us the Holy Spirit would reveal and, in revealing, protect our Church from all error.

As to what is *essentiis* and what is *dubiis*, there may be lively and even hot debate, but if we remember the last part of the aphorism *in omnibus caritas*, in all things love, then, in the words of the song, we can work it out, we can work it out. With the help of God.

2

JIM FOREST

Coming to Know
the Mercy of God

Jim Forest is a peace activist and has served as general secretary of the International Fellowship of Reconciliation since January 1977. Forest has been in prison several times for peace actions. For several years he edited Fellowship *magazine. His friendship with Thomas Merton led him to write* Thomas Merton: A Pictorial Biography *(1980). He has also written* Thomas Merton's Struggle with Peacemaking *(1983) and contributed a chapter to* Merton by Those Who Knew Him Best *(1984). His most recent book is* Love Is the Measure: A Biography of Dorothy Day *(1986). He is contributing editor of* Sojourners *magazine and often writes for* The Other Side, Fellowship, *and other publications.*

At the great turning point in his life, Saint Paul was struck blind on the road to Damascus. What marvelous drama! It is embarrassing for me to confess that the equivalent moment in my own life occurred at the movies. It was in the late summer of 1959. At the time I was seventeen years old, not yet half a year in the U.S. Navy, and was studying meteorology at the Navy Weather School in Lakehurst, New Jersey. The film was *The Nun's Story* (with Audrey Hepburn in the starring role), which I later discovered had been criticized in Catholic publications for its portrayal of loneliness and of the abuse of authority in religious community. In the end, the nun became an ex-nun. The reviewers seemed not to notice that it was one of the rare films in which conscience was at the heart of the story: conscience leading a young woman into the convent and eventually leading her elsewhere, but never away from her faith.

If it had been Hollywood's usual religious movie, on a level with *The Bells of St. Mary's*, I doubt it could have been an instrument of grace in my life. Fortunately it was an honest story, honestly told, with no happy ending; rather, apparent failure. But in that failure remained both integrity and faith. Against the rough surface of the story, I had a haunting glimpse of the Catholic Church, with its complex structures of worship and community. Ritual and prayer had always seemed dead and boring; now I realized they could be alive and astonishing.

After the film I went for a walk, going away from the buildings and sidewalks, needing to be by myself. It was a lovely August evening, the sun long set and the sky filled with stars. During that walk, I was overtaken by joy. Bliss rose up through the grass on the hillside and showered down on me in the starlight. I had never known such uncomplicated and overwhelming happiness as I experienced that night — and have rarely known it since. I felt I was being carried in God's love, floating on it like a cork in the water. I had a sense of being outside time and in a state of utter connectedness. I didn't think very much about the film, except for a few words of Jesus that had been recited to the novices during their first period of formation and that seemed to recite themselves within me as I walked: "If you would be perfect, go, sell what you have, and give it to the poor, and you will have great treasure in heaven, and come, follow me."

I went to sleep that night with the conviction that I must become a Catholic and eager to go to Mass the next morning. I had gone once before in my life, when I was a Boy Scout and our troop (Catholic-sponsored) had to be present at Mass — for me a bizarre experience. But I expected to experience it in a very different way this time.

I did go to Mass in the morning at a church near the naval base, but it was no less bizarre for me than it had been when I was a Boy Scout. I had no idea what was happening. Much of the time the priest had his back to the congregation. Most of the worship was in mumbled, hurried Latin, except for the sermon, which perhaps I would have preferred had it been in Latin. Throughout the Mass, other people in the pews either seemed bored or were concentrating on their rosaries. At least they knew when to stand, when to sit, when to kneel: there was much more of all these things in the pre-Vatican II liturgy. I awkwardly struggled to keep up with them. There seemed no contact between people. Even at the end of Mass, no one said hello. Catholic worship seemed to have all the intimacy of supermarket shopping or being together on a commuter train. On the way out I bought several of the Catholic newspapers and magazines in the back of the church. What impressed me most in these were ads for rosaries that glowed in the dark and garish Mary statues with electric lights inside that could be placed on top of the television.

I had immediate second thoughts about my urge to become a Catholic but not about being a Christian. I remained intent on finding a church where there was engagement and beauty and at least something of what I had imagined I would find in Catholicism. A fellow sailor was a devout Episcopalian, and "High Church" as it turned out. He shared his Book of Common Prayer with me, and in the weeks that followed we occasionally read its beautiful services of morning and evening prayer together. The Episcopal Church presented itself to me as the obvious alternative.

I spent my two-week Christmas leave in an Episcopal monastery that I had heard about through my friend in the navy. It was a joyous experience in which I thought I had found everything I was hoping for in the Catholic Church: liturgy, the sacraments, religious community combining prayer, study, and service. On Christmas Day, one of the monks gave me my first rosary, a precious gift indeed.

Stationed with a navy unit at the Weather Bureau in Washington, D.C., I joined a local Episcopal church in which the Book of Common Prayer, and especially its Service of Holy Communion, little by little became grafted into my life. I was in the church for services several times a week.

That Easter I went for a second visit to the monastery where I had stayed at Christmas. One afternoon while praying in the chapel, I felt as if I were in a river of light. Opening my eyes, I found that indeed I was. Light of a deep golden color was pouring through the lancet window over the Mary altar on the right side of the church, and I was in the center of its narrow path. I closed my eyes and enjoyed being bathed in light. Only after I had finished praying and the light was gone did I realize how mysterious an experience I had had, for it was late in the day, and yet the light had come through a low window set to the east. Searching for some rational explanation, I looked outside the church expecting to find a shiny surface that could have served as a mirror, throwing the late light of the day through that little window. But I found only trees.

Those months were full of grace. Why didn't I remain an Episcopalian? It isn't easy to give an answer. One piece of it was that I had never quite let go of the Catholic Church, despite that first disappointment. In Washington, I often went into Catholic churches to pray. Through the Episcopal Church, I had developed a deep love for the Eucharist, Christ's presence in bread and wine, and was drawn in the doors of any church where the consecrated bread was reserved. I found it easy to pray or simply to sit or kneel in stillness. A hallmark of the Catholic Church was that the Blessed Sacrament awaited anyone who came into any church, and the doors seemed always open.

Another important part of my attraction to Catholicism came through reading. I had happened upon Thomas Merton's autobiography, *The Seven Storey Mountain*, in a bus terminal and read it with the attention my children give to dessert. No less important was the series of Image books that were sold in the back of many Catholic churches. This was a remarkable line of books by Catholic authors. I first read Ronald Knox, G. K. Chesterton, and Dorothy Day in Image editions, as well as some of the classics such as Thomas à Kempis's *The Imitation of Christ*.

My work at the Weather Bureau was going on all the while— agreeable, even fascinating employment that involved use of the first weather satellite and two live television broadcasts a day to the War Room of the Pentagon. There were also grim reminders of what the future might hold; one of our jobs was to do fallout predictions for nuclear explosions. It was work with long and odd hours, but allowed much free time—we had seventeen days off each month. Much of that personal time I spent helping at a home for emotionally disturbed children sponsored by the Episcopal Church; my main project was setting up a carpentry shop in one of the basements where the main product manufactured was little four-wheel push-carts that were made to look fit for the Indianapolis 500.

Among the institution's salaried staff, there was a Catholic who had only recently left the seminary after six years of preparation for the priesthood. We often got together for a few glasses of beer at the end of the day and inevitably ended up talking about theology. Though he had decided not to be ordained a priest (actually a decision against celibacy), he had left the seminary with his love of Catholicism intact. (I realized only in writing this that he had a lot in common with the Belgian woman whose autobiography had been dramatized in *The Nun's Story*.) I had not experienced such a lively passion for one's faith among the Episcopalians I had met, even in the monastery. He helped me to see something beautiful, even adventurous in Catholicism despite the drabness and ordinariness when compared with the Episcopal Church that I had come to know.

When someone was needed to take the Catholic children in the institution to Sunday Mass, I offered to accompany them. The nearest Catholic parish, it turned out, was a particularly vital one: Blessed Sacrament, on the northwest edge of the city. Here the congregation took a very active part in the liturgy, singing the Latin responses. The sermons were intellectually lively. After Mass people stopped and talked.

But the most remarkable blessing of that parish was the fact that it had a first-class library. It was open after Mass and I never failed to browse. I borrowed often and heavily. It was there that I started reading *The Catholic Worker*, Dorothy Day's eight-page tabloid that I later helped edit but initially regarded with cautious fascination.

Mainly I was reading books. The Catholic writers that I discovered that summer, whether in that library or in Image books bought elsewhere, were at least as interesting to me as any of the mountains or canyons I had so joyously explored earlier in my life. Catholic writers impressed me for their clarity of thought, their surprising definitions of key words (I have been a reader of dictionaries and etymologies ever since), and their insistence not only in their words but in the spirit of their writing that faith is *the* great adventure and that it ignites the whole of life. I avidly copied down a quotation from Chesterton (perhaps from *Orthodoxy* or his book on Saint Francis of Assisi): "Christianity has not been tried and found wanting. It has been found difficult and left untried. Even watered down, Christianity is still hot enough to boil the modern world to rags."

·Perhaps the single most important book I found in the Blessed Sacrament library (though I felt found by the book, as if it had flown from its spot on the shelf into my hand) was Eric Gill's *Autobiography*. Gill was a man on fire, whose stone carvings and wood engravings brought together the modern and the Romanesque, who communicated in word and even more in his craft an amorous, joyous, spiritually charged sensuality that I hadn't imagined was possible within Christianity. His work provided me with the first clue that not only was Jesus the Incarnation but that the spiritual life is incarnational—lived not outside the flesh but in the flesh. If God had wanted us to be fleshless creatures like the angels, we would have been made angels. Through Gill's work I began to realize that we are blessed in being both flesh *and* spirit and needn't suffer angel envy. It was a motto of Gill that "it all goes together." Everything is connected: body and soul, ourselves and our enemies, life and death, prayer and action, the visible and the invisible, the distant past and this very moment, the ordinary and the extraordinary, the way we live now and the way we live forever. There was something else remarkable about Gill. He was one of the rare Christians of his day, Catholic or otherwise, to argue that modern war could not possibly be reconciled with a life shaped by the Gospels—a disquieting opinion for a reader in military uniform.

What was most exciting in my religious reading and even in much of my religious experience was coming from Catholic sources. And yet I had already put down some roots in the Episcopal Church. Much that kept drawing me toward Catholicism existed in the Episcopal Church as well, if not in every parish at least in many parishes. I was living with an Episcopal family who had close ties with the magnificent Washington National Cathedral, a place I wandered in freely and often, day and night. I cherished the Book of Common Prayer and had learned to sing the monastic offices in English plain chant. (In recent years I have returned to frequent use of the Book of Common Prayer, and I never stopped singing the English plain chant, even if mainly in the shower.)

Perhaps if it hadn't been for a particularly unhappy experience at the Episcopal monastery I occasionally visited, I would now be writing a chapter for a book on why I am an Episcopalian. At very least, I would have found my way to Catholicism more slowly. Visiting the monastery again, one of the monks asked to see me in the visiting room after the liturgy one Sunday morning. Once in the visiting room, he pulled me into a closet and embraced me. I pulled myself free and left in great confusion. At the time I said nothing about it to anyone in the community. But once back in Washington, I decided to write to the prior of the community, hoping that something could be done to help the particular monk or at least to make it unlikely that other guests would have similar experiences. In his reply, the prior did not point out to me that monks, like everyone else on earth, suffer loneliness and sexual longing of one sort or another, and sometimes don't manage it very well. What he did say was that homosexuality is often an indication of a monastic vocation. As my own sexual orientation was of the more common variety, I wondered if the prior meant I wasn't the right sort of person to be visiting monasteries, at least this monastery. Certainly, after that letter, I had no desire to return.

There may be readers of this text who have memories of comparable events occurring in Catholic monasteries or convents, or who have read letters from those in positions of Catholic religious leadership that were similarly unresponsive and evasive. Tales of woe are not hard to find in the Catholic Church. Among other things, there are quite a lot of desperately lonely Catholics, by no means only laity. But at the time I was quite young, had little experience in any church, and was experiencing a steady tug toward Catholicism anyway. Little was needed for me to take a new step toward actual membership in the Catholic Church.

How well I remember putting down one of those Image paperbacks (an anthology of Chesterton's essays and poems) one sunny Saturday morning in the summer of 1960 and walking from the house where I roomed near the National Cathedral to the rectory adjacent to a church where I often stopped to pray, the Church of Saint Thomas Apostle on Connecticut Avenue. When I rang the doorbell my knees were shaking and my teeth were almost chattering from the tension I felt. Why was it such a drama? Perhaps it was anxiety about what my parents would think, what others would think. Perhaps I sensed I was taking a big step into the unknown and that my future would be very different and much less secure. Perhaps I was rehearing all the criticism and hatred of the Catholic Church that I had encountered from time to time. (I had an uncle who, when I was about ten, had given me a booklet about the Spanish Inquisition, vividly illustrated with prints of sadistic Dominicans torturing young men and women. The family I was staying with, noticing how many Catholic books I was reading, had told me about tunnels connecting convents and rectories and aborted babies buried in clerical cellars; they spoke with the conviction of people who had been in the tunnels themselves and had dug up the little bones.)

The rectory housekeeper, a no-nonsense woman with a feather duster in one hand, opened the door. I stammered, "I would like to talk to a priest about becoming a Catholic." She nodded her head as if that was a sensible thing to do and showed me into a sitting room where a photograph of the recently elected pope, John XXIII, dominated the wall in front of me. After a little while a priest came in, Father Thomas Duffy, and we had the first of many conversations.

Once I had knocked on the rectory door, I don't think I knew a moment of doubt about the fact that I would become a Catholic, though in the study of the Church and its teaching that Father Duffy led me through during our weekly meetings, I sometimes found my questions and objections were not swept aside by my desire to be a Catholic. I was deeply troubled with the doctrine that unbaptized infants would not be in heaven but rather in a region of eternity outside of both heaven and hell called limbo. I was still more disturbed at what was implied by such teaching: that heaven would only be for those with the right ecclesiastical membership and the correct theology. Such doctrines made God into a grader of tests and a border guard—not the God I was experiencing, mercy within mercy within mercy. I was dismayed with Catholic attitudes toward non-Catholics just as much as I had been put off by anti-Catholicism among Protestants. Fortunately such attitudes were totally foreign to Father Duffy.

Struggling with all my objections, I can remember thinking: I will do my best to understand, but if I can't understand, even if I cannot at certain points agree, I will simply go forward in faith. And I did.

In fact most that I found in the catechism, far from being an obstacle, inspired assent, as had all that Catholic reading that had preceded my arrival at the rectory door.

The most potent force in my conversion, however, was the delight and gratitude that was flooding my life. The catechism was part of that general happiness. (There were events at the time that, had that happiness not been so huge, would have been quite depressing. For example I was ordered out of the house where I had enjoyably been living, for my hosts could not bear to have a Catholic under their roof. I moved back into the navy barracks and gave the rejection little thought.) During that year of conversion, I had come to love being in churches. I was especially happy in Catholic churches, felt particularly alive in them, and was no longer arguing with my happiness. (A year later, when I was part of the Catholic Worker community in New York City, I saw a text of Leon Bloy written on the office wall, "Joy is the most infallible sign of the presence of God," and found that said perfectly what I had experienced in being drawn into Catholicism.)

On November 26, 1960, after Father Duffy heard my confession, I was baptized. It was a very quiet event attended only by a few friends. My beer-drinking Catholic friend from the Episcopal Home for Emotionally Disturbed Children had now become my godfather. I remember the water being poured on my head and the tears running down my cheeks: tears of rapture and unspeakable gratitude.

"Would you do it again?" a student asked me more than a decade later when I was teaching a theology class at a college. She had been born and raised a Catholic, felt estranged from the Church, and could not imagine anyone actually joining it.

Yes, I said. Yes, and yet again, yes. But I assured her it had not been easy for me. In the years since coming into the Church, I had several times tried to give it up, generally because of brokenness and failure in my own life, or disappointment and anger with various people in the hierarchy, or some mixture of both. But I found it was impossible to get along without the Eucharist. I became homesick for Mass and never could manage more than a few weeks without it. But in those hungry weeks I managed to become a bit more compassionate about both bishops and even myself (or myself and even bishops), and hopeful that God hadn't given up on any of us. I also learned, crisis by crisis, that I could no more renounce the Catholic Church than abandon my parents.

I find myself lucky to have come to faith during one of the great ages of reformation in Christianity. Perhaps this has been especially true for the Catholic Church. The changes in form and structure are astonishing, but still more astonishing are the changes in spirit and theological stress—less dogmatic, more pastoral. There is a more compassionate climate, more emphasis on forgiveness and reconciliation, more stress on love and service, recognition not only of private sin but public sin, the evils we do in defense of wealth or in the grip of collective fear and hatred. Most of all, it has become a Church much more emphatic about what Jesus said is the final measure of His judgment: "I was hungry and you fed me. . . . What you did for the least person, you did for me." To have been witness to such change occurring in what was a magnificent but quite petrified religious body makes it possible to hope for even greater miracles of conversion. Increasingly we Catholics have come to know the mercy of God and to let that mercy pass through us into the world.

3

JUDY VALENTINE GERTH

The Persistence of the Paraclete

Judy Valentine Gerth graduated from Michigan State University in 1959 with a B.A. in communication arts. She has been deeply involved in community service as well as professional life, which currently finds her as executive director of Catholic Church Extension Society in Chicago.

Right around the corner. That's where the Baptist church stood. There were no streets to cross so my parents knew their six-year-old daughter would be safe walking alone to the neighborhood's closest house of worship. My parents did not attend church on a regular basis, although my father considered himself a Unitarian and my mother was raised a Christian Scientist. The nearby church seemed a convenient way to round out the religious upbringing of their only child.

By quiet example my parents provided excellent Christian grounding for my young faith. Their words and actions gave true meaning to "loving neighbor as self." Never did I hear a disparaging word spoken about another person — no expressions of prejudice or criticisms of others made in my presence. I grew up wonderfully naive, totally unaware that some people made judgments based on race or religion.

Their tolerance, however, weakened when it came to the intolerance of others. When I repeated my Sunday school teacher's warning that they would go to hell for drinking and smoking, my Baptist church attendance abruptly ended.

Turning to the faith of my mother, my parents enrolled me in the Christian Science Sunday school, which remained my religious touchstone until I was twenty.

Other than memorizing the books of the Bible at the Baptist church, I really had no substantial religious education. I had no understanding of the context of the Old and New Testaments — no idea of what Christianity was and no sense of just who Jesus was. Ten years in the Christian Science Sunday school did little to help me. Our readings in Scripture were accompanied by abstract interpretations that had no practical relationship to daily living. The only message that was clearly communicated to me was that we have the mental power to physically heal ourselves. Jesus was not divine, but the perfect example of how man, through faith in God and our having been made in His image and likeness, could overcome sin and sickness: "Man is not material, he is spiritual."

In retrospect, what seems to be most significant during those early years was my faithful attendance at Sunday school. I had no friends there or sense of community. When my parents did not drive me, it took two buses and more than an hour to get there all by myself on those Sunday mornings.

A still, small voice seemed to nudge me along.

After graduation from high school, my spiritual pilgrimage began in earnest. Happily, college did what it was supposed to do, exposing me to new ideas. It made me think, and gave me an understanding of history. Classes in humanities and philosophy revealed the past and the possibilities of the future. It was a glorious time for learning. I was the tabula rasa; that blank tablet spoken of by philosophers, open to new facts and ideas, which I explored for the first time.

One reading assignment was Saint Augustine's *City of God*. I was particularly struck by his comment that the happiness we experience here on earth is no comparison to that which God has in store for us in heaven. What hope that passage gave me! I took it all in with wide-eyed enthusiasm.

Spiritually awakened by many of these courses, I decided to take a class in comparative religion. It became my first brush with Catholicism, and I became aware gradually that there were "Catholics" out there. This brief introduction gave me a sense of the scope of this universal religion and provided a glimpse of its long and eventful history. I found it all very intriguing. I was impressed by its beliefs, size, and authority.

Even though Catholicism was so foreign to my upbringing, it held a compelling fascination for me. What was it that prompted me to pursue my study of the Catholic faith in spite of my radically different background?

As my sophomore year ended, I entered the most pivotal part of my journey. My job that summer brought me under the wing of a recent convert who handed me a copy of *Father Smith Instructs Jackson*.

I have to chuckle when I look back at that old-fashioned catechism book. Not even the updated version is in favor with current religious educators. At the time, however, its basic, straightforward question-and-answer format was, quite literally, a godsend. This simple book presented the Catholic faith clearly and logically, integrating everything I was learning and questioning. For years I had coasted, spiritually, suspended by faith but not firm belief. Now, all those nudgings of faith were gaining a solid foundation.

As I recall reading that book, I now recognize something I did not realize then. The primary issues were not the questions I asked or even the answers I received. The most important part of my pilgrimage was the underlying motivation of my search. It was something that had gently covered and encouraged me in my spiritual struggles. It was the loving embrace of the Holy Spirit.

Back then I had no idea, beyond a written definition, of who or what the Holy Spirit was. I was just learning about the Trinity. God the Father had always been my refuge for prayer. Of course I remembered Jesus from my Baptist Sunday school days. But the Holy Spirit? It was something mystical, incomprehensible, and far removed from my personal experience — or so I thought.

Almost imperceptibly, however, various instruments of the Spirit converged upon me, continuing to guide, direct, and nudge me on my journey.

A priest I met by chance one weekend handed me a copy of *The Road to Damascus*. This small paperback contained the inspiring stories of fifteen Catholic converts. Many passages from those narratives touched me deeply. I felt a kinship with the writers in their search and ultimate discovery of faith. Gretta Palmer's conversion story was especially meaningful. I retyped it and carried it in my wallet for years. "A conversion," she wrote,

is like trying to open an old, heavy door that has been closed for many years. Dust and grime have glued its edges fast, and the oil in the hinges has long since dried away. The first heave doesn't budge it, nor the second. Sometimes it is so tightly sealed that we are tempted to say, "There isn't really a door here at all. It is just a pattern on the solid wall that looks like a door." And then we may stop pushing and relapse into despair. But something still assures us that there is a door and that it is worth while battering at it with our raw knuckles and straining with our tired shoulders in the hope that it will finally give way. When it does yield, we do not notice how or remember the

> sensation of the final shove. For by then we are staggering out,
> our half-blind eyes still blinking in the unfamiliar sunshine.*

During that summer when I was reading *Father Smith* the woman who had given me the book would often give up her lunch hour to spend time with me in the chapel of a nearby Catholic church. The experience of kneeling and praying in church was new to me. The chapel was old, dark, and musty and there were numerous statues and candles. Just being there was comforting. I focused my thoughts and carefully repeated newly learned prayers and devotions like the Hail Mary and the Stations of the Cross. I soaked up Catholicism in that quiet chapel.

When I returned to college in the fall, a Catholic friend regularly accompanied me to early-morning Mass on campus. Knowing she could have used the extra sleep, I was impressed by her devotion to her friend and her faith. Even though I could not participate fully in the Mass, I still felt at home. I was amazed that so many other students got up so early to attend daily Mass. I had to believe something was going on for them, too.

Then came a doubtful, dry period. Nothing appeared to be falling into place. I felt I was making no progress in my spiritual life. I examined Eastern religions, Judaism, and, disheartened, even considered agnosticism. The enthusiasm I felt the year before seemed to have evaporated. I was confused because I thought I should feel more definite, more convinced that Catholicism was "the answer." Without the assurance, I lapsed into spiritual apathy. A persistence within me, however, would not go away.

I tried again. I took the catechism course for the second time, and although the priest pronounced me ready, I remained hesitant, a state of indecision that continued for weeks. I felt spiritually stuck—I simply could not move. But I did not forget to pray.

One day as I knelt at the altar the following words came to me: what are you waiting for? Go ahead. I stood up and felt the doubt slip away. I was ready.

I was baptized at Saint John's Catholic Church in East Lansing, Michigan, on April 25, 1959.

I wish I could say my faith life was changed at that moment. I wish I could say that my First Communion and confirmation had the spiritual highs I expected them to have, but it wasn't so. My conversion was not the end of my pilgrimage. It was only the beginning.

---

*Gretta Palmer, "Escaping from an Atheist's Cell," in *The Road to Damascus*, ed. John A. O'Brien (New York: Image Books/Doubleday, 1955).

In this pre–Vatican II Church I was caught up in the ceremony of the Mass, the Latin prayers, and a still alien feeling of being part of the Catholic culture. In fact, I had taken on the externals of the Church but had not matured in a true understanding of the meaning behind them and in the true mission of God's Church. The same quiet, persistent nudgings I had felt from childhood kept me going through the motions.

The years after my baptism were filled with a preoccupation with my profession and then marriage and the birth of five children within six years. The emotional intensity of my conversion had somehow evaporated into perfunctory Catholic obligations. The stresses of raising a large family and assisting my husband through law school and a subsequent new career were my primary and immediate concerns.

Occasionally I would long for the spiritual feelings of the past. I wrote a poem to myself that probably only a mother of small children could understand:

> *My mind strains with the burden of time*
> *Thoughts stand waiting their turn*
> *Just the living of life claims me now*
> *Identity I cannot discern.*
> *Ideas pass unrecognized*
> *Modest talents remain untried*
> *Who has time for the spiritual life*
> *When the body is occupied.*

On our eleventh wedding anniversary my husband and I attended a Marriage Encounter. At the time, the inducement for me was a vacation from the children. The weekend was presented by a priest and three couples who related personal stories about their own lives, their marriages, and their faith. Personal reflection and private couple dialogue led us from questions of basic self-examination to more profound considerations, questions of life, death, and faith. And it was all done in a loving, spiritual atmosphere.

For the first time in years I felt my soul being touched. And for the first time both my husband and I were able to share in the same loving and enveloping spirit of our faith. We left the weekend enriched in more than our marriage.

A year later we decided to become one of the presenting couples for Marriage Encounter. The training weekend to prepare for this responsibility became yet another turning point. This weekend, too, was a wonderful shot in the arm for our marriage. But it was the

Mass at the end of the weekend that was most significant. As we all stood in a circle around the altar, each holding a candle, I looked up from my prayer and was overwhelmed with what my spirit saw. Moving from one person to the next, I sensed the Holy Spirit washing over each of us with an intense feeling of love I had never before experienced. I was awed as I felt it passing from person to person around the circle. That moment has become one of my most precious and inspirational memories.

Because my life-style was not one of quiet reflection but rather of constant activity, it took a structured event like a retreat to jar me to the next step in my pilgrimage. It was just such an event that brought Scripture into my life.

The occasion was one more Marriage Encounter–related weekend. Called "Retorno," this weekend focused on the scriptural dimension of our personal and married lives. We were each handed our own Bible and given a private room for reading and contemplation. What tremendous release and revelation I found that weekend! Passages in the Bible seemed to spring out at me. I underlined the verses and made notes and stars next to the passages that were the most meaningful, most of which were about the Holy Spirit. One verse seemed to guide all the rest: "the Paraclete, the Holy Spirit whom the Father will send in my name, will *instruct* you in everything, and *remind* you of all that I told you" (John 14:25, NAB, emphasis mine). That is exactly what has been happening, I marveled. The Holy Spirit has been behind me. Instructing. Reminding.

Something else happened that weekend.

God, the Father, had always been a "friend." Someone I could talk to. Someone who cared about me. I found it puzzling when other people expressed a feeling of distance from the Father. Instead, their relationship was through His Son, their brother. I envied them their closeness to Jesus. It just wasn't there for me.

During my prayers one evening, I envisioned God slowly coming toward me with someone in tow. Coming close, He put His arm around me and said, "I want to introduce you to someone very special. This is Jesus, my Son." I felt overwhelmed with His love at that moment.

That was nearly ten years ago. In the years since then my faith seemed to be slowly turned outward toward others. Gradually I was coming to realize the meaning of one very basic and simple message of the Gospel: "God is love, and he who abides in love abides in God, and God in him" (1 John 4:16, NAB). The extension of that message, then, was the "greatest" commandment: Love God and love neighbor as self—the message lived out so beautifully by my parents.

In 1979 my work in media and marketing dovetailed with a Catholic religious education video project for the Catholic Television Network of Chicago (CTN/C). Then, when CTN/C decided to produce a national Catholic television series, I was asked to promote and manage its distribution. The series featured a Jesuit priest, Father John Powell, a well-known speaker and author of many best-selling Christian books. His presentation of faith and personal stories of Christian challenge were as meaningful for me as they were for his millions of readers. He possessed the special knack of capturing the essence of an idea and then communicating it in such a way that you were able to make it your own.

One of his key messages was that in all of life's situations a person of faith should ask: "What is the loving thing to do?" This, for me, is the essence of the gospel message and our mandate to love one another. Putting this into practice, however, is something else. Compromise, anger, frustration, and pride continually threaten to overwhelm me. Many times I forget to just stop and ask myself that simple but critically important question.

But spiritual vigilance seems destined to be my never-ending occupation. Whenever I let up, or take my faith for granted, I am assured of another slip into complacency. For all the beautiful faith experiences I have had, I find it incredible that periodically I am still confronted with spiritually empty feelings. Somehow I feel I should be past all of that.

Finding myself in that state of mind several years ago I attended yet another retreat. This one was sponsored by our parish and consisted of presentations by other women in the parish and then questions for sharing in small groups. By this time I had tired of group retreats. Instead I longed to go off privately somewhere to be alone. I thought I could only be filled by God's Spirit in quiet contemplation. I felt I had heard enough of other people's spiritual problems. I found myself telling God exactly what I needed and how it should be delivered. I was like the man who stubbornly sat in front of the cold potbellied stove and demanded, "First give me some heat and then I will give you some wood." Give me the consolation I am looking for and then I will feel more like praying.

During the retreat we had an opportunity to participate privately in the sacrament of reconciliation, my first "face-to-face" confession experience. I had always preferred the confessional boxes and the anonymity of a large downtown church.

What I had expected to be routine became another powerful experience. The power was not in my conversation with the priest, which was pleasant enough. But rather, as I bowed my head to pray and receive the priest's blessing and absolution, I felt a very powerful, deep sense of God's love surrounding me.

I sat quietly in my room in reflection and I began to understand that perhaps I had to stop trying to look for and define faith in my own terms. I pictured myself holding up a small box to God, saying, "Here, this is what my faith looks like. Please pour yourself into it." Instead, I needed to lay aside my little prescribed prayer box, open my arms in total surrender, and pray, "Here I am, Lord."

Over the last few years I have found my life slowly wending more closely to the Catholic Church in a formal way. My responsibilities at CTN/C enabled me to establish contacts in diocesan offices all over the country and brought me in touch with many Catholic organizations. One of these was the Catholic Church Extension Society. Founded in 1905, Extension is a national fund-raising organization that supports the "home missions," those areas of the United States that are too poor or too remote to sustain a Catholic presence. After two years as a consultant, Extension asked me to assume the newly created position of executive director.

My work at Extension enables me to see firsthand how important the faith is to thousands of American Catholics. Their prayers and financial support help bring the healing presence of their Catholic faith to this country's poor, isolated, and lonely. It has been wonderfully inspirational for me to learn and actually be a part of home missions.

My work, therefore, has placed me squarely into the lap of the Church. I feel, with great enthusiasm, that I have been given the opportunity to help make a difference in supporting and extending the Catholic faith. I could never have conceived the scenario that led me from that small Baptist church around the corner to the bosom of the Catholic Church in America.

And where has my pilgrimage taken me today?

My constant prayer is that I can be a worthy instrument of the Holy Spirit. To discern the loving thing to do is both a challenge and opportunity every day of my life. I know I must keep growing in my understanding of my Catholic faith. I need to appreciate more fully the many blessings it has been and the comfort it continues to be.

But, admittedly, I sometimes still feel unsteady. Life's problems continue. At times I feel uncertain and doubtful. Has my conversion really made a difference? How would things be different if I were not a Catholic?

When my mind explores such questions, that persistent Spirit of love and faith explodes within me, saying simply, Yes, you were ready and it was right. You are loved. You are mine. Peace.

4

JAMES J. THOMPSON, JR.

A Wink of Heaven

James J. Thompson, Jr., holds a Ph.D. in American history from the University of Virginia. He has written three books: Tried as by Fire: Southern Baptists and the Religious Controversies of the 1920s *(1982),* Christian Classics Revisited *(1983), and* Fleeing the Whore of Babylon: A Modern Conversion Story *(Westminster, Md.: Christian Classics, 1986), from which the following testimony is excerpted with permission. He has published articles and reviews in the* New Oxford Review, Chronicles of Culture, *the* University Bookman, *the* Mississippi Quarterly, *the* Southern Humanities Review, *the* World Quarterly, *the* Southern Humanities Review, The World and I, *and other journals and magazines. He is at present the book review editor of the* New Oxford Review.

> *I have had a tremor of bliss, a wink of heaven,*
> *a whisper,*
> *And I would no longer be denied; all things*
> *Proceed to a joyful consummation.*
>
> T. S. *Eliot,* Murder in the Cathedral

On a Thursday morning in mid-September 1975 I knocked at the door of the rectory of Saint Bede's parish in Williamsburg, Virginia. When a priest appeared I said, "Father, I want to become a Catholic." If the choirs of angels burst into rejoicing at that moment I did not notice, for I felt more apprehensive than joyful. I knew what this decision would cost: shock from kinfolk, incomprehension from friends, alienation from the culture that had bred me, and clucks of pity from colleagues at the College of William and Mary. I knew something else as well: there was no turning back—I must become a Catholic.

Three weeks short of my thirty-first birthday I had reached a decision that did not square with my upbringing. No wonder some of my friends viewed my sudden penchant for papistry as an indication of incipient derangement. After all, I had been born into the thoroughly Protestant and energetically anti-Catholic culture of rural Maryland. That I had been raised in the Seventh-Day Adventist denomination made my choice of church all the more perplexing: former Adventists may stray into atheism or take up sheep molesting, but they rarely head for Rome. Unlike Saul of Tarsus, I had no Damascus Road to explain my conversion—no voice from heaven, no darting flash of celestial light. Nor could I claim that I had followed the example of such converts as John Henry Newman or Ronald Knox, Englishmen who poped only after arduous and systematic study eventuated in intellectual certitude. Yet I was ready to enter the Catholic Church (ready at that moment had the priest been willing); if that struck my friends as preposterous I could only reply that it was the most sensible step I had ever taken.

Before answering the question "Why Rome?" I must respond to another: "Why not Takoma Park?" Almost a decade earlier I had repudiated Seventh-Day Adventism, thereby abandoning my appointed role in the cosmic drama that culminates in the triumph of the fundamentalist saints. That I was a graduate student at the University of Virginia when my apostasy occurred explained everything to the Adventists back home in Takoma Park; they sorrowed over the loss of yet another young man of promise who had succumbed to the beguilements of secular learning. Suitable as that explanation was for home consumption, it bore little resemblance to the truth; my disillusionment with Adventism had in fact arisen during my undergraduate years at Columbia Union College, an institution dedicated to the three R's of Religion, Righteousness, and Republicanism (of the Barry Goldwater variety). There, surrounded by Adventist students and taught by Adventist professors on a campus that lay only a mile from the world headquarters of the denomination, I had begun to question the dogmas of my faith.

Oddly enough, the first stirrings of rebellion coincided with my formal reception into the denomination. Like Baptists, Adventists condemn infant baptism as a nonscriptural practice foisted upon Christianity by the Catholic Church. For Adventists, baptism (in this case, total immersion) does not occur until one reaches "the age of accountability," usually somewhere between the ages of ten and thirteen. Although thoroughly indoctrinated in the faith by my grandmother and by the teachers at John Nevins Andrews Elementary School, I had passed through the critical period of emergent accountability without seeking baptism. Why, I cannot say for certain. Perhaps my reluctance arose from the fact that my mother was

not an Adventist, and when we moved to Takoma Park my grandmother's vigorous influence began to carry less force. Then, too, I
bridled at the pressure our schoolteachers exerted upon us as we
approached the brink of accountability. By the time we reached the
sixth grade they had begun to bombard us with appeals to seek
baptism. Twice yearly the school's principal would invite an evangelist to conduct a "Week of Prayer," which would reach a crescendo on
Friday mornings with students marching to the front of the assembly
hall to declare their readiness to take the fateful step. One by one my
fellow juvenile miscreants renounced their lives of sin and succumbed to the overwrought emotionalism that pervaded these sessions. Whether from nascent rationalism or an overdeveloped case of
adolescent obduracy (most likely the latter), I resisted the siren song
and refused to follow my schoolmates into the baptismal tank. I
suspect as well that the prospect of being dunked in a pool of water
while an assembly of Adventists stared at me was repellent; like the
practice of footwashing, public baptism struck me as an embarrassing display of forced intimacy.

Though I refused baptism, I continued to consider myself an
Adventist; I diligently attended weekly services and, moreover, I
believed the church's teachings. It came as a shock, then, when in
my senior year in high school my girl friend, the daughter of a
preacher, informed me that we could never marry because I was not
an Adventist. I stalled, hoping she would relent, but when my hope
of reprieve evaporated I steeled myself for the ordeal. Besides, I
knew that baptism would fulfill my grandmother's urgent desire to
see me assume full fellowship with the church. On November 24,
1962, toward the end of my first semester in college, I descended into
the waters to take what had become by then an anticlimactic step.

Baptism failed to forestall a mounting dissatisfaction with Adventism. I would prefer to remember those first heady days of skepticism
as the product of a high-minded search for truth; the image of the
earnest student combing his books, thrilling to new insights, and
then acting upon his convictions appeals to one's self-esteem. Unfortunately, candor will not permit this; my rebellion stemmed most
directly from a motive so commonplace as to be a cliché: the young
man's ineluctable urge to tweak the orthodoxies of his elders. Armed
with a smattering of learning, a vaunting self-confidence bred of
ignorance and immaturity, and an ill-defined sense of grievance
against authority, I sallied forth to do battle with the established
powers. The sixties were upon us as well and we of the blessed young
were rapidly discovering that everyone beyond the age of thirty was
irredeemably corrupt.

The symptoms of this malady flared up initially in a psychology course I took in the second semester of my freshman year. At the first class meeting the professor announced that we could earn extra credit by sampling (to the tune of one hundred pages a week) the writings of famous psychologists. We could eat freely of all the trees in this bountiful garden save one: with a gravity commensurate to the imminent danger, the professor proscribed the works of Sigmund Freud. I could have cared less about the wicked Viennese doctor, but once warned is twice tempted: I headed immediately for the forbidden fruit. Clutching the Modern Library edition of Freud's *Basic Writings*, I plunged into the abyss, and for an entire semester I wallowed with ids, egos, superegos, complexes, maladjustments, sublimations, and a profusion of delectable neuroses. I emerged from this orgy relatively unscathed. I did not contract satyriasis nor renounce Christianity; I did not even latch onto the catchwords of Freudianism as a means of impressing my less-learned friends. But I had discovered the sweet delight of defying the mossbacked guardians of orthodoxy. What ecstasy to be young and freethinking!

If my fling with Freud left my religion intact, my introduction to Charles Darwin took a more ominous turn. I entered college firmly convinced that all decent people adhered to a literal reading of Genesis and that only reprobates and perverts credited the pernicious theory of evolution. This tidy dichotomy collapsed when I took a course titled Philosophy of Science, taught by a jocular herpetologist who boasted of having survived the bite of virtually every variety of poisonous snake that had fallen into his (perhaps careless) hands. Professor Harris nursed no heretical notions, but he insisted that in pursuit of the truth one must give the devil his due. His devotion to this principle meant that not only did we scrutinize creationism but that we also read *The Origin of Species* in its interminable entirety and listened to the lectures of visiting evolutionists. In search of additional reading I discovered Loren Eiseley's *The Immense Journey*, a lyrical rendering of evolutionary progression written by an anthropologist who possessed the soul of a poet. Encountering the enemy at his most attractive, my enmity began to dwindle; and if I knew too little to call myself an evolutionist, I had learned too much to rest comfortably with the official version of Genesis.

With my critical eye growing ever sharper I began to spy out the fallacies and inconsistencies embedded in the faith of my childhood. I focused on Adventism's weakest point: those moralistic strictures and prohibitions with which it abounds. That drinking should be denounced as a grievous sin struck me as incongruous when one considered that Christ Himself had transformed water into wine at the wedding feast at Cana. ("Grape juice," retorted the orthodox;

"Christ turned the water into grape juice.") Could a puff on a Marlboro or a chaw of Red Man really cost one eternal life? Would the eaters of pork chops go to hell? Would the illegitimacy rate soar if we danced? Would the angels weep if I stepped inside a movie theater? ("Bad people frequent theaters," a preacher once told me.) How I loved to catch the saints in their little hypocrisies! Never, for example, would the pious Adventist matron adorn herself with a necklace, a bracelet, or even a plain gold wedding band, but somehow she and the church saw nothing amiss in a swank diamond brooch displayed on a basic black Sabbath dress. Most Adventists could not intelligently defend their culture-bound proscriptions; when cornered they resorted to two defenses: the Bible says so ("Strong drink is a mocker"—so there!) and the church teaches it. But their Bible was a truncated handbook of legalisms and their church a small sect that had arisen out of the heated fantasies of nineteenth-century millenarians.

When Adventists asserted that "the church teaches it," they really meant that Ellen G. White, the denomination's founder, had issued a dictate on the matter. This lady's omnipresent authority began to oppress me. Her spirit hung like a thick fog over the comings and goings of Adventists. One could sit through an entire sermon and hear scarcely a mention of Jesus Christ, but find Mrs. White quoted repeatedly on everything from toilet training to the Second Coming. Beginning in high school I had read assiduously in her voluminous writings; two of her books— *The Desire of Ages* and *The Great Controversy between Christ and Satan*—were, I had learned, to be ranked only slightly below the Bible, for they completed the revelation contained in the Scriptures and schooled us on how we as Adventists differed from other Christians.

Mrs. White and her writings permeated the instruction at Columbia Union College. Sociology: "What does Mrs. White teach about the ills of modern society?" Psychology: "How does Mrs. White refute the theories of atheistic psychologists?" Phys. ed.: "Mrs. White offers the soundest principles for good health that the world has ever seen." My English teachers shied away from assigning novels because Ellen White had decried their deleterious effects, and my religion courses were often little more than glosses on her writings. Most infuriating to me, because I had chosen history as a major, was the way she intruded upon our study of the past. Whether in courses on European or American history, a religion major ("preministerial" would be more apt, for they were all headed for the Adventist pulpit) would invariably inform the class of what Mrs. White had declared about a given event. God, said Mrs. White, had brewed up a storm to destroy the Spanish Armada, thereby preserving England as a Protestant stronghold. God, said Mrs. White, had intervened in the struggle between France and England in the eighteenth century to ensure a Protestant triumph in North America. God had even taken sides in the American Civil War; prim New Englander that she was, Mrs. White had discerned God's hand in numerous Union victories. Groaning audibly was my only defense against such arrant non-sense—that, and a mounting aversion to the very name "Ellen White."

One of the crucial events in my rejection of Adventism occurred in a course on Christian ethics. In the midst of a discussion one day an irritatingly self-righteous young woman blurted out that it infuriated her to sit in the same Sabbath congregation with flagrant sinners. As she prattled on about her offended sensibilities my rising discontent took a new turn: for the first time I saw clearly the arrogance of the Adventist conception of the Church—this huddling together of a handful of saints who cling to their list of niggling do's and don't's while the rest of humanity gropes blindly toward perdition. Had Christ died only for my smug classmate and those she would deign to sit with on Saturday mornings? Although I possessed too little theology to refute her, I was certain of one thing: I was more comfortable in the company of sinners than in the embrace of self-proclaimed saints.

Despite my dissatisfaction with Seventh-Day Adventism, I was unprepared as yet to leave it, and had I remained in Takoma Park it would have taken many years to make the break; the dictates of that tightly knit society would have been disregarded only with strenuous effort. But I was not to linger in that environment, for in late February 1966 the University of Virginia awarded me a fellowship to study American history. Three months later, accompanied by my bride (the preacher's daughter), I headed for Charlottesville.

With Takoma Park and the threat of censure one hundred miles away I undertook to discard the remnants of my faith. I felt immense relief at ridding myself of a burden, but at times a pang of remorse would stir up memories of the security and certitude of the fellowship I had abandoned. Carol shed her Adventism even more easily than I did; for her, it had always been bound inextricably with the rigid authoritarianism of her father, and without him to enforce belief, her belief vanished. Out of a mixture of habit and residual guilt we continued to attend services at the small church in Charlottesville; other than that we had no contact with Adventists, for the church members left us alone—largely, I suspect, because I attended a university that they regarded (not without justification) as a sinkhole of drunkenness and fornication. Our observance of Adventist mores could not hold out once the doctrinal foundations crumbled. We began to sneak off to movies and to violate the Sabbath by watching television on Friday nights. Occasionally I would return to my studies on Saturday afternoon instead of awaiting sunset to signal the conclusion of the day of rest. Most egregiously, we began to skip church services, at first only sporadically, then with some frequency.

Carol and I dwelled half in the faith and half out until the fall of 1968, when a new pastor took over the pulpit of the Charlottesville church. Had he been one of those crusty, crotchety old preachers molded in the Adventism of an earlier era he would have scolded us for our waywardness and threatened us with expulsion if we failed to mend our ways. This one, however, was a modern and enlightened preacher, so fresh from seminary that his diploma was still unframed. His courses in pastoral psychology had taught him to eschew old-fashioned coerciveness in favor of friendly persuasion. He would, he decided, entice us back into full fellowship by dangling a carrot instead of thrashing us back into the fold with a stick. Playing on Carol's interest in social work, he asked her to assume leadership of the local Dorcas Society, an organization of Adventist women devoted to aiding the poor and sick. Carol accepted, but only reluctantly, for we knew that implicit in the bargain was the understanding that we would resume regular church attendance. A week later the preacher returned with a quid pro quo: because Carol's wedding band offended the women of the church she would have to remove it, if only, he hinted, when she participated in church activities. That settled it: we never returned to church, and at my insistence we demanded that our names be struck from the membership rolls.

I did not fully comprehend the implications of my rejection of Adventism until the spring of 1969, when I received a letter from my former mentor at Columbia Union College, who was now the academic dean at Andrews University, an Adventist institution located in Berrien Springs, Michigan. He informed me that a job had opened up in the university's department of history; he would be passing through Charlottesville in June and he wanted to discuss the position with me. Dr. Joseph Smoot had exercised an immense influence upon my college career. He had inspired me to aim for a Ph.D., had given unsparingly of his attention in fostering my budding intellectualism, and, most important, had furnished me with a model to emulate. Widely read, erudite, blessed with a powerful and probing mind, humorous, compassionate, and deeply committed to the idea that teaching is a vocation and not simply a job, he had become my hero and, I suspect, something of a replacement for the father whose absence I had keenly felt.

Dr. Smoot came to Charlottesville that June. We walked the grounds of the University of Virginia and admired yet again the elegant buildings of classical grace and symmetry; we talked of their architect, Thomas Jefferson, a man whom we both venerated; and we excitedly plied the range of topics that had formed the meat of our conversations in my undergraduate days. Finally the purpose of his visit, which I had been skirting, could be avoided no longer. Did I want the job? Never have I found it more difficult to admit to an Adventist that I had left the faith. A deep sadness entered Dr. Smoot's eyes: "I feared that, Jim; I feared that we could not hold you." There was nothing more to say: he was an Adventist, I was not, and not even the affection we felt for one another could heal the rift that had opened between us.

With Dr. Smoot's departure my last tenuous ties with the church were cut, and I relegated religion to the outer edges of my life. Yet I never ceased to believe in God's existence, nor did I disavow the Incarnation, redemptive death, and bodily Resurrection of Jesus Christ. In this sense, I suffered no crisis of faith; the blandishments of atheism and agnosticism failed to sway me. If asked my religious affiliation in those days I would reply, "unchurched Christian," a term whose ring of fearless independence pleased my fancy. I was fooling myself, though; in reality, my soul shriveled. Save for an occasional wedding, I avoided churches. I stopped praying as well— gladly, I might add, for I had been a fumbler at what the country folk of my childhood had called "talking to Jesus." My Bible lay unread and unopened, certainly not rejected, but certainly ignored. Calling myself a Christian, I drifted into a secular view of myself and the world; God still existed, but I effectively told Him to mind His own business. Who needed God? I had a wife who loved me, a Ph.D., and, as of September 1971, a job at the College of William and Mary. A future of success and happiness lay waiting for me to grasp it.

To those who knew me in those first euphoric days at William and Mary I must have appeared one of the blest; outwardly I had every-thing, or, at least, if I lacked anything it would surely come in time. I flourished in the classroom, winning student approbation with a combination of ebullience, hard work, youthfulness (the students, barely younger than I, welcomed me as an ally in the war against stodginess and mental decrepitude), a quick wit, and an intuitive grasp of what it takes to entertain an audience of adolescents. I had found my vocation and I assumed that it would reward me with continuing pleasure. But it didn't: by the middle of my second year at William and Mary the delight had vanished and an inexplicable sadness had replaced it. No one guessed my secret; I told no one—could have told no one even had I wanted to. How could I explain my sadness when my sadness had no name?

There was one name I might have given it: a disintegrating marriage. Carol and I had met when we were sophomores in high school and, in the parlance of those antique days, we had started going steady at the age of fifteen. We capped our long and tempestuous courtship—one rife with betrayals, fights, breakups, and reconciliations—with a union destined for disaster in the opinion of more than one observer. I neglected her from the start as I immersed myself in a world of books and ideas, which she—a practical and unbookish woman—had no desire to enter; in return, she vested her time and energy in her thriving career as a social worker. We drifted apart, and though we continued to profess our devotion to one another, we both increasingly realized (but refused to acknowledge openly) that beyond some vague and immature idea of love we had no grounds for a lasting marriage—no shared interests, no children (and no plans for any), no mutual joy in each other's company, no comfort in the other's presence. The move to Williamsburg only exacerbated matters. We shared a house like antagonists caught in unwelcome propinquity, stepping gingerly around one another lest a fragile peace flare into savage warfare. At times this game of mutual self-delusion would fail and our frustrations and meticulously refined grievances would plunge us into bouts of lacerating recrimination.

With both marriage and career on the skids, I looked for solace and found it in alcohol. I had never been a serious or even regular drinker. In high school I had sampled only sparingly the dubious exaltations of teen-age inebriation—that state of ecstasy induced by three beers and followed by a two-day hangover. Seventh-Day Adventism proscribes all alcohol, and though sneaking a beer in defiance of such intransigence had been exhilarating, it had been hardly worth the trouble or risk. In graduate school, largely out of deference to Carol's inbred hostility to drinking, I had teetotaled—to the utter amazement of my fellow students. As if to confirm Father Ronald Knox's quip that the Catholic loses his morals first and belief last, while the Protestant reverses this order, Carol relinquished her faith but refused to compromise her opposition to alcohol. As our marriage disintegrated I ceased to care what she thought. Late afternoons would find me in a bar, washing away the dissatisfaction with teaching and anesthetizing myself for the evening's combat. My drinking goaded Carol to new outbursts of rage, and her fury in turn reinforced my conviction that only by dulling my senses could I continue to live with her.

I hit bottom on a Friday in October 1974. As yet another week of teaching, drinking, and marital discord drew to a close I headed to my favorite hideout, a dank and noisome bar called the Cave. I drank far past my usual time to leave, but the alcohol only deepened my gloom. Late in the evening I left for home, but I never reached there that night; once in the car I kept driving, heading for nothing, escaping nothing, but propelled onward by a restless urge to keep moving. I remember only fleeting and blurred images of that long night: losing my way in a maze of highways in Arlington; drinking coffee and listening to lugubrious country songs at 4:00 A.M. in an all-night diner in Warrenton; buying a six-pack of beer at a market in Charlottesville; stopping by the side of the road to watch the sun rise over Monticello; and finally returning to Williamsburg, admitting that I could not flee the sadness because wherever I went I carried it with me.

I made two decisions in that night of aimless wandering and on Monday morning I acted on both of them: I submitted my resignation to the dean of the faculty and I called a psychiatrist for an appointment. Although my resignation would not be effective until the end of the academic year in June, I was relieved that I would soon be free of a profession that had bitterly disappointed me. I was less pleased with my second decision; I did not relish the idea of subjecting myself to the ministrations of psychiatry, whose practitioners I ranked slightly below snake oil salesmen in the hierarchy of humanity's benefactors. But I needed help and since alcohol had failed I decided to give psychiatry a chance to ply its magic.

I found no magic, but I did discover in Dr. Ann Stewart a psychiatrist of insight and wisdom. Though semiretired and reluctant to accept new patients, she agreed to take me on, her affinity for dilapidated college professors (she had over the years salvaged the psyches of more than one of my colleagues) persuading her that I was worth the effort. She promised no miracles; all I could hope for was mitigation of the misery that plagued my days and nights. After several months of weekly sessions with Dr. Stewart I reached a conclusion I had desperately sought to avoid: peace of mind would be purchased only at the cost of my marriage. In mid-April 1975 Carol and I parted, convinced at last that our shattered marriage was beyond repair. There were tears on both sides; it was not easy to accept that our love had ended in sorrow and separation.

To my surprise the pain of loss subsided quickly; in its place came, at first, relief, and then — greatest surprise of all — serenity. I rented a two-room furnished apartment four blocks from my office and set about restoring some semblance of order to my life. With the encouragement of the dean of the faculty I withdrew my resignation, for I suspected that my discontent with work had come not from teaching itself but from the general disarray of my life. Had I solved my problems? Had I at last banished the sadness?

This mood of hopefulness was lovely while it lasted, but it could not hold reality at bay for long. By early June the examinations had all been graded, the students had departed, and the professors had scattered for vacation and research; I was at loose ends, left to the mercy of the hordes of tourists who descend upon Williamsburg with the first sign of summer. The loneliness I had dreaded now seeped into my days; it became a palpable presence, there in the morning when I awoke, there at night when I drifted off to an uneasy sleep. The loneliness brought the full shock of what had happened: I had lost the woman whom I had loved for half my life. She might as well have been dead, for I knew that she was gone forever: the emotional wounds we had inflicted upon each other, especially in that last appalling year of our marriage, precluded reconciliation.

I spent much of that summer stumbling through a fog of drunkenness, longing for death but clinging to life, shrinking from suicide but afraid to live. Often at 2:00 or 3:00 A.M. — after a night of solitary drinking — I would head in my Fiat for the deserted serpentine roads in the countryside around Williamsburg where I would push the car toward the razor's edge where a split second's mistake leads to twisted wreckage. Back home I would wash down a handful of Valium with a can of beer and in drugged sleep seek an obliviousness from which I hoped never to return.

Catholicism saved my life. Graham Greene facilitated the rescue. A friend loaned me a copy of *The Power and the Glory* and I entered Greene's bleak and chaotic world of sin and redemption. The book seized me with a violence that shook my determination to surrender to hopelessness; I read it hungrily and then I read it again. I followed this with *The Heart of the Matter, The End of the Affair*, and *A Burnt-Out Case*. In Greene's bedraggled and Christ-haunted characters I discerned a reflection of my own anguish, and as I pondered the meaning of their lives I understood fully for the first time — understood in heart as well as in mind — the meaning of that brutal execution on Calvary nearly two thousand years ago: Jesus Christ had died for even the most forlorn of sinners. The Protestantism of my youth had implied that only the godly deserved to be numbered as Christians; Catholicism, by contrast (at least as filtered through Greene's sensibility), provided a hospital for ailing souls. As Christ said, "They that be whole need not a physician, but they that are sick."

Though encouraged by Greene's rendering of Catholicism, I resisted the idea of joining the Church; I had carried away from Adventism a distaste for organized Christianity and I had no intention of leaping from the Adventist frying pan into the Catholic fire. Curiosity, however, prompted me to slip into Saint Bede's one Sunday morning to observe a Mass. I was ill prepared for what greeted me; expecting something along the lines of a small-scale Saint Patrick's Cathedral or Shrine of the Immaculate Conception (my idea of typical Catholic churches), I found instead a sanctuary of shocking simplicity. To my untrained eye, only the presence of a statue or two and a canopy over the altar betrayed the church's identity; there were no stained-glass windows, no votive candles, no holy water stoup, no confessionals—none of that creepy-mysterious atmosphere that had both repelled and allured me on previous excursions into Catholic churches. The Mass was disappointing; not for Saint Bede's any of the smells and bells that Protestants with a hankering for Rome have always wanted and expected and, until recently, found in the Roman Church. I entered Saint Bede's that morning in search of Baroque or Gothic splendor; I left trying to decide if even a Southern Baptist would be offended by what I had witnessed.

I thought, Well, that takes care of that; unless someone offers me the equivalent of Henry IV's Paris I'll not be returning to Saint Bede's. But my preoccupation with Catholicism refused to abate; to the contrary, it compelled me to seek out books on Catholic history and doctrine. As the stack of carefully read books—Chesterton, Belloc, Pieper, Maritain, Guardini—mounted, so too did the conviction that the Catholic Church was the greatest repository of Christian truth; other churches had bits and pieces of the truth (even *important* bits and pieces), but nowhere outside the Roman Church could one find such richness and plenitude. The next step was obvious: I returned to Saint Bede's, there to find in the Mass the liturgical expression of the doctrines I had noted in my reading. I began to frequent the church at odd hours as well, and there, in the stillness of the empty building (no, not truly empty; the burning candle before the tabernacle reminded me of a divine presence) I rediscovered how to pray. I even accepted the neo-Protestant bareness of the church, for I had come to realize that the ultimate value of Catholicism lies not in its Gothic or Baroque magnificence—in the trappings that Protestants so often mistake for the essence of Catholicism—but in the simple fact that it is true.

On a morning in September I awoke knowing that the time had come to act. I sought out the parish priest, and three months later—on December 14, 1975, amidst the piercing loveliness of the season of Christ's birth—I walked to the railing in Saint Bede's to receive my Lord.

5

DALE VREE

A Less Traveled
Road to Rome

Dale Vree is editor of the New Oxford Review, *a monthly magazine published in Berkeley, California, which is the primary forum for the new generation of converts to Roman Catholicism. A former Marxist-Leninist, he is the author of* On Synthesizing Marxism and Christianity *(1976) and* From Berkeley to East Berlin and Back *(1985). Dale writes a regular column for the* National Catholic Register.

"**A**ll roads lead to Rome," it is said. One way of understanding that dictum is to say that there are many routes to Rome, some well traveled and some less traveled. I suspect my road is of the latter variety—though some may see that road as more of a maze, but if so, let's hope it is "a maze in grace."

Having been raised an evangelical Protestant (Dutch Reformed/Presbyterian), my path to Rome was long and arduous, for the distance between Calvinistic-*cum*-evangelical Protestantism and Roman Catholicism is immense.

Consider what I was up against: as a small boy in the late 1940s, early 1950s, I was told by some relatives that, centuries ago, Spanish Catholics persecuted Christians in Holland—this being a major issue because all of "my people" were Protestant immigrants from the Netherlands. Moreover, I was informed that Catholic countries in Latin America continued persecuting Christians.

Catholics persecuting Christians? This may sound contradictory, especially to the Catholic ear, but I was reared in a milieu that generally thought that Catholics are *not* Christians (although this view is enjoying a resurgence in the 1980s, I am confident that my relatives abandoned it for good long ago). I was introduced to this view in the deceptively simple terms a small boy could easily grasp: since Catholics call themselves Catholics while we Protestants call ourselves (simply) Christians, Catholics are not Christians — after all, they don't call themselves Christians! And later I would learn that only we Christians are "saved." Christians believe in Jesus Christ, but Catholics believe in Mary, popes, saints, and worship idols in their churches. Catholicism and Christianity were, you see, different religions.

But even as a small boy I didn't quite believe it. I had noticed that Catholics had crosses (not crucifixes, but *crosses*, with which I as a Protestant was quite familiar) on top of their churches. I even realized that Jesus Christ was the central figure in Catholicism.

Later, in high school, I wandered into Catholic churches a couple of times at odd hours. We Protestants correctly talked about our church buildings as "God's house," but our church interiors resembled auditoriums, whereas I was immediately struck by a different ambience inside Catholic churches: there was a permeating "divine presence" (even when no worship service was in progress). Perhaps it was the flickering candlelight, or the occasional pilgrim kneeling and genuflecting, or the statues and the "color" and the altar — I don't know exactly — but being inside a Catholic church elicited my primitive sense of worship and my desire to kneel and pray (only much later would I learn about the reserved sacrament).

In 1960, when I was sixteen, the Catholic John F. Kennedy contested the Protestant Richard Nixon for the U.S. presidency. Virtually all my relatives and the members of my church were against Kennedy — and the most frequent charge against him was that he was Catholic. But my father and I were for Kennedy (not that we were pro-Catholic, but we weren't anti-Catholic either). This deviation from the norm was significant and deserves an explanation.

My paternal grandfather, an immigrant from Holland, began his working life as a mechanic and sheet metal pressman, and he taught my father (who didn't graduate from high school, but finished his education at a trade school) to respect the common man — his culture, his economic concerns, and his trade unions. My father passed this "proletarian consciousness" on to me. He taught me always to look at things from the point of view of the "little guy." Seeing society from a working-class point of view was a factor that, although I didn't realize it at the time, set me (as well as, I suspect, my father and grandfather) somewhat at odds with my Protestant environment.

As I've indicated, my kinfolk were Dutch Calvinists, and they were part of a wave of Dutch Calvinist immigrants who came to America after the turn of the century and settled in the Midwest. They became overwhelmingly Republican — and not surprisingly.

Calvinism, many believe, was the progenitor of capitalism. Certainly it was an ideology well suited to the nascent bourgeoisie. It is individualistic and oriented to self-improvement. Success is thought to be a result of hard work and a sign of God's favor, lack of success a consequence of laziness and a mark of God's disfavor. The connection between poverty on the one hand and discrimination, exploitation, or inherited financial, social, and educational disadvantages on the other is generally overlooked. To be blunt, the social implications of Calvinism (individual pursuit of prosperity) and proletarian consciousness (the idea that to be disadvantaged is not necessarily shameful, and that the disadvantaged should struggle *together* for a better world) are antithetical.

That my tightly knit ethnic subculture was so heavily, even so naturally, Republican meant that it took a lot of conviction on the part of my grandfather and father to be strong populistic Democrats. The working-class issue was responsible for this. I well remember being instructed by them during the 1948 presidential election that the Democratic party is the party of the workingman — and so, at the wee age of four I knew that I too was a Democrat. The proletarian consciousness I learned was a far stronger influence on me than the anti-Catholicism of my general milieu. Hence in 1960 it was not hard for me or my father (my grandfather by then being dead) to have strongly favored a Catholic Democrat over a Protestant Republican.

By 1959–60 I had become deeply troubled by the lack of concern for social justice in my particular Protestant affiliation (then a large middle-class Presbyterian church). Being a Protestant, I was taught to read the Bible. Thank God for that! And from my readings I instinctively picked up a sense of God's "preferential love for the poor" (as many Catholics now call it). One of the most poignant passages in Scripture for me was where Jesus warns the outwardly righteous that they stand in danger of judgment. To them, Jesus will say when He comes in glory at the end of the world: "Depart from me, ye cursed, into everlasting fire." Why? "For I was hungered, and ye gave me no meat: I was thirsty, and ye gave me no drink. . . . Verily I say unto you, inasmuch as ye did it not to one of the least of these (my brethren), ye did it not to me" (Matt. 25:41–45, KJV).

Then, I surmised, Christ will often come to us in the guise of the least advantaged of people. To want to aid them is to want to aid Jesus. So in addition to simple proletarian consciousness, I felt I had another reason to be a Democrat and be concerned for social justice.

Now, this was not merely an abstract matter. In the late 1950s and early 1960s the civil rights movement—led and supported by many Christians, black and white—was gathering national momentum. Racial justice, which was also a matter of economic justice, was a burning issue for me. But the folks at my church seemed utterly oblivious or indifferent to the plight of "the least" of our brethren.

Although my Protestant background gave me a strong sense of the authority of the Bible, the importance of a personal relationship with Jesus, and the value of adherence to traditional Christian personal morality—for which I remain eternally grateful—I sensed something missing.

As a boy I would swing erratically between my orthodox religious convictions and my political interests—but I could never integrate them. For example, an evangelistic rally would come to town and impel me to put religious pictures on my bedroom wall. But then a Democratic political campaign or a liberal political cause would come along, and the religious pictures would go down and political posters would take their place. Then, after going off to a church summer camp, I would switch the pictures and posters again.

In college I tried to resolve this conflict by becoming an Episcopalian. A side attraction was that, like the Roman Catholic Church, the Episcopal Church *did* elicit my sense of worship. But the more salient attraction was the social justice witness of Episcopalians. (At the time, it would have been much too large a leap for me to have become Roman Catholic.)

However, the hoped-for integration of orthodoxy and (what is now called) orthopraxy did not occur for me, for being an Episcopalian quickly got me—unintentionally—tangled in the web of modernist theology. My hero of the moment, Bishop James A. Pike, was not only speaking up for social justice, but also publicly jettisoning central Christian doctrines such as the Incarnation, the Trinity, and the physical Resurrection of Jesus Christ.

Through the influence of Episcopalians like Pike, I was led to read Paul Tillich, Rudolf Bultmann, and other theologically liberal Protestants. I noticed that, for some reason, the social action emphasis went hand in hand with doctrinal skepticism. Although I didn't particularly want to surrender my belief in a supernatural God, miracles, an afterlife, and all the rest, that seemed to be the required thing to do if one was serious about social justice. That one could combine theological orthodoxy with working for social justice didn't seem to be an option. I knew of no compelling role models among either Episcopalians or evangelical Protestants for orthodox social action.

In the early to mid-1960s my participation in the civil rights and peace movements deepened. In 1964, while a senior at the University of California at Berkeley, I was arrested for my involvement in the Free Speech Movement. As I drank deeply from the wells of modernist theology, my faith in Christ weakened, and my "proletarian consciousness" was redirected into Marxist philosophy. Then I abandoned Christ and became a Marxist-Leninist.

To make a long story short, in 1965 I traveled to Berlin to make a new life in East Germany — what I thought would be a true workers' state. I was searching for an egalitarian social order and the New (Communist) Man. I didn't find either.

While living in East Berlin in 1966, I was, to my surprise, converted to Christ (for details, see my book, *From Berkeley to East Berlin and Back* [Nashville, Tenn.: Thomas Nelson, 1985]). The conversion was rather sudden. It occurred on Easter Sunday in a Protestant church as a result of hearing a sermon proclaiming the physical Resurrection of Christ.

There are three things that need to be said about this:

1. I saw firsthand the inadequacy of communism, which is the preeminent and most determined form of human self-salvation in our time. It was deeply impressed upon me that man cannot save himself. So, when I converted to Christ, I did so on *His* terms. For me, modernist Christianity had been a slippery slope on the way to outright atheism. Modernism's assumptions were atheistic: man need only believe what he finds believable, and nothing miraculous or paradoxical is included. I knew modernism to be a shrouded atheism. I knew that, as a modernist, I hadn't believed in Jesus Christ in any significant sense — nor had I had any relationship with Him. So I would have no more of the "pick-and-choose-what-you-want-to-believe-or-not-believe" of modernism. It had led me farther and farther from Christ; I could no longer trust its subjectivism. I would therefore embrace Christ without prevarication. I would adhere to the Bible — both the teachings I liked and those I didn't particularly like.

2. Part of what turned me to Christ in East Berlin was the witness of the Christians there. Looking for the Communist New Man, I ran into the Pauline New Man instead. Searching for the dictatorship of the proletariat, I found the primitive Church instead (the pre-Constantinian Church where Christians are a persecuted minority). In America, I had found Christians to be comfortable, complacent, smug. In East Berlin, it was the Communists who were that way, whereas the harassed Christians were dedicated and willing to suffer hardship for Christ. This was a Christian witness I had never really seen before. In retrospect, it would almost seem that for *me* to really find Christ I *had* to go to a place like East Germany to do so.

3. In becoming a "born-again" Christian, I did not become anti-

Communist, much less antisocialist; nor did I experience a conversion to capitalism or the American Way of Life. After all, the
American Way of Life—and the bourgeois captivity of American
Protestantism—had been great obstacles to faith for me, whereas the
Communist persecution of religion had shown me another—a more
primitive and, I dare say, more authentic—face of Christianity, and
had actually ignited my faith.

All three of these factors, I now realize, had a bearing on my
eventual turn to Rome. But before getting to that, I need to say
something about the seventeen years that intervened between my
turn to Christ in East Berlin and my becoming a Roman Catholic.

Upon returning to Berkeley later in 1966, I began looking for a
church to attend. Since I had been an Episcopalian, I picked up
where I had left off and looked for an Episcopal parish. But this time
it could not be one infected with modernism. It would have to be
orthodox, which I thought then meant evangelical (there is a small
contingent of evangelical Episcopalians in the United States). But in
the Berkeley area I couldn't find an evangelical Episcopal parish.
The only satisfactory Episcopal parish I could find was Anglo-Catholic. As with much of my life, I found something I wasn't exactly
looking for. Was it grace?

I don't know for sure. But what I do know is that I could never
have become a Roman Catholic without a long sojourn in Anglo-
Catholicism (which is why I can only be grateful to it). For among
Anglo-Catholics I would learn the Catholic understanding of Christianity: the importance of justification *and* sanctification, of faith *and*
works; the value of suffering; the authority of tradition; and the
meaning of priesthood, the seven sacraments, Mariology, purgatory,
the intercession of the saints, the incarnational principle, and more.
As for good works and suffering, I had already had a glimmering of
their significance in the Christian life, but the rest was new to me.

The most important new thing I would learn as an Anglo-Catholic
was that the corporate Church—through her tradition—possesses
teaching authority. The Bible is not our sole rule of faith because the
Bible was assembled by the Church. The New Testament did not fall
out of the heavens whole. Before there was the New Testament there
was the Church. In the early years of the Church, there were numerous gospel accounts and other documents circulating that claimed to
be authentically inspired. But not all of them were, and the Church
had to determine which ones were to be accepted into the New
Testament canon (as well as determine whether the Old Testament
was still to be included in what we call the Bible).

Since the Church was deciding which books were inspired and

which were not, it was obvious to me that the Church had to be inspired by the Holy Spirit in this portentous undertaking. Moreover, once this undertaking was accomplished, it was quite natural that the Church would feel competent to make authoritative interpretations of the Scriptures.

As we can see vividly from Christian history, the Scriptures lend themselves to a multitude of theological, ethical, and social interpretations. Their meaning is not transparent — which is why there have been so many quarrels about their meaning. For example, Christians believe in the Incarnation of Christ and the Holy Trinity; but although it certainly implies these doctrines, the New Testament does not even mention these terms (nor does it define these doctrines unambiguously). It was the Church through her tradition that spoke *authoritatively* on theological, ethical, and social matters. So, thanks to the Church we have the Christian Bible, and thanks again to the Church we need not quarrel endlessly about the Bible's meaning.

The Church believed that while the Holy Spirit spoke through the Scriptures, the Spirit would continue to guide the Church in her function of articulating the truth. After all, in the latter days of His ministry Jesus said to His disciples: "I have yet many things to say unto you, but ye cannot bear them now. Howbeit when he, the Spirit of truth, is come, he will guide you into all truth" (John 16:12–13, KJV). Since the Holy Spirit does not contradict Himself, the ongoing teaching function of the Church would not contradict, but rather clarify and deepen and amplify, what was revealed in Scripture. The result, most notably in the first millennium of the Church, was the anathematization of heresies and the formulation of creeds and doctrines — in short, the development of doctrine.

From a purely biblical point of view, the idea of development of doctrine makes a lot of sense. For example, when one contrasts what seems to be the tribal, vengeful, forbidding, and warlike God of the Old Testament with the universal, forgiving, loving, and peace loving God of the New Testament, one can easily see how doctrine develops in the Bible itself. (Indeed, because of this contrast, some early Christian heretics held that the Old Testament should be omitted from the Christian Bible. In effect, they could not see that doctrine develops.) T. S. Eliot, an Anglo-Catholic, said with great wisdom that man cannot stand too much reality. God's truth is the ultimate reality, but in His kindness God only seems to show mankind as much of His awesome reality as mankind can assimilate at a particular time in history.

That the Church possesses teaching authority makes sense in another way. When Christ ascended into heaven, He did not leave behind a book; he left behind the Church. And it was *one* Church he left behind. Moreover, he *intended* to leave behind one Church. Again in the latter days of His ministry, Jesus prayed to His Father: "keep through thine own name those whom thou hast given me, that they may be one" (John 17:11, KJV). When the new-fangled notion of *Sola Scriptura* ("Scripture is our sole authority") broke out at the Reformation, the results ran directly — and flagrantly — against Christ's will that His Church be one. The Reformation has spawned thousands of churches and sects and cults and conventicles (according to the *Oxford Encyclopedia of World Christianity*, published in 1982, there are more than 28,000 recognizable denominations of Christianity). Most of them base their belief on "the Bible alone." But *Sola Scriptura*, as a principle of authority, is unworkable and self-defeating because the Bible can be interpreted in thousands of different (and often mutually exclusive) ways.

If Christ willed that his Church be one, it is inconceivable that He would have authorized the principle of *Sola Scriptura*. Indeed, He never did: that principle is not in Scripture!

Now, the only viable alternative to *Sola Scriptura* is Scripture and Tradition. This latter principle makes sense because what Christ left us with was the living tradition that is the Church, and the Church gave us the Bible, as well as herself as the guardian and interpreter of divine truth. So, if one wishes to conform one's will to the teachings of Christ, but if those teachings are not unambiguously presented in Scripture, then one is forced to look toward ecclesial tradition and the teaching authority of the Church's bishops. The Church possesses the authority to teach by virtue of her tradition — which is the life of the Holy Spirit in the Church — and by virtue of the authority Christ gave the seventy Disciples when He sent them forth with these words: "He that heareth you heareth me; and he that despiseth you despiseth me" (Luke 10:16, KJV).

Until 1976 I was content to remain an Anglo-Catholic while accepting the above understanding of the Church. But by 1976 it was apparent to me that the Episcopal Church had broken with the apostolic, Catholic faith on two decisive counts. That church (1) approved the ordination of women to the priesthood, and (2) had by then already adopted a permissive position on abortion.

When I say "broken with the apostolic, Catholic faith," what do (or did) I mean? Anglo-Catholics generally understand Catholic orthodoxy in terms of Saint Vincent of Lérins's rule, that it is "that which has been believed everywhere, ever, by everyone." That means that Catholic orthodoxy is that which has always been believed by all Catholic Christians. Anglo-Catholics understand "Catholic Christians" as those Christians who stand in the Apostolic Succession of bishops—primarily Roman Catholics, the Eastern Orthodox, and Anglicans.

I will leave it to theologians far more competent than I—whether Roman Catholic, Eastern Orthodox, or Anglo-Catholic—to explain why the two departures from Catholic faith noted above are violations of Catholic tradition rather than "developments" of it. Suffice it to say that of the two departures, the ordination of women is the more far-reaching for Anglo-Catholics. In one sense, of course, abortion is the more grievous departure because it involves something the ordination of women manifestly does not—that is, the killing of innocent human life. But when I say the ordination of women is more momentous for Anglo-Catholics I mean that in a strictly ecclesiological sense. In *this* sense it is more far-reaching for two basic reasons:

1. If a woman cannot be a priest, then her priestly ministrations are invalid. Hence, when one receives communion consecrated by a woman priest, one is *not really* receiving Christ. It is just make-believe. Moreover, when a woman becomes a bishop, the priests she ordains (whether male or female) are not priests either, and the whole Apostolic line of Succession inevitably becomes hopelessly compromised at a minimum, or totally defective at a maximum. One way or the other, the ordination of women puts one on the road to Catholic self-destruction—that is, to the destruction of the priesthood and episcopate. Of course, Roman Catholics hardly ever worry about such a thing as Catholic self-destruction in some ultimate sense. For them, the Catholic identity of their Church is given. But for Anglo-Catholics, the Catholic identity of the Anglican communion is not a given. Anglo-Catholics have had to fight for their Catholic identity ever since the English Reformation—and concomitantly, it is something they have persistently feared they could lose.

2. While a church's stand on abortion can be reversed, it is inconceivable that after thousands of women priests have been ordained, a church would or could realistically reverse itself and undo what it has done. It is like squeezing toothpaste out of the tube and then trying to get it back in the tube. Or, to switch the imagery, if the ordination of women puts one on the road to Catholic self-destruction, it is a road that, once taken, one can't get off or turn around on; one must follow it to the bitter end.

Even if one wishes to withhold an opinion on whether a woman *can* be a valid priest, from an Anglo-Catholic point of view one "branch" of the Church Catholic is not entitled to act unilaterally in the vital area of sacramental theology. Thus, that the Episcopal

Church did so essentially placed that church outside the Church Catholic (as Anglo-Catholics understand it). It also meant that in the United States the Episcopal Church's *via media* between Protestantism and Catholicism had broken down irretrievably, as the Protestant wing of that church finally triumphed over its Catholic wing.

From an Anglo-Catholic viewpoint, the only way such a stark departure from Catholic tradition as ordaining women could conceivably take place is if a grand ecumenical council of Roman Catholics, the Eastern Orthodox, and Anglicans (as well as the Old Catholics) jointly agreed to do so—that is, if it became a practice accepted "everywhere" and "by everyone" (by all Catholic Christians). Needless to say, that such a council would ever take place and that it would come to such a decision are both extremely unlikely prospects.

So, because I wanted to remain a Catholic (indeed, could not become a Protestant again, if only because of my understanding of the nature of the Church sketched above), 1976 began a process in which I had to consider whether—or how long—I could remain an Episcopalian.

For Protestants the question of Rome is usually framed as "Good heavens, why *Rome?*" But for Anglo-Catholics, the question is usually, "Why *not* Rome?" Even before 1976 this was a perennial question. After 1976 in the United States it became quite an urgent question for many Anglo-Catholics. Over the years, I have known countless Anglo-Catholics who have said, "Someday I may have to cross the Tiber." Many who say that have not crossed over (or at least, not yet), and many of them never will, but since 1976 in the United States increasing numbers of them have been crossing over.

The question is "Why *not* Rome?" for an Anglo-Catholic because in so very many ways the Anglo-Catholic believes exactly what the Roman Catholic believes, and so—in light of the will of Christ that His Church be one, and the sense of the very word "Catholic" as "universal"—he must ask why he chooses to remain separate from the vast majority of Catholics who owe obedience to Rome. So, I too asked myself, "Why *not* Rome?" and over the years found my qualms about Rome pale in comparison to my qualms about invalid women priests and permissive positions on abortion. It became harder and harder for me to justify my separate existence as an *Anglo*-Catholic. (Anglo-Catholics regard themselves as members of the "Western Church" as opposed to the "Eastern Church" and so the question is seldom "Why *not* Constantinople?" As such, I will not try to answer that question here.)

Furthermore, the more I thought about Rome and the nature of the Church, the more I realized that if (as stated above) the Church is authorized to teach, the Church must also have an intact teaching authority—that is, a magisterium. Anglo-Catholics, holding to the maxim of Saint Vincent Lérins, tend to believe that with the schism between the Western Church and the Eastern Church in 1054, the Church's teaching authority essentially went into limbo for the next thousand years. But could this be? The Catholic tradition is a *living* tradition. Could or would the Holy Spirit take a thousand-year vacation from, as Christ said, guiding us "into all truth"? I didn't know the answer for sure, but to my mind, it seemed unlikely.

I also came to realize that a magisterium not only guides us into all truth, it protects the truth we already have. Surveying the wreckage of the Western Christianity of the last couple of centuries, I could see that old and new heresies were running rampant in most of the major Western churches. Indeed, for a time it seemed to me, as an Anglo-Catholic, that Rome herself might one day succumb to the disease of modernism (or what Roman Catholics call "neomodernism"). But when Karol Wojtyla assumed the Chair of Peter as John Paul II, I no longer worried about that. Furthermore, I could see that the Roman Catholic magisterium is truly alive—and its newfound vigor was most assuring to me. And more, I could see that the only thing—in this modern world of skepticism, false messianisms, relativistic morality, and consumerism—that can safeguard Christian truth is a magisterium. And then I saw that the Anglican communion's lack of a magisterium is no minor deficiency.

Which brings me to the three salient points about my conversion to Christ in East Berlin and how they relate to my turn to Rome:

1. When I converted to Christ in 1966, I did so on *His* terms. No longer would I set myself up as the arbiter of religious truth. I would submit to Jesus and the truth about Him in Scripture—I would even accept those things in Scripture that weren't particularly appetizing. So, the Christianity I had converted to was a kind of generic orthodox Protestantism. But there was a lingering problem here. Integral to orthodox Protestantism is the belief in the supremacy of conscience. Yes, orthodox Protestants hold that the Bible is the truth—but it is true only relative to the individual's interpretation of it. There is, finally, no authority above the individual who can say *with recognized authority*, "Your interpretation is wrong." It was the very lack of such authority that, in my judgment, had led to the modernist erosion in the leading Protestant churches. When I became an Anglo-Catholic, I learned that Anglo-Catholicism had a different view—but I would later see that without a living magisterium it had no credible or durable way of implementing that view.

If I had converted to Christ on His terms, how could I find out what His terms really were? In Protestantism, the individual is thrown back upon himself and his fallible and highly subjective judgments—or upon the ersatz (and, from a strictly *Sola Scriptura* point of view, illegitimate) traditions of Calvin, Luther, Wesley, and a multitude of others, or worse, upon the ersatz and elusive authority of the modernist theology professors and their shifting opinions. In seeking the living faith of Christ's Church, I was compelled to consider seriously the Roman Catholic magisterium.

Now, there were a few things Rome taught that didn't much appeal to me. But ironically, my qualms about Rome made Rome attractive in a way that seemed fitting. That is, it seemed that if Rome were the authority I thought her to be, I *should* have some qualms. For it would be awfully arrogant of me to think that my own natural preferences would be in perfect harmony with the will of Christ. If the quest for Christian truth had driven me to *submit* to Christ and the revealed Word of God in East Berlin, then it might also drive me to *submit* to the magisterium. Christ asks us to believe and do things we might not really want to believe or do, and so it seemed symmetrical that Christ's teaching authority in the Church would do so too. A Bible-believing Christian doesn't "pick and choose" from the Bible what he wants to accept—no, he is under authority. The same applies to the magisterium. If in accepting Christ in 1966, it was necessary for me to accept even Christ's hard sayings, then if the necessity of the magisterium became apparent to me, I would have to accept even its hard teachings.

So, the very difficulty of "submitting to Rome" made such a submission seem appropriate—as well as consistent with my original decision for Christ in 1966.

2. In East Berlin I ran into the Pauline New Man and the heroic primitive Church. What attracted me to Christ was, in part, the selfless witness of Christians. Is persistent hardship therefore indispensable to authentic Christian living? I hope not, but I don't know for sure. Be that as it may, my experience in East Berlin gave me a profound appreciation for Christian suffering and mortification—themes I saw more powerfully represented in the Roman Catholic Church than in any other Western church. The Protestantism I had been exposed to as a youth stressed the "blessings" (often quite self-centered, even materialistic) that follow from accepting Christ. What was lost sight of was the potentially greater blessings that follow from adversity and suffering. Seldom in Protestant churches did I hear about these inconvenient words of our Lord: "Blessed are ye, when men shall revile you, and persecute you . . . for my sake" (Matt. 5:11, KJV).

Saint Teresa of Avila said, "We always find that those who walked closest to Christ our Lord were those who had to bear the greatest trials." Protestants often overlook the connection between holiness (or sanctity) and suffering (whether voluntary or involuntary). What Protestants derogate as the "cult of the saints" I saw as just another of Rome's strengths. The saints *are* the New Men, and I came to see that one of the primary purposes of the Roman Obedience is, with grace leading the way, to create this new humanity. Which is not to say Roman Catholicism is an elitist form of Christianity—far from it! Rome has a well-deserved, if often misunderstood, reputation for embracing even the weakest of (repentant) sinners. Nor is it to say Rome believes in creating a Pelagian heaven on earth. Rather, the saints are the very embodiments of Love; in their sacrificial charity they dramatize for us the very nature of God; and by their examples they point us to the New Jerusalem, which is ultimately beyond this world.

3. When I accepted Christ in East Berlin, I did not surrender my "proletarian consciousness" or my concern about "the least of these my brethren." I did not become a champion of America (where the Church is suffocated with respectability) against communism (where the Church lives, as she first lived, in agony). I did not resolve to join the middle-class merry-go-round, become (what is now called) a "yuppie," or forget about social justice.

In the balkanized Protestant world, one must usually choose between embracing orthodox theology and right-wing politics on the one hand, and modernist theology and left-wing politics on the other hand. As early as my teen-age years, I couldn't quite make that choice. For decades I would search in vain for a way of combining theological orthodoxy and populistic political views. But the more I studied the Roman Catholic magisterium, the more I realized that it was offering what I had been looking for all along, that essentially it taught the unusual mix of convictions—socially Left, theological Right—I had carried with me since boyhood. And it did so *with authority*. As a Roman Catholic, my theological and social views would not seem idiosyncratic—peculiar to me.

So, in Roman Catholicism I found a church in which I could emphatically affirm both the rights of labor and the ancient creeds, reject both abortion and the use of nuclear weapons, affirm both lifelong marriage and the dignity of the poor, reject both laissez faire capitalism and do-your-own-thing morals, and stand apart from both the philosophical materialism of the East and the practical materialism (consumerism) of the West—and do so in full harmony with the teachings of my church.

Finally, I have always felt that if I were a Christian, my loyalty to Christ would have to transcend my temporal loyalties—whether to nation, ethnic group, or social class. Most non-Roman Catholic churches have identities forged by nationalist preoccupations or affected by national conditioning. Only Rome has been able to stand above nation rivalries and relativities. Moreover, of all the churches, the Roman Catholic is least affected by class and ethnic provincialisms. The Roman Catholic Church is the most "catholic"—that is, the most universalistic, most international, most all-embracing—of all churches.

When I became a Roman Catholic in 1983, many Roman Catholics greeted me with a "Welcome home!" It was meant in an ecclesiological sense. But in ways my greeters did not know, I would feel *very much* "at home" indeed.

6

ELENA M. VREE

Home at Last

Elena M. Vree is the mother of four children and managing editor of the New Oxford Review *in Berkeley, California.*

In September 1983 my family and I were received into full communion with the Roman Catholic Church. My personal odyssey into the Church began a few years after I was orphaned at the age of four and my maternal grandmother undertook the unexpected chore of raising my older brother and me.

I recall an early longing to be part of the Church when, at the age of eight, I attended my best friend's First Communion. Although she and I spent almost all our free time together, this was the only occasion I was allowed to visit her church. My grandmother was shielding me from exposure to the Roman Catholic Church. Why, I did not know. But that first introduction was the beginning of a lifelong love.

The memory of a company of cherubic little girls (I'm sure there were little boys, also, but they had not yet captured my attention) veiled and dressed in white and carrying candles reminds me now of the parable of the wise virgins who meet the bridegroom and accompany him to the marriage. I watched my friend and felt such admiration for her. I also felt envy. I sensed the Bridegroom beckoning to me, but I did not know how to respond. I wanted to be part of the company. I wanted to say yes and receive the life-giving bread. But that desire would not be fulfilled for at least three decades. I was not yet prepared.

My grandmother was a good Christian woman. She saw to it that I was baptized and raised in the Presbyterian Church. We were faithful churchgoers. We had no car and would spend well over an hour on foot and on the streetcar getting to church. Occasionally friends would give us a ride, but usually we made our slow way to church and back home. As she grew older, and as walking became more difficult for her, we found a church closer to home. Saturday evenings were usually spent singing, praying, studying the Bible, and preparing our clothes for church.

Although she was a good Christian woman, my grandmother had a great enmity for the Catholic Church. She told me she was born in Chihuahua, Mexico, but beyond that she shared very little of her childhood with me. There seemed to be a great sadness about her life that she never shared with me. She had one son who died young, the victim of a childhood disease. Her older daughter died of tuberculosis shortly after having given birth to her second child. My grandfather died when his children were still young. And my mother died at the age of thirty. On top of family tragedies, my grandmother had to work hard to support her children and then her grandchildren.

I'll never forget my cousin asking me to be the flower girl at her wedding. I was young and full of anticipation. I asked my grandmother to make my dress. But she informed me that I would not be permitted to participate in the wedding. My cousin had converted to Roman Catholicism and was being married in the Catholic Church. For that reason I would not be allowed to take part in the ceremony. I did not understand and I dared not question her decision. I tried never to cross my grandmother. She was quick to anger and slow to forgive. I worked especially hard to earn her approval.

After my grandmother died I discovered the reason for her anger toward the Church. She had been raised a Roman Catholic in Mexico and was married in the Church; however, she divorced her husband and remarried, falling out of communion with the Church. She was very resentful that the Church would no longer receive her as a full communicant even though she felt her remarriage was justifiable. She dissociated herself completely from the Church and withheld approval from any of her grandchildren who later associated with Catholicism. Her resentment and anger never abated.

Over the years, both before and after my grandmother's death, I spent weekends and summer weeks with my Catholic cousin. On Sundays we never missed Mass. It was through these visits that I grew closer to the Church. I made quiet mental comparisons to our Presbyterian church and I came to the conclusion that God isn't always on the watch to catch us in a sin and punish us, but that He loves us and forgives us if we love Him. Although I knew nothing about the Real Presence, I felt the presence of Christ whenever I worshiped with my cousin and her family. He seemed somehow nearer, and I felt more responsive to him. Gradually I came to love the saints and felt it was possible to call on their help.

I discovered a wide variety of humankind all worshiping God

under one roof. My experience had been that individuals and families of like national origin and socioeconomic status attend the same church. In my cousin's church, people from various national origins and socioeconomic classes worshiped together. I observed the universality of the Catholic Church. (I remember an instance in our Presbyterian church when an unkempt stranger wandered in and immediately came under the careful scrutiny and interrogation of several churchmen before he was politely escorted out the door. Was God offended by his appearance? Was he the Stranger whom we did not take in?) I wanted to be a part of a church where all were welcome, where Christ lived, where the saints prayed for us, but I felt somehow restrained. I still was not ready.

I made an important discovery while spending time with my cousin during Lent. I knew nothing of Lent or the disciplines one makes for Our Lord's sake. It was a foreign and novel practice, yet I was drawn to it. The more I thought about it, the more I began to understand. It no longer struck me as odd to purify myself in preparation to receive the Risen Christ. We had never fasted in my grandmother's home and there were no disciplines to commemorate Christ's temptations in the desert. I never imagined that small acts of self-denial could bring me so much closer to Christ. And although my cousin was not always successful in keeping her disciplines (she usually tried to give up smoking), I admired her efforts.

After my grandmother died my new guardian was my other cousin, a Presbyterian. Although I became lax in my church attendance, my cousin made it clear to me that I was to be received into the church because it was our grandmother's wish. There was to be no more hesitation. After all, the primary reason I was put under her care was because our grandmother was reassured I would continue to worship in a Presbyterian church on a regular basis, which I thereafter continued to do. I was cooperative and acquiescent, attempting to be as accommodating as possible.

By the time I left my cousin's home I was anxious to unload all religious baggage — not unexpected for an eighteen-year-old. Yet, when I met my husband, Dale, I prayed fervently that God would allow this romance to flourish. He did.

Dale and I were married in the Episcopal Church. Dale had also been a Presbyterian and had converted to Episcopalianism while at the University of California at Berkeley. Since I had fallen away from active churchgoing and had never felt that the Presbyterian Church would be my permanent church home, I moved easily from the Presbyterian to the Episcopal Church.

I had not lost my faith at that point in my life, but had put Christ on hold. I called on Him only when I needed Him. He had ceased to be an active part of my life. Or so it seemed. As it turned out, He was actually a very active presence in my life. In spite of my indifference, He protected and cared for me during those young adult years. But I placed my faith in man, looking for the perfect man-made society—a society where good people looked after one another and where injustice did not exist.

Dale and I searched for this society together. We wanted to be active participants in such a society, to be nourished by it and to contribute our youthful energy and idealism. Above all, we wanted to raise our yet unborn children in such a place.

It was clear to us we would not find that perfect society where the New Man—that paragon of virtue—prevailed, here in America. So Dale and I set off to find him where we thought he would most likely be found, in East Germany. Unlike Diogenes, we needed no lantern to find an honest man; we had the certainty of our ignorance.

It was both a revelation and a disappointment not to find the New Man in a Communist society. Although the sloganeering and party rhetoric decried the soft, decadent West, the goal of the party, at least in East Berlin, appeared to be the establishment of a showcase Communist society wherein all would share more or less equally in the material benefits usually reserved for the upper middle classes in Western countries. People would not receive according to their needs, but according to their desires. This would not be a society establishing social justice for all. Rather it was a society attempting to create comfort and excess and lethargy for all. The Communists wanted to become precisely that which they denounced. There was no new consciousness.

There was, however, in the midst of this acquisitive society an example of great devotion to the otherworldly kingdom of God. Initially, from a sociological and political curiosity, Dale and I visited a Lutheran church in our East Berlin district. Whereas we had occasionally visited churches in West Berlin, we began attending our small East Berlin Lutheran church on a regular basis. The churches we had visited in West Berlin had been large and impressive structures, but poorly attended. But our East Berlin Lutheran church was another story entirely.

There were no state funds to maintain the inside of the church (the exterior was state-maintained) and even the casual observer could not overlook the peeling plaster, the large cracks in the walls, and the choir loft that looked in danger of falling onto the congregation below. Yet Sunday after Sunday this church was packed with the faithful. These people were so filled with the love of God that the church was transformed into a place of warmth, light, and beauty. The presence of the Holy Spirit was almost palpable. I had never witnessed such love and devotion. This small church made Christ come alive for me in a new way. It was so clear that Christ was the center of these people's lives. Here, in this church, we found the New Man we had been seeking. We had to learn anew that the kingdom of God cannot be established without God and at our behest. Only God brings us to the new consciousness; only He establishes the new order of the New Man.

After we returned to Berkeley, however, it was virtually impossible for us to find the same intensity and quality of worship. We visited various Protestant churches in our search to recapture our East Berlin experience. The persecuted church seems purified through its suffering; we know so little of being persecuted for our faith. Eventually we returned to the familiarity of the Episcopal Church, eventually attending a "high-church" parish where we shared concern for orthodoxy and traditional values with the priest.

As an Episcopalian I had not considered myself a Catholic but, rather, a Protestant. However, in this parish I learned about Anglo-Catholicism. Unlike our former Episcopal parish, here we were Anglo-Catholics. We had incense every Sunday, we never had morning prayer, confessions were heard every Saturday, we observed Lent and we venerated Mary. I began to feel that this was the church I had longed for in my youth. In fact, I once mentioned to one of our priests that I had always wanted to be a Roman Catholic. He told me that I was, in fact, now more Catholic than the Roman Catholics. After all, our altar still faced the wall, did the Roman Catholics'? We used incense every Sunday, do the Roman Catholics? He recited a litany of comparisons for me. Since I was still having some difficulty with a few Roman Catholic teachings, I allowed myself to be convinced. He must be right, I thought. I am more Catholic than the Romans. I accepted the form rather than the substance.

It became apparent, however, that I was not quite the Catholic I fancied myself to be. I lacked the authority of the Church and the Church's concern and love for the poor. I was beginning to understand exactly why I needed to be a Roman Catholic. I needed the Church of the ages; the Church with consistent teaching authority. I needed, for my children, a reliable moral authority, an authority not subject to the prevailing world view but bound by Scripture and Tradition.

In time, the shine of Anglo-Catholicism began to dull for me. I was becoming more and more aware of my peculiar status in Anglo-Catholicism. I learned, for example, that "Anglo"-Catholicism, for some, means that one must ethnically be "Anglo," which I am not. My mother was Mexican and my father Filipino. Anglo-Catholicism, for many, is not something one converts to, but is a birthright.

It also became evident that I was out of step politically with my fellow Anglo-Catholics. Generally, Anglo-Catholics are political conservatives. Although I no longer held romantic notions about communism and the perfect society, I still had the same concerns: the welfare of the poor, American nonintervention in the internal politics of other countries, protection of all human life, containing the arms buildup and reducing the nuclear threat. These concerns were shared by very few of my fellow Anglicans. In fact, one Anglican friend once said he hadn't any idea how I ever happened to become an Anglo-Catholic; didn't I feel out of place there? That made me stop and think: What *was* I doing there? I was out of sync politically, my race was unbecoming, and I still wanted to be a Roman Catholic.

But Anglo-Catholicism is still very dear to me. I shall always regard it as a sort of godparent. Anglo-Catholicism introduced me to the mystery and beauty of the Mass and cleared my path toward Roman Catholicism. It was as an Anglican that I made my first petitions to Mary, attempted my first confession, observed my first Lent, lit my first Advent wreath. It was as an Anglican that I learned the centrality of the sacraments and the fullness of Christ's redemptive love.

Soon the inevitable became inescapable. The Roman Catholic Church represented and embodied most of what was dear to me: orthodoxy in matters of faith; justice in social matters. Although I loved the Anglican liturgy and its rich ceremony, I needed a more satisfying spiritual food — maybe not something quite as rich, but something more basic and substantial. I once scoffed at the Roman liturgy for its plain music and unadorned Mass, but I began to see that the Roman Catholic Church is truly universal. She is able to address and embrace a wide range of humanity around the world. She draws this humanity to herself just as Christ draws us all to himself, loving the poor and the rich, the politically conservative and liberal. All are drawn together into one family at the Mass.

The event that brought me to the realization that I should become a Roman Catholic was the election of the current pope. He has been an irresistible force to me. He is such a fervent, right-minded, charismatic leader — a man who warms the hearts of millions; a man who inspires Catholics and non-Catholics; a man who travels far and wide to make himself known to his flock; a man who represents Catholic orthodoxy *and* the Church's special concern for the poor and oppressed. If the Holy Spirit could move the College of Cardinals to elect this man to the papacy, then the Holy Spirit, through the Pope, could energize me and stir me from my complacency and move me into action. This is a man who symbolizes, for me, the persecuted Church. A man who, I hoped, would invigorate the Catholic Church with the powerful faith and worship I had witnessed in East Berlin. Not only would he shake me from my complacency, but he would, I hoped, energize the whole Church.

There seemed no reason for further hesitation when, at the urging of a small group of Anglo-Catholic priests, the Pope authorized a program whereby married Episcopal and Anglo-Catholic priests would be accepted into the Roman Catholic clergy. This demonstrated to me that the Pope did indeed understand the special position of many Anglo-Catholics. He was inviting us into the Catholic Church; he wanted to share with us the full benefits of Catholic substance. I could resist no longer.

In September 1983 my family and I were received into the Church. We were later often greeted by fellow Catholics with the salutation "Welcome Home!" Indeed, we were home. It was a long journey, but the arrival would not have been half as sweet without having taken the long and seemingly circuitous route. In our arrival we came not to the end of our journey, but to a new beginning.

7

PETER K. WEISKEL

Drawn to the Sacramental Mysteries

Peter K. Weiskel was graduated from Yale University in 1974 with a B.A. in geology. After completing a M.A. in religious education at Boston College, he served as editor and administrative assistant to Father Henri J. M. Nouwen. Love in a Fearful Land: A Guatemalan Story *(1984) is a fruit of their collaboration. Presently, Mr. Weiskel is doing graduate study and research in groundwater hydrology at Boston University.*

When I was first asked to tell the story of my spiritual pilgrimage, I was filled with foreboding. Knowing how the *New Oxford Review* thrives on controversy, I was reluctant to expose myself to the firestorm of criticism that, I was certain, would break out no matter *what* I might write. Nevertheless, encouraged by Saint Peter's exhortation to "always be ready to give an account of the hope that is in us" (1 Pet. 3:15), I offered an account of my hope and how I came to it.

I was born the son of a Congregational minister and raised in the fold of New England Protestantism. My earliest years were spent in a white clapboard parsonage in southern New Hampshire; when I was six we moved to the Boston suburb of Newton. My parents, as I now realize, were (and are) people of extraordinary integrity and Christian commitment. Having come to maturity during the pit of the Depression in the 1930s, they knew the reality of suffering and injustice, and learned early to trust God for everything. My two older brothers and I grew up knowing God's stern and tender love, and the story of our salvation in Christ. We learned as well that the poor have a claim on our time and talent. I can still hear my parents repeating Jesus' admonition, "From those to whom much has been given, much will be required."

However, several other powerful creeds competed for our allegiance during the self-confident era of the late 1950s and early 1960s. Chief among them was the suburban gospel of success, which declares that success and failure are meted out in this life to the hardworking and the lazy, respectively. The short form of this gospel reads: "God helps those who help themselves." Subscribing to the academic interpretation of this gospel, my brothers and I firmly believed that eternal happiness would be ours if we applied ourselves at school, impressed our teachers, and gained admission to an Ivy League college.

Though I cannot speak for my brothers, Tim and Tom, each of us has stories to tell concerning how we lost faith in this simple creed. My story begins in 1966. As I said, my parents had a deep sense of social responsibility. It was rooted in their own experience of hardship and nurtured under the influence of my father's teachers Douglas Steere of Haverford College and Reinhold Niebuhr of Union Seminary in New York. Dad was also greatly moved by the witness of Martin Luther King, Jr., and in the mid-1960s made some modest attempts to engage his congregation in the civil rights movement. They rewarded him for his efforts by (very politely) throwing him out of the parish.

Needless to say, this event shook us to the roots. We faced exile from our home (the church owned it), our friends, and all visible means of support. Suddenly the world began to look different. My eyes were opened to the racism that lay below the surface of even the most enlightened suburbs. I also began to realize that, contrary to my expectations, hardworking and righteous people like my father sometimes get crucified. Bad things do indeed happen to good people.

Nevertheless, old creeds die hard. I clung to a desperate hope that getting into the right college would set my world aright. And after a few years of nearly monastic devotion to my prep school studies, my wish was granted: I arrived at Yale in the fall of 1970. I assumed I would be able to spend my days in calm and edifying conversation with the other saints in light (my classmates). Instead, Yale turned out to be a competitive arena more imposing than any I had known before. Too few of us in the class of '74 took time to enjoy ourselves, and like the good preppies we were, we staked all our hope on school. The more adventurous upperclassmen dubbed us "the grim professionals" years before the word *yuppie* was coined.

This was so in spite of the fact that Yale's principal chaplains were distinguished Protestants who did their best to propose to us an alternative vision to the suburban gospel. University chaplain William Sloane Coffin, Jr., was (and is) an astonishing preacher who packed Battell Chapel with all kinds of people week after week. A

Freedom Rider during the early days of the civil rights movement, he was also a vocal critic of U.S. policy in Vietnam. Bill always had the greatest solicitude for my family, and for my father especially. On some level I think he knew that his patrician background (and a supportive Yale president named Kingman Brewster) protected him from the sort of persecution that hit my father. Associate chaplain J. Philip Zaeder was an even greater influence on my life and remains a friend to this day. I now realize that I was exposed to the very best of liberal Protestantism while at Yale, and I thank God for those years.

However, the "identity crisis" through which I was passing on my way to adulthood was protracted to an almost ridiculous degree. By the time I finished Yale and a year of graduate school, it was nearly impossible for me to sustain meaningful connections with people, partly because I had come to see all people as potential rivals. I began to run out of gas emotionally and spiritually.

In the midst of this period, my brother Tom fell through the ice of a half-frozen pond while trying to rescue his drowning daughter, Shelburne. Both succumbed to the frigid December waters. A promising young scholar of English literature, Tom was my best friend and chief model. His death threw me back on my own resources, and I was forced to admit that those inner resources were scant indeed, or at least beyond my reach.

My faith in the suburban gospel of success fell through the ice with Tom and Shelburne. I think God knew I might have been ripe for something more substantial, and He began to invite me to it.

I won't recount all the years it took me to respond to this invitation. Suffice it to say that I was living in Greenfield in western Massachusetts and working as a house painter when I was stopped in my tracks by the laughter of a child who lived next door. I had never witnessed such a jubilant little girl at play. Her laughter pierced the layers of fear and resistance I had piled on top of myself and tapped a reservoir within me that I could not name. I got to know her family and soon discovered three things about them that both shocked and attracted me: they were full of joy; they were disciplined and full of purpose; and they professed a plain and simple faith in Jesus Christ. I had never encountered people who so fully embodied both duty and delight. I thought one had to choose for one or the other and be either a dutiful Christian or a happy, irresponsible pagan. At the time I was trying my best to be the latter, but wasn't succeeding too well at it. I began to suspect that their well-ordered, joyful lives had something to do with their unadorned faith in Christ.

One Sunday I joined them for worship at the local evangelical church. I was struck by the spirit of hope that filled the air. Church members welcomed me warmly, and extended true kindness and hospitality. I went back a few more Sundays and was greatly inspired and encouraged by a brand of preaching that was new to my ears. Then, one Sunday, a young man approached me and asked if I was saved. Not knowing quite what to say, and feeling somewhat cornered, I responded by saying I wasn't sure. When he started to ask prying questions, I began to eye the door and then bolted out at my first opportunity. My admiration for my next-door neighbors continued, but I knew that for better or worse I would never be able to squeeze myself into their version of the Christian life. I would have to look elsewhere for duty and delight.

One Saturday afternoon a few weeks later I was walking down Main Street in Greenfield, when, for no apparent reason, I decided to step into Holy Trinity, the local Catholic church. From the outside it was as white and plain as the southern New Hampshire meeting house where I went as a child. But upon entering, I knew I was in a different kind of place. It was almost dark, for one thing, and racks of candles flickered away in front of various statues. A few people loitered in the pews — sitting, kneeling, praying.

Gradually my attention became fixed on a very simple statue of the Virgin on the left side of the church. I enjoyed watching the candlelight flit across her wooden surface. After some time, I decided I'd been there long enough and began to rise from my seat. I then found to my amazement that I was actually pinned to the pew, or rather, held there in a calm embrace I had no impulse to resist.

A few minutes later a priest walked into the sanctuary and began to lead us in the celebration of Mass. In his homily he pleaded with us to respect and love our neighbor, because Christ is hidden in all people. I was captivated by the whole scene — the bright green vestments, the stone altar, the priestly apparatus of chalice, paten, and sacramentary, the bread, the wine. The liturgy appealed to something in me much larger than my intellect. I had the sense that something was happening here, something was being enacted in which we, the congregation, were invited to participate. I knew not what that action might be, but I resolved then and there to find out.

I moved back to Boston and began to participate in the life of a student parish called Saint Clement's. I went to Sunday liturgy and soaked in the color, the music, and made many new friends. I was welcomed, but never cornered. The Catholic Church was big enough, apparently, to include inquirers like myself. I wasn't forced by the third week to declare myself in or out. There was, so to speak, a warm vestibule near the door where I could wait, pray, and talk things over with people.

While waiting there, I discovered the writings of Thomas Merton and Dorothy Day. That they both had converted freely to Catholicism fascinated me. Each, in a unique way, held together the paradoxes that had ripped American Protestantism into liberal and evangelical/sectarian pieces. For example, Merton chose a highly "sectarian" option — the Trappist order — while passionately denouncing injustice and indiscriminate warfare. Dorothy Day was an activist-journalist in the social gospel tradition who also wrote with mystical fervor about the "primacy of the spiritual life" and never stopped searching for her crucified and risen Lord among the broken ones she served. My experience in liberal Protestantism had been social concern with little spirituality, whereas the evangelicals had a spirituality that didn't seem to address itself to the transformation of unjust social structures. But both spirituality and social concern were present in the Catholic Church, and in a way I'd not seen before.

I encountered in Merton and Day, and in many other Catholics I was coming to know, a certain kind of awareness or spiritual wisdom. Specifically, they knew themselves in all of their weakness, sinfulness, and giftedness; and they knew God in the depths of his mercy and healing power. I knew precious little of my own sin, even less of my own giftedness, and by then I knew God only by reputation. How could these Catholics probe their own inner recesses so fully, as fully as any Calvinist or Freudian, and yet not succumb to despair? How could they be so optimistic about the eventual redemption of the entire cosmos, and yet be sober about the exact cost involved?

More and more, I found that the answers to these questions had something to do with the mystery of the Eucharist, and the sacramental life as a whole. The action I stumbled upon in the Greenfield church, the action I vowed to try to comprehend, was the mutual exchange of gifts that is the Eucharist. God invites us to offer ourselves to Him (our actual selves, not our ideal or "religious" selves), and in return He gives us the most precious gift imaginable: Jesus — Son of Mary, Son of God. The Mass begins with a penitential rite, in which we ponder our sin and God's mercy. At the Eucharistic prayer we lift up, as a community, the fruits and gifts of our lives, our brokenness, and our very selves. At Communion, we get them all back again, transformed, along with the Real Presence of the Lord, who comes among us to feed, heal, reconcile, and to call us to works of healing and justice.

Each of the sacraments is a different way of enacting the divine-human exchange, which is an image or symbol of the eternal exchange taking place among the three Persons of the Holy Trinity. There is no question here of bargaining or manipulation. The initiative is all on God's side, and God is the source, finally, of everything we have to give, including the very desire to give at all.

The Eucharist, especially, is structured in such a way as to dispel both our presumption and despair. We are invited to accept both the fact of our own frailty and the wonder of God's stupendous love, made incarnate before our eyes. As a lapsed believer in the suburban gospel of success, I was prone to presumption on some days and despair on many others. I knew that I needed to find a more sane and realistic way to live. I knew I needed the Eucharist and a church that was founded on it.

God was calling me to leave the vestibule and make my way to the sanctuary. I joined the catechumenate at the Paulist Center in Boston and was received into full Catholic communion at the Easter Vigil there in 1978. Since that time, the Lord has nurtured and challenged me in many ways, principally through the people of my parish, Saint Ann's in Boston. Chief among those instruments is the woman I later married, Kathleen Sheehan. She has a penchant for doing the truth rather than merely talking or writing about it. Her laugh could lighten a heart of lead, and her love, enacted daily, is God's major grace in my life.

I have also had the privilege over the past few years of working with Father Henri Nouwen, a priest and writer I first met while we were both at Yale twelve years ago. Our friendship has helped me grow in many ways, and I stand in awe of his ability, as a writer, to share his own inner struggles with complete honesty and trust — and in a way that speaks profoundly to the needs of Christians across the entire ecumenical spectrum.

I am grateful to be a Catholic Christian in the late twentieth century. It is exhilarating to be part of a body so full of paradox and so blessed with opportunity. At the same time, I would never deny that we are beset with certain weaknesses and lacunae: for example, our peculiar tendency either to exalt or degrade women, and thus deny their full humanity; also our tendency toward authoritarianism, which has periodically broken out in the form of uncharitable, even cruel, behavior toward Jews, dissenters, and nonbelievers. These and other failings are not paradoxes, but contradictions against the gospel of Jesus Christ. We must carefully distinguish paradoxes from contradictions and repent of the latter, lest we be blind to our own failings and forever project them upon others. The corollary to this, of course, is that we must be quick to acknowledge the gift of sanctity wherever it appears, whether inside or outside the Catholic fold.

Nevertheless, the authentic, life-giving paradoxes of Catholicism are many and diverse. For example, the Catholic Church is both a local, even tribal, phenomenon and a transnational institution with a global reach. It is inclusive: every social class, race, and level of ability is represented. "Catholic" means "including everybody." Moreover, Catholicism is both a sanctuary for adoration and contemplation and an animator of political and social reconstruction. We honor those who surrender everything to devote themselves to prayer and penance, and those who labor patiently as husbands, wives, parents, and workers in the secular arena. We are a vast repository of historic wisdom, culture, and tradition, which is also committed to "reading the signs of the times" and bound by our Lord to look with hope toward the future. We have a clear, coherent, and authoritative body of moral teaching, as well as a long history of pastoral clemency and solicitude toward human failure. We affirm the dignity and goodness of the human body, and indeed of the entire created order, yet we look toward the transfiguration of all things in the kingdom of God.

We must embrace these paradoxes, celebrate them, and bear them in our very flesh and bones. This is our vocation. I pray that God will help us remain faithful to it, for the sake of our own salvation and that of the world.

8

JOHN MICHAEL TALBOT

On Becoming a
Radical for Christ

*Formerly a successful rock 'n' roll recording artist, John Michael Talbot is now a
Franciscan brother living in the Little Portion prayer community he founded in
Arkansas. His religious recordings have sold in the millions.* He has also written
several books, among them Changes *(1984),* The Lover and the Beloved
(1985), The Fire of God *(1986), and* Reflections on the Gospel *(1986).*
*He has generated hundreds of thousands of dollars for the poor through his concert
appearances. He is honorary chairman of Mercy Corps International and founder of
Franciscan Mercy Corps, agencies that together assist the world's homeless and
hungry.*

I sat at the end of our long driveway throwing pebbles into a
pool of water that had collected in the gravel. The water was
muddy, the color of the red Oklahoma clay. The warm summer
breeze blew through the leaves of the oak trees in the yard around
our comfortable, suburban ranch house.

It was the house of our family's dreams. There were plenty of trees
and open space to satisfy any small child's adventurous fantasies. We
three kids had a room to ourselves in one end of the house with Mom
and Dad situated at the other in a large master bedroom. They were
far enough away for privacy but not too far away — we felt the security of their love. Two rock fireplaces always warmed the house on
winter evenings.

My father was successful in public relations and sales. He had
worked for Braniff Airlines at its beginnings after World War II and
seemed always ahead of his time. My mother was a housewife, the
daughter of a Methodist minister. Both were always there when
needed. All seemed safe. All seemed secure. We felt blessed by God
and very happy.

My dad often spoke to me of God, usually during those warm,

summer nights when we would sit looking up into the immensity of the stars, knowing that God created them all. My mother, too, spoke to us of Jesus, sometimes singing a religious song at the piano. She wasn't too "churchy" though. Perhaps she got too much of that as she was growing up.

I also have fond memories of the children's Bible stories we heard at Sunday school. And I liked to hear the people sing, I mean *really* sing the hymns at church. I recall my older brother, Terry, always being able to sing the choral harmonies—I was proud to be his younger brother. I don't, however, remember much about what was preached. During that part of the service I would usually draw imaginative action scenes of airplanes and ships at sea. Wisely, my mother didn't object.

All seemed right in my childhood world. I was loved and I loved. We were not rich, but we were comfortable. We seemed secure in the hands of God.

I suppose it was at the end of the driveway on that warm summer afternoon that the reality of God first dawned on me. I looked into the water and up at the trees. I felt the wind blow across my face. It was then that I realized that God loved me.

I emphasize this childhood account to bring out the significance of my baptism as a child. Today many "born-again" Protestant Christians belittle infant baptism, saying that it isn't important until one is an adult. I once felt the same way. Granted, adult conversion to Jesus Christ is important for both the baptized and the nonbaptized, and some outer symbol of that adult conversion is often necessary and good. But I don't believe this negates the grace bestowed upon a child who has been baptized as a Christian.

My religious upbringing was not an intense one. Some would have called my family's faith "nominal." But I believe I experienced a grace I would not have otherwise had by being formally baptized into a professing Christian family and faith community. I believe God gave me the grace of Jesus in my childhood baptism.

I say this to encourage young Christian parents. The Scriptures say, "Raise a child in the way he should go and when he is older he will not depart from it." It is good to baptize your children in Christ. Even if they depart for a time, the grace bestowed by God through the faith of the family and the church community will not be in vain. Even if it is minimal, it will offer Jesus to your children in a way they would not otherwise experience.

This is not to limit God's grace in baptism to the faith of the family or the believing community. God is sovereign. He moves when He wills. Practically speaking, we can see that He often works through the faith of those around a young child who is baptized. Mystically, God is able to move as He wills, like the wind that blew through the oak trees in my yard on that summer afternoon so long ago. Who is to say my perception of God in that wind was not the direct result of my baptism? This is true especially since baptism is a direct command of Jesus Christ.

Scripture commands all followers of Jesus to be baptized. It also depicts the entire households of adult converts as being baptized. The experience of the early Church confirms a nearly universal practice of baptizing, not only adult converts, but their children as well. Only Tertullian disagreed. Infant baptism simply wasn't an issue in the early Church. It was a normal practice.

Still, I fell away from the faith, for a time. Despite my baptism and good Christian upbringing, I began to go the way of most young American boys in the 1960s. I began replacing God with secular interests. First it was baseball, which seemed innocent enough, but soon it occupied all my dreams. I can remember my uncle reaching down to tickle my ear with his little finger. "Ol' John," he would say with a typical Oklahoma drawl, "I believe if we opened up your head, little baseballs would fall out." Obviously, those around me thought I was a bit preoccupied!

Soon, however, music began to become my primary preoccupation and desire. It became my very life. It became my God.

At eight I picked up the drums because drummers seemed somehow "athletic." Then I saw a banjo player on television. His music was happy and, besides, he was an earthy-looking character and I loved cowboys and mountain men. The banjo appeared to be a snare drum with a guitar neck and strings on it so I figured the switch from drums to banjo would be easy. I was wrong.

The strings of a banjo are made of thin steel. The end of a string is not unlike the end of a sewing needle. I can remember long hours of painful practice as my tender fingers went through a seemingly endless series of blisters, cuts, and calluses. The loud, not-so-musical sounds from my long practice sessions must have driven my mother crazy.

As soon as I learned about five chords, I joined a folk group called the Quinchords, started by my older brother and sister about a year earlier. We placed high in the Indiana State Fair "hootenanny" competition—a nice professional start. In the course of playing all the favorite folk songs of the early sixties for a seemingly endless array of Rotary Clubs, Knights of Columbus dinners, and Methodist Youth Fellowship gatherings, I also picked up the guitar. It would later become my primary instrument.

With the onslaught of "Beatlemania" in 1964, folk music went into a nose dive. After a short regrouping, the Quinchords became Sounds Unlimited, and the Talbot family began "folk rocking" their way across the midwestern United States. First place in the "battle of the bands" at another state fair competition won us a small-time recording contract.

By 1968 we experimented with a new idiom in American music called "country rock." We reintroduced the banjo into our rock 'n' roll sound with a new kind of twist. I also picked up several other instruments: the pedal steel guitar, the dobro, and a working knowledge of bass and drums. With our versatile and novel sound we soon landed a national recording contract with a not-so-impressive label under the "wing" of the Flying Tiger Corporation, called Happy Tiger Records. Soon we had some FM radio hits and found ourselves on the national concert scene of the late sixties. Later, we recorded a number of albums for Warner Brothers Records.

There definitely is no such thing as an "overnight success." We played dive after dive in order to expose our music to people around the country. We slept on floors. We ate truck-stop food. We worked hard for the success we enjoyed. At an early age I was subjected to things I never should have seen.

All this put me in an unusual situation. Suddenly, at age fifteen, I was able to see the reality of success. I saw in person many rock and folk stars I had idolized. Most of them were miserable. They had everything I wanted — money, success, fame — yet most of them were personally frustrated and terribly unhappy. I saw many of the so-called "greats" break down in tears because of the mess their lives had become. Some even took their own lives in a final outcry of loneliness and despair. God allowed me to see the end of the course I was pursuing before I personally arrived there myself. This, too, I believe was an unmerited grace.

I began praying again. I started reading an old Revised Standard Version of the Bible my grandmother had given me. I also started reading other religious literature, the Vedic literature of Hinduism and books on the American Indian Medicine Wheel, among others. In all these books I found elements of truth *about* God, but I did not actually enter into a personal relationship *with* God.

I began to pray: "God, I want to know you. Are you a 'he,' a 'she,' or an 'it'? I don't care! I just want to know you."

After about a year of daily prayer, God answered my prayer in the person of Jesus Christ. I didn't understand any of the theology about the divinity and humanity of Christ, or the awesome mystery of the Trinity. All I know is that I prayed for a personal love relationship with God and that prayer was answered in the person of Jesus.

This all occurred as a visionary experience. In this vision, I saw the classical Christ figure: a figure of transparent, bright light holding His arms out to me. I could not make out the fine details, but this figure had long, dark hair and a beard and was robed in light. I immediately understood and knew it was Jesus.

I sensed at this moment a total expansion of my awareness, like someone had thrown open the windows of my soul to let in the light. I sensed that this figure was God, that He was an all-powerful, all-knowing, perfect being. I was immediately aware of my own imperfection and that the very being of His perfection judged, by its simple nature, all of my sins in stark reality. I knew that He, in His perfection, could judge me as easily as I judge the life of a fly before I swat it. Yet, at the same time, I sensed that Jesus chose to be gentle and patient with me. He chose to spare my life. He could easily have condemned me in the truth of justice. But he chose to forgive. Somehow I knew Jesus had, in fact, forgiven my sins!

People often say that visions are only a psychological phenomenon. I do not fully understand the ramifications of my experience. I only know it happened. God created me with a psychology—if He wants to use it in order to reach me, that is His business. The argument as to whether a vision might be psychological or not is entirely beside the point to me. I only know that I had a personal experience of God's love in the person of Jesus Christ through this vision. That is enough for me.

At this point I began calling myself a "Christian" once again. I didn't understand denominational theology. I only knew that Jesus was God and that He had forgiven my sins. This experiential knowledge bore much fruit in my life. At that time I became more completely human. My friends say I became a better friend. My family says I became happier and more cheerful. My fellow band members said I became very easy to work with. Jesus said you will know the source of a spiritual reality by its fruit. Perhaps that should be the primary test of any so-called vision.

It was at this time that I met, and soon married, my wife. I was barely seventeen. She was a "grown woman" of nineteen. She was beautiful, tanned, and blond; she seemed like the incarnation of purity. I suppose, subconsciously, she symbolized to me the truth and beauty my soul sought. I was too young to know the difference. Later I would discover I had substituted a relationship with this wonderful woman for a deeper relationship with God. It was unfair to the woman. It was unfair to God. The marriage would later end in divorce and would be annulled by the Church.

Then came another trial—I met other Christians! First I saw them in airports, an intense look in their eyes and religious tracts in their hands. They began coming up to me after my concerts. They were filled with inquiries and demands; did I have the right kind of Bible? A Revised Standard would never do. I simply *had* to have a Scofield Reference Bible. A Barcley's Commentary wouldn't do either. I *had* to have an Unger's Bible Dictionary. Of course, all of these "Bible tools" were really "Bible interpretations," each with its own theological interpretation.

Yet, the Christians who seemed to be most outwardly excited about their faith were the media-proclaimed "Jesus freaks," who adopted this fundamentalist theology. Having come from the highly existential, free-love world of hippiedom, they adopted the theological extreme of Protestant fundamentalism in order to give their spiritual and moral life clear, concrete direction.

I gradually accepted a similar Protestant fundamentalism to objectively guide my life with Christ, and I must say that it seemed to work for a short time. It gave me a clear direction concerning some basic beliefs common to all Christians. Likewise, it gave me a clear path to follow regarding personal morality. The issues of drugs and sex and the violence of war all seemed to be addressed by this theology. In a world where the basic theology of God, Jesus Christ, and the human being were so vague and unclear in much of mainline Christianity, fundamentalism provided the searching soul with clarity.

But the crystalline clarity of this theology soon degenerated into cold and lifeless legalism. I studied the Scriptures for hours every day. My relationship with God and people became less and less personal as I crammed all life's experience into my narrow interpretation of Scripture. If you had a personal problem, I had a Scripture for it. I became like a little Scripture computer constantly giving Scripture "readouts" to people in need. The life-giving love of Jesus Christ was slowly disappearing from my newfound Christian faith. I was committing the sin of "bibliolatry."

The picture of Jesus I was portraying degenerated from a masterpiece of life-filled hue and color into a lifeless, colorless cartoon. I would have to say that, due to the absence of color, the artists who were drawing this picture of Christ began to distort the placement of these lines in order to achieve at least some artistic impact. Soon even the basic lines became distorted. So the fact became clear and remains clear: instead of being a life-filled oil painting of Jesus Christ, the fundamentalist version of Christ is a distorted cartoon.

Ironically, my initial conversion to Christ was spurred by seeing other people's breakdowns. But suddenly, as a Christian fundamentalist, I was experiencing a breakdown of my own. Without the colors and hues of Jesus, my Christianity became lifeless and empty.

Because I had no life, I could not minister life. Soon my friends and family began to write me off. My wife of six years left me. I was devastated. I cannot say she was without cause. My Christianity had backfired. Soon all of my family and friends were gone. I was left alone.

It was at this point of despair that a friend gave me a copy of a book about Saint Francis of Assisi called *The Journey and the Dream*, by Murray Bodo. In the pages of this short book I read about a man who lived some eight hundred years ago; yet his story inflamed my soul with God's love. He had what I had lost and sought to regain. God used this *poverello*, this little poor man from Assisi, to transform and renew the Western Christian world with the original fire and fervor of the Holy Spirit.

He was a radical Christian, but he was not a fanatic. A radical is one who is rooted firmly and deeply in the gospel. A fanatic is hung up on mere externals, emphasizing one or the other points of the gospel to undue extremes.

Francis's life demonstrated that Jesus doesn't make freaks out of people; he makes people out of freaks. Francis was a "Jesus freak," a "charismatic." He was "born again" in the fullest sense of the phrase. Yet he avoided all the fanatical pitfalls into which I had apparently fallen headlong. He understood the gospel of Jesus Christ in the same way I did at the beginning. For Francis, the gospel was alive. It was a living word from a living God to a living people. In Saint Francis of Assisi I saw a way back to my first love. Like a prodigal son, I wanted to come back home.

There was just one small problem: Saint Francis of Assisi was a Catholic! His home was "Mother Church." He was a radical reformer, but he always carried out renewal with a humility that kept him ardently submissive to the authority of the Church. Francis was a "papist" through and through. He was a radical Catholic, but he was not a fanatical fundamentalist.

I had been theologically trained to believe that the Roman Catholic Church was the "whore of Babylon" spoken of in Revelation 17 and 18. I knew all the arguments against the Catholic Church. I had "saved" many people from the clutches of her "apostasy." It was easy! Just quote a few Scriptures out of context, turn the head of some unsuspecting Catholic, and one, two, three, I left them stammering, unable to explain their faith.

Yet here stood Francis, ministering the love of Jesus in a way both gentle and true to renew my parched soul. He was a contemplative, yet a fiery gospel evangelist. He was a social activist for peace, but he was never a rebel against authority. He was a gospel literalist, but never a fundamentalist. Francis was not a theologian, but he had a deep and abiding love for the rich mystical theology of the Church. Francis fulfilled all the legitimate spiritual desires of the radical fundamentalists, but he did it in a way that was fully Catholic.

Then I came face to face with another dilemma: the obvious disunity of the professing faith communities of Jesus Christ. I would talk to one seemingly intelligent, well-meaning group of believers, yet they often disagreed with other groups of believers who seemed equally intelligent, well meaning, and Spirit filled. All claimed the Scriptures as their primary source of knowledge about Jesus and the church. All were educated, often holding high degrees in theologically related areas. All were well meaning, genuinely wanting to see unity among Jesus' followers. All manifested various fruits and gifts of the Spirit. Yet, try as they might, they could not agree among themselves. They could not bring unity. This disagreement was not about some irrelevant, speculative theological issue. It was about the basics of the faith. Who is Jesus? What did He say and do? Who does He want us to be?

We could not find agreement about the one thing Jesus commanded us to do when we assembled together in His name — the Lord's Supper. Obviously, if we could not agree on the meaning of Communion, sharing it would destroy its credibility. It would be like consummating the union between lovers before they agreed on the real meaning of marriage. It is something Jesus commanded us to do, but we cannot do it. How sad, yet how fitting that this great sacramental sign of unity is prohibited precisely because we are still divided.

What, then, is the answer? There had to be an additional God-given dimension to discerning the truth of the gospel as a united people.

It was here that I stumbled upon universal truth: if the Scriptures came forth from God through the Church, they can only be properly interpreted through the Church. Failure to recognize the God-given authority of the Church destroys the authority of the Scriptures themselves. So, if there is a debatable passage of Scripture that divides Christian communities today (and there are many) it only makes sense to go back to the early Church from which the Scriptures came to see how they interpreted that same passage. If a substantial agreement can be found among them, then application can be made to the modern world in a developed way.

I tried it. But to my chagrin, I found out that the Fathers of the early Church were Catholic! The primitive seeds of all modern Catholic doctrines were firmly planted in the soil of the Church of the first centuries. The doctrines about Mary, prayer to the saints, purgatory, the role of the pope — all were clearly visible and accepted in the early Church, at least in their primitive form. Most especially, the place of Eucharist, or the Lord's Supper, as both a symbol and the real presence of the Body and Blood of Christ, was central to the common worship and prayer of the assembled Christian Church. Furthermore, all these beliefs and practices were centered squarely on the Jesus all Christians hold dear. Every doctrine, every sacrament, and every structure began with Jesus, were centered on Jesus, and led to Jesus. They existed for no other reason. There was no other conclusion for me to reach: the early Christian Church was Catholic! For me, the conclusion was clear. Fundamentalism leads to Catholicism because if you zealously fight to guard the authority of Scripture, you must fight for, respect, and even submit to the authority of the Church. Otherwise you deny the very authority of the Scripture upon which you base and guide your Christian faith. Ironically, the true fundamentalist must become a Catholic and, as a Catholic, can no longer be a fundamentalist.

So there I was, a staunch Protestant fundamentalist, anti-Catholic to the core, being confronted by the Catholic Church at every turn. It was the Catholic Church that brought me Jesus again. Fundamentalism had failed me; it was the Catholic Church that was saving me. I was finding the heart of Jesus Christ through Saint Francis. I was finding the mind of Jesus Christ through the early Church Fathers. Both sources were Catholic through and through! Quite literally, I was being "reborn" in Christ through the Catholic Church.

I retreated into prayer at the Franciscan Retreat Center of Alverna in Indianapolis, Indiana. I walked the secluded paths through the woods and sat for long hours next to the gently flowing creek and simply listened to the voice of God. Here He spoke to me in the quiet recesses of my heart and I will never forget what He said: "John, the Catholic Church is my first church. I love her most dearly. She has been sick and has nearly died. But I am going to heal her and raise her to new life. I want you to be a part of her." At that point I could only say, "Amen."

Some say that the conflicts in today's Church and many seemingly "dead" parishes clearly demonstrate a sick Church. Indeed, I would agree that it takes a miracle of grace for us to overlook these externals and instead see the underlying value and faith of the Church.

But what about the Anglicans and the Orthodox? What about the Lutherans? Don't they all consider themselves "Catholic" too? What about the phenomenon of the small new sects trying to return to the catholicity of the Church Fathers by an awareness of liturgy, sacraments, and Apostolic Succession in their church structures of bishop, presbyter, and deacon?

I would answer these questions by a simple appeal to the reality of the pope. All of these catholic-oriented expressions claim to have the Apostolic Succession and structure that Jesus ordained to insure unity in the Church. Yet none of these expressions can accomplish that hoped-for unity. They might even have valid bishops, with a continued succession of apostolic antiquity or history (such as the Patriarchs of Constantinople, Jerusalem, Antioch or Alexandria). But none of these bishops who succeed even the greatest and best-known apostles have been able to bring unity without a leader who can claim the objective authority of both Scripture and apostolic tradition.

The Orthodox are still divided among themselves. The Archbishop of Canterbury cannot exert the needed authority to unite the Anglicans. The Lutheran approach to things "catholic" is still only hesitantly accepted among this church's members.

Only the Bishop of Rome can claim the full authority of both Scripture and Tradition to unite the Church. Only Peter was universally understood in the Early Church to stand in Christ's place as the leader of the Apostles, ordained by Jesus Himself. Only the Bishop of Rome was seen as Saint Peter's legitimate successor. Common sense and experience deemed that someone had to take the place of leader. Otherwise, even the best college of apostles and succeeding bishops could be deadlocked in controversy and debate. That "someone" was the Bishop of Rome, the successor of Saint Peter, the pope. Only he could claim an authority based on both Scripture and apostolic tradition that, objectively and historically, link and unite the Church of Jesus Christ with the authority of Jesus Christ.

The mere existence of the Roman Catholic Church argues in favor of this position. There is no larger unified group of professing Christians on the face of the earth. Yet the people would not be united without the pope and the pope would not carry such weight in proclaiming the gospel to the world, without the people. Think of it: no other Christian leader has such impact in spreading the gospel of Jesus Christ. Billy Graham has never preached to so many. Pat Robertson has never received such widespread television coverage. Bishop Tutu has never had such profound effect on peace and social justice. There is no group of pentecostal charismatics so large. There is no parish renewal movement so diverse and strong as the various renewal programs and teams that branch out through our parishes. All of these renewals stand ultimately united in the Church because of the existence of the pope.

Today we are at a turning point. Never before has the world possessed the potential for bringing God's blessings to so many, yet never before have so many faced poverty, war, and ultimate destruction. The issues that face us are awesome and vast. Widespread sexual immorality breaks down the human family. Abortion, global poverty, and the ever-present threat of nuclear war are problems set deeply within our modern society. They require a radical Christian response. I believe it is the Roman Catholic Church that lifts up its voice most radically for Jesus Christ as it meets the challenges of our modern world. No other institution has spoken out so loud and clear since the beginning of the atomic age, that the nuclear arms race is an immoral option for the just defense of the nations of this world. No other institution on the face of the earth has spoken out so consistently for a preferential option for the poor, speaking out prophetically against both atheistic Marxism and the immorality of the materialism of the West. No other institution can match the Catholic stand against the devastation and devaluation of human life through abortion.

Ironically, it is that much-debated document of Pope Paul VI, *Humanae Vitae* (Human Life), that is proving to be most prophetic. Standing in uncompromising reverence of God's creation of human life, it calls forth a sophisticated and consistent moral theology of life to the Church and the world. It is also proving to be fundamental in all areas concerning basic human rights and reverence of *all* life. I believe this document will prove to be one of the most prophetic works of this era. Once again, it is an encyclical of a pope.

Furthermore, the Catholic Church calls people to a balanced political involvement in shaping the future of this world. While respecting the separation of Church and State in America, she calls all Christians everywhere to stand up for both freedom of religion and a basic human morality that is consistent with both the laws of nature and God's revelation of just government through Holy Scripture. Recognizing the limitations of any human government in this age, she still calls all people to follow Christ's command to be peacemakers.

All of this has profound social and political ramifications, starting within the community of the Church and reaching out to spread the gospel of Jesus Christ to every living soul. This means that the Church itself is called to live the gospel radically. It means that Catholic Christians must raise their voices in appropriate political ways to insure the basic human rights of all the people throughout the world.

The Catholic Church brings the gospel of Jesus Christ to our modern world in a way that challenges us to radically respond to God's call. It is time to be radical for Christ. It is time to be on fire for God. It is time to begin the gentle revolution that can transform the entire earth in the peace that passes all understanding. If we do not respond, the world will perish. If we do not take our role as "leaven" seriously in these times, the "dough" of the world will fall flat.

I propose the following slogan: "Be a radical. Be a Catholic!" The world faces a darkness that only the light of Christ can dispel. I feel that if you look realistically around this troubled world, you will find no other institution so fully shining Jesus' light as the Catholic Church. It was the Catholic Church that first brought the gospel of Jesus Christ to the world. Today is no exception. It is also the full instrument of God's salvation in this lost and troubled time. Never before has it been so apparent that the salvation offered by Jesus Christ to the world is brought forth most fully through the Catholic Church.

If you want to get radical for Jesus, if you want to be on fire with the Spirit, if you want to join this gentle revolution, then look into the Catholic Church. If you are a Catholic already, then really *be* Catholic. If a Catholic simply obeys the teaching of the pope and bishops, that person will be radical enough to shake this world, and spread the gospel of Jesus Christ wherever he or she may live.

I recall an incident that occurred during one of our Franciscan community's itinerant parish missions. We had just returned from street ministry when I heard a woman's scream coming from the highway. Running outside, I found a young girl of twenty or so lying flat on her back in the road. A semitrailer had sideswiped her as she returned home from work on her motorcycle. In an instant her life had been drastically changed. The bone protruding through her flesh indicated that she had a compound fracture in her lower right leg; she also had a broken collarbone and possible internal injuries. She lay helpless in the middle of the sunbaked pavement, which must have been at least 150 degrees on this hot summer day. Drifting in and out of consciousness, she alternated between screams of pain and threats of vengeance against the trucker who had unknowingly hit her and continued down the road. All I could do was comfort her a little and pray.

It was here that my Catholicism was most tested. There were no theological arguments to be shared. No global crises to be overcome. There was only me and this newly crippled girl. Here I stammered for words of love in the face of her anger and fear. Here I prayed for courage to overcome my normally weak stomach as I confronted this broken, bloodied person. I prayed that the Jesus of history, the Jesus the Church has proclaimed for some two thousand years, would somehow work through my own frail human attempts of love and concern, to bring salvation to this thoroughly modern young girl. This is what all of our sacraments, all of our doctrines, and all of our structures are ultimately for. This is where "the rubber meets the road."

I honestly don't know if I succeeded. I held her hand. I told her to hold on and be calm. I supported her mangled leg. I don't recall that I said a word to her about Jesus or God. She only knew that a Franciscan friar, a "monk," was there to love her and care for her. Ironically, everything I am as a Catholic Christian Franciscan brother went into this wordless proclamation of the gospel of Jesus Christ.

Later I visited her in the hospital. She was asleep. Her broken bones had been set in heavy casts. She was going to be okay. In the quiet stillness of her hospital room, I prayed over her. Then I left a tape of my prayer songs by her bed. I still pray for her, although not as much now as immediately after the accident. I pray for her health. I pray for her soul. I honestly believe that this is the most effective way I can share my Catholic Christian faith. This is what Catholicism, ultimately, is all about. It is the way of love, the love that comes from God through His Son Jesus Christ.

9

THOMAS HOWARD

Lead, Kindly Light

Thomas T. Howard, Ph.D., has taught English at the Kingsmead School, Cheshire, England, at Saint Bernard's School, New York, and at Gordon College, where he twice received the Excellence in Teaching Award. Since September 1985 he has been teaching English at Saint John's Seminary College in Brighton, Massachusetts, and at Our Lady of Grace Seminary in Boston. Dr. Howard has written numerous books, including Christ the Tiger *(1967),* The Liturgy Explained *(1981),* Evangelical Is Not Enough *(1984), and* Christianity: The True Humanism *(with J. I. Packer; 1985). His articles have appeared in such periodicals as the* New York Times Magazine, Redbook, New Oxford Review, *and* Christianity Today. *The following narrative, in which Professor Howard describes what first drew him to explore Catholicism, appeared in the religious journal* Communio *(vol. 8, no. 4) in winter 1981. At the Easter Vigil in 1985, he was received into the Roman Catholic Church.*

During the summer of 1980 there occurred in Thailand a congress. It did not attract the attention of the Western news media, so most of us are unaware of it. It was called the Congress on World Evangelization. Nearly two thousand Christians from well over a hundred nations, and representing literally tens of millions of Christian believers, came there to talk seriously about the apostolic task given by Our Lord to His Church just before His Ascension. Many of these delegates were from places like Hungary, Russia, North Korea, Southeast Asia, Uganda, South Africa, and other places where to be a Christian means to know what suffering and even martyrdom mean. Just to read the statistical reports from the congress was to have one's heart strangely warmed, not to say broken.

I have often been asked to set down as well as I can just what it is that keeps driving me closer and closer to the ancient Church of Rome. The above paragraph would seem to be an unlikely way to begin such an account, except that on at least two levels that congress dramatizes with terrible clarity the difficulty that lies at the root of any ecclesiastical pilgrimage I might contemplate.

My twofold difficulty is this. First, the entire congress was carried on with virtually no consciousness of the questions that loom so gigantically in the landscape of my own religious vision — questions of sacrament, liturgy, antiquity, catholicity, unity, apostolicity, and so forth. Oh, to be sure, there were many Anglicans there, and Anglicans are supposed to take these questions seriously. But in the areas of the world, especially the Third World, where we find a robust, growing, suffering, faithfully witnessing, and vigorously evangelistic Anglican Church, we find that it is usually Low Church, that is, that its concerns are with getting people saved and grounded in the Bible, not with teaching them liturgy, hagiology, and sacramental theology. If "low" is a term of obloquy in the opinion of any Anglican, then he had better pack his bag and make his pilgrimage to Uganda; his mouth will be stopped forever. I say this as a man whose own pilgrimage has led him steeply toward what many people would jocularly call Anglo-papism. But as a Christian I must ponder what was visible at that congress: tens of millions of my faithful, zealous, even suffering brothers and sisters in Christ who are mature, biblical, articulate Christians, who live their whole lives never once contemplating these questions that I (or, say, Saint Augustine and Saint Benedict and Saint Thomas and Cardinal Newman and Ronald Knox and Yves Congar and Gregory Dix and David Knowles and John Paul II) struggle with. Those Christians love and serve Jesus Christ, they know the Scriptures, they nurse no heresies, they win others — thousands and thousands of others — to belief in Him, they exhibit a transparent integrity and holiness of life that more worldly Christians might try to pass off with an airy comment about "pietism" or "anabaptist." Whatever it is, it is right bang on the New Testament target — or, if we don't like talk of the Bible, since that is too fundamentalist, then the apostolic target.

This is the first level of difficulty: here are all these Christians who seem to me to exhibit virtually all the qualities that Christ looks for in His people. Shouldn't they be my model? How can I possibly set my concerns, so luxuriously pursued in the quiet of my study, over against their priorities — priorities tested in decades of patient endurance, humility, fortitude, and suffering?

The second level is this: I know that crowd. My own spiritual nurture came from that wing of Christendom. My "Catholicism" has grown from a deep matrix of years and years of nothing but the Bible. I know hundreds, even thousands, of those people. Of countless ones of them I would have not the slightest hesitation about saying to angels, demons, and men, "What? You want to see what a true Christian looks like? Here, I'll show you." But it is closer than that. Not only was my whole family of this ilk (not snake handlers or even holy rollers, but plain, blue-stocking Philadelphia Christians), but one of my own brothers is the man who ran that Thailand congress. He is a man whose sheer sobriety, wisdom, integrity, and sane biblical common sense I trust utterly. He travels round and round the globe, meeting with pastors from embattled churches in hostile societies, and lay people who carry on year after year on less than a shoestring, and bishops (yes, even Anglican bishops) and others whose whole intention is getting people *saved*. Nary a conversation about the liturgy, the sacraments, the nature of episcopacy, the saints and angels, or least of all the claim of the Apostolic See in Rome.

The other half of all this, of course, is that for hundreds of millions of Christians down through the centuries this latter set of topics has furnished, if not necessarily the stuff of conversation, then at least the fabric of the vision that they assume. The whole set of assumptions at work in this vision is so vastly remote from those at work in the imagination of the others of whom I have been speaking that no one at all has ever been able to bridge the distance between the two. The last irony, of course, is that both crowds would walk straight into the lion's jaws singing the Nicene Creed and meaning every syllable of it.

The dilemma presents itself to me in the following way: does any of this matter? Shouldn't a man just hang his hat on such and such a hook in Christendom and stop rending his garments about questions that everyone else has got quite happily settled? I mean, neither the Roman priest in my home town nor the Baptist minister (nor, may I add, their respective clienteles) is the slightest bit worried over these questions. Each of them knows the answer, never mind that the two answers cancel each other out. Why should I, a mere layman, bother? And the stakes are somewhat higher than this: there is something pettifogging about a man who forever pecks away at the questions that *divide* Christians. My great mentor C. S. Lewis fiercely refused to do this, ever. What is more tiresome than some zealot who hauls every single conversation round to Calvinism versus Arminianism, or pedobaptism versus believers' baptism, or premillenialism versus amillennialism, or Gallicanism versus Ultramontanism? From pedants and partisans and bores, and all their strident blatting, Good Lord, deliver us.

So, for me, the question is not a nice easy "Should I pope or not?" but rather, "Aren't you wasting your time chasing fox fires?" Look again at the plain, sturdy job of work in the kingdom that is getting done by all these Christians who never in their lives come across the questions that dance along in front of you.

But I have used a very strong word here. To pope: to submit oneself to the Roman Catholic Church. The word was used, pejoratively sometimes, sometimes jocularly, of Newman and people like that. Why should I want to do so at all? As an Episcopalian, am I not the fortunate member of the best of all possible churches? Here one can be Catholic while being innocent of Roman excesses. One can be Reformed without having lost the Apostolic Succession and tumbled into the free-church ditch. One can flirt with Byzantium, even hanging up icons if one likes, and also read the spiritual books of such starkly evangelical Anglicans as Charles Simeon, Bishop Handley Moule, John Stott, and J. I. Packer. Surely there is no more prudent place to be?

Perhaps so. Perhaps I may die an Anglican. I know—heaven knows I know—all the arguments.

My free-church friends and colleagues have the simplest solution of all: the Church—the entire Church—went off the rails about A.D. 95, and so Church history is a farce. Only the faithful (read "evangelical") remnant matters. My difficulty with this line of thought has been settled forever by Saint Augustine's argument against the Donatists: no matter how mucked up the Church is, you can't start anything new. It is the only church we have, and Christ calls it His Spouse and sanctifies it with His Holy Spirit, not with the right livin' of its members. I am aware that this raises the awesome question of Apostolic Succession. The only comment I might venture here is that the notion of there being any such succession apart from the *physical laying on of apostolic hands* is unknown either to the New Testament or the Early Church. You couldn't just hive off and start something *else*.

My Anglican friends take two different lines. If they are evangelical and Low Church, they cannot see the problem. What do I think the Reformation was all *about*? The Anglican heritage is Protestant, man: why dilly-dally with all this popish frippery? (Quite seriously, it is excessively difficult to get many people to grant that the questions that bedevil me are not just that: frippery.) For them the liturgy is just a nice orderly way of organizing a worship service; the sacraments are merely helpful aids to memory; the Apostolic Succession is a succession of doctrine only.

My "Catholic"-Anglican friends argue that I am already fully Catholic, and what's the point in dodging into that hopeless Roman cul-de-sac with its absurd claims? And besides, they urge, look at Rome anyway: the old ship is full of holes. You'll pope and wake up the next morning in a lifeboat.

The one line of argument that carries the most daunting force for me is the Orthodox. One has only to read the work of Alexander Schmemann, Georges Florovsky, John Meyendorff, and Kallistos Ware, to realize that here, really, is something to be reckoned with. Alas. And on this point I find myself dodging behind two patently bogus defenses: first, how am *I* going to sort out primacy and *Filioque* when a thousand years has not sufficed? *Kyrie, Kyrie, eleison.* And second, I am a Westerner. This is like T. S. Eliot's reason for not becoming a Roman: "I am an Englishman"—no good theologically, but nonetheless almost insurmountable psychologically and emotionally.

It will long since have occurred to the reader that I have not yet got round to the question at hand: what is it that attracts me to Rome?

Here, then are the factors.

First, *attracts* is the wrong word. I am more *attracted* to Anglicanism, if we are thinking of things like music (imagine leaving King's College Chapel behind); and the way the liturgy is done (my parish in New York was Saint Mary the Virgin); and Cranmer's and Coverdale's matchlessly sublime prose; and architecture (fancy exchanging Norwich Cathedral, or even any tiny Norman or Perpendicular parish church among the hedgerows, for some ghastly shrine all done up in blonde wood, pastel plaster statues, and linoleum); and hymnody (must I leave forever J. M. Neale and John Bacchus Dykes, and "Christ Is Made the Sure Foundation," and "Vigiles et Sancti," and "Who Are These Like Stars Appearing," and "See the Conqueror Mounts in Triumph"? One could weep at the prospect).

The fundamental question, of course, is whether the Roman claim is true. There are only two possible answers to that. If I say no, then I have Augustine and Bede and Gregory and Aquinas and Erasmus and Thomas More and Ignatius and Bellarmine and Bossuet and Suarez and Newman and Chesterton and Knox against me for starters, and that makes me nervous. But infinitely more serene than that, I have the colossal *securus judicat orbis terrarum* looking passionlessly at me. "The calm judgment of the whole world" is against me. The Roman Church has, as it were, nothing to prove. Everyone else has to do the sleeve plucking and arm pawing to validate their cases.

I know the clamorous rejoinders to everything I have said so far. Libraries have been written pro and con. I would interpose the following books between my own remarks here and any agitated letters to the editor: J. H. Newman, *An Essay on the Development of Christian Doctrine*; Ronald Knox, *A Spiritual Aeneid*; Louis Bouyer, *The Spirit and Forms of Protestantism*; Henri de Lubac, *Catholicism*; Dom Bede Griffiths, *The Golden String*; and the Baltimore Cathechism. Demolish them before you demolish me.

Second, there is the intractable question of authority. Here again we all know the whole discussion before we start. The items that stick in my imagination on this point are these: Christ's words giving authority to His Apostles, and especially His words to Peter, come first, of course. He did *not* say that the Church would be built on Peter's *confession*, and it takes jiggery-pokery to make the text say that. He even named Peter Cephas, a stone. Furthermore, Christ founded one Church: He did not ascend leaving behind a book that anyone could take up and run off with (although as an evangelical, I will defend against all comers the authority of the Bible). That Church was built on the foundation of the Apostles, and in the apostolic Church it was the bishops in council who defined doctrine and anathematized heresy. All the heresiarchs believed in the inspiration of the Bible, but it took the Church to say, "This is orthodox" or "That is heterodox." The notion of *Sola Scriptura* is a new-fangled and disastrous one: we have only to look at the jumble of Protestant sects to see this and the stranglehold that the riddle of "verbal inerrancy" has on every evangelical seminary and theologian. They never talk of anything else at all.

On this point of authority, as an Anglican I am despondent over the bleak fact that there is no magisterium in my church. The bishops have thrown in the sponge on the whole question of heresy. Not that one relishes anathemas flying about, but what sort of a church is it where a bishop, from under his very miter and with his crozier in his hand, may wonder aloud to the faithful whether Jesus was a bastard, or whether God exists at all in any sense ever imagined by Jews or Christians for four thousand years; or where a vastly popular priest "comes out of the closet" with stunningly self-congratulatory panâche, and shrilly plumps for homosexual promiscuity as a deeply Christian style of life, and the church refuses either to silence or to unpriest him? To be Anglican these days is to be massively urbane at the very least, apparently: we wink at all. But how do I defend this to my Brazilian pentecostal brethren, or my fundamentalist colleagues? They call it apostasy. How shall I correct them?

This is perhaps the point at which I should touch on a difficulty I have with the Anglican position, one that is not easy to classify. It is this: most Anglican clergy and theologians will either chuckle in an avuncular way or argue quite earnestly that "the glory of Anglicanism" is its very lack of definition, or better, its comprehensiveness. It does not worry them at all that two neighboring parish churches, both claiming to be Anglican, will have irreconcilable views on such matters as the priesthood, the Eucharist, the Apostolic Succession, the nature of the sacrament itself, and let's face it, on the church itself. The nice old Anglican phenomenon is here, cranking along after 450 years, to silence any anxious protestings on the part of any fevered layman that this sort of thing is at the very least nonsense, and at the worst cynicism. If this is a quality that we must call "Anglican," then I am appalled at being an Anglo-Saxon. It makes it sound synonymous with "cretinous" or "wooly-minded."

Third, there is the sheer question of antiquity and catholicity. I know the Anglican case is that we did not begin with Henry, and that the extreme Anglican case is that we and not Rome represent the true Church of the Fathers. So be it. But *something* started in the sixteenth century in the scuffle, and it wasn't Rome. I myself am not disposed to chase the argument into such narrow defiles as the Nag's Head business, but a certain amount of tinkering is necessary to get the Anglican phenomenon steady on its course. It begs the question to say insouciantly that Anglicanism is simply English Catholicism. (Even the Gallicans have never made quite that claim for France.) Are we prepared to write Basil Cardinal Hume off as primate of a nonentity? If Anglicanism can claim catholicity in the sense of being widespread geographically, that claim is snowed under by the sheer magnitude of the comparable Roman data.

But I must confess that it would never be this sort of Anglican-Roman tit-for-tat quarrel that would budge me in either direction. I am too Saxon and too Anglican in my marrow, and too sentimental about all that Anglicanism means, not to bristle over that sort of thing. After all, do I really want to abandon Lancelot Andrewes and John Donne and George Herbert and (skipping a bit) T. S. Eliot and C. S. Lewis and Charles Williams? They are *my* men. If it's good enough for them . . . And all waggery aside, this rejoinder does, in fact, carry some weight with me.

Fourth, there is a factor that I can only call splendor. I do not refer to ceremonial dazzle. The Anglicans are generally better than the Romans on this front, with the exception of what goes on in the basilica in Rome itself. I mean the sheer splendor of the Roman Catholic *vision*. It is immense. It is full of glory. It is unsupportably bright. But not only this: it is *present*, in the Mass. Any Christian, of course, can reply, "Oh, but I believe in all that about the *mysterium tremendum* and the seraphim and the mystery of the cross and so forth." But it is only in the liturgy (pace the Reformed churches) that the whole drama is unfurled and the scrim of temporality is pierced and we begin to see both the abyss and the Sapphire Throne. It is very hard to keep this vision alive in nonliturgical worship. The Anglican rejoinder here, of course, is, "But what's the problem? We have the liturgy as well." Yes. But the thing I am speaking of seems, somehow, to show itself in that sense of the ineffable sublimity and sheer plenitude that animates not only such phenomena as the liturgical music of Palestrina, Victoria, and Mozart, but also the serene sense in which Roman Catholic philosophy may claim that the Catholic faith, rightly understood, is *absolutely satisfying* to the human intellect. One immediate example of what I am speaking of here is my own experience of trying to salvage brilliant and restless students over the last decade for the ancient faith: I despair of finding anything outside of Roman Catholic thought and spirituality that is big enough, with the possible exception of C. S. Lewis. I have to send them to Newman and Knox and Romano Guardini and Gerald Vann, not to say Merton and John of the Cross. That vision seems to open onto vistas that dwarf Reformational horizons. But it is *Roman*. We Anglicans snatch at it here and there, with only intermittent felicity. We have it by derivation. We have generated very little that can match what was there before us. And I speak as one who teaches, and who loves passionately, Donne and Herbert.

This brings me to my last point, and Romano Guardini would embody what I would like to say here. There is something about what one finds in Catholic spirituality that is—what is the word I want?—ripe. It believes in the Incarnation, and in the limitations of our mortal flesh. It is wise. It talks of day-to-day matters with an authority that is both high and charitable. It speaks to us not in terms so much of "Jesus can help you" or "I'm just a poor wayfaring stranger" or "Are we weak and heavy laden, cumbered with a load of care"—although those are all legitimate sentiments as far as they go—but rather in terms of transfiguration. Transubstantiation even: the miracle whereby the ordinary stuff of our lives, including the ambiguities and conundrums and death, are changed into glory. The Eucharist is the great paradigm of this. It is very difficult for me to chase down, even for my own satisfaction, just what this quality is. If one reads Guardini's *The Lord*, one will see what I mean. Perhaps I ought to phrase this last point as a question, then: if the Roman Church has nourished that sort of thing (*and* the writings of the Lady Julian and Richard Rolle and Bernard of Clairvaux and Saint John of the Cross and Saint Teresa of Avila and ten thousand others whose work towers above the terrible flea-market junk filling religious bookstores these days), then I must ask myself whether that source is worth finding. Nearly all mere *arguments* — about Petrine claims, about Loreto, about indulgences and the Immaculate Conception and the Perpetual Virginity and infallibility and the Infant of Prague and bingo and the Mafia and horrible Mexican cults and Borgia popes and Torquemada and the Duke of Alba — die away in the light of this question of spirituality. Not that doctrinal questions do not matter. But one pauses before some such syllogism as this: "If the Church that makes *those* claims has nourished *this* spirituality, then what is one to make of it?" Of course there are riddles and horrors. Anything as old and enormous as the Roman Church is bound to be a horror show. But then one remembers how Christ insists on calling His poor Church, who paints herself up like the Whore of Babylon sometimes — how He insists on calling her his spotless Bride.

I am still Anglican. I may die an Anglican. And I will take up arms in defense of the holy and faithful Christians I know of, by their tens of millions, for whom every word I have said would be either incomprehensible or reprehensible.

Meanwhile I can only pray, with one of my chief mentors, "Lead, Kindly Light."

10

CELIA WOLF-DEVINE

From New Age Christianity to the Catholic Church

Celia Wolf-Devine received a B.A. from Smith College and completed her Ph.D. in philosophy at the University of Wisconsin, Madison, in 1984. She is currently teaching at Stonehill College, and has taught at many other colleges and universities, including Tufts University, Simmons College, the University of San Francisco, and Saint John's University/College of Saint Benedict. Her publications have appeared in the Review of Metaphysics, *the* National Catholic Register, *and the* New Oxford Review.

In the mid-1970s I was living in Boston, teaching part time, and trying vainly to finish my dissertation in philosophy; each time I sat down to work on it I became totally blocked and panicked. Emotionally I was drained by conflicts with my family, and my periodic relationships with whatever man was most insistent in his pursuit of me at the time added to my turmoil. Spiritually I felt I was being worn down, herded in some inexorable way into a narrowing path—dying. I was grasping desperately for ways out; I learned transcendental meditation and began using the *I Ching* for guidance. Through it all, two old-timey country songs began to run through my mind, one about Jonah and the other about the prodigal son. "I believe I'll go back home, acknowledge I done wrong."

I met a woman at a party who told me about a wonderful man she'd been to who did psychic readings and gave spiritual guidance. Not wanting to get involved in any black magic, I asked if he was a Christian, and she replied that he was, or at least he read the Bible and had a crucifix and pictures of Christ. Encouraged by the *I Ching*, which gave me "turning point leading to abundance," I made an appointment and set out alone on the several-hundred-mile trip to Rochester, New York.

The night before the reading I went to one of the regular meetings of his students. The lecturer spoke about the importance of forgiveness for spiritual and physical health, and following this we had a healing meditation in which we concentrated healing energy on several members in turn. At one point during the meditation, I suddenly saw a woman's face dissolve as though seen through undulating water, and be replaced with the face of a bearded man. As we went out afterward for food, I felt an electric feeling, as though dormant mental powers had been awakened.

The psychic did readings in the basement of his unassuming suburban home. While I sat in a chair, I could see him dimly as he paced up and down behind a black curtain, smoking cigarettes. He told me a great deal about myself—my inability to trust my own judgment, my lack of emotional self-control, my negative thought patterns, my overemphasis on sex, my talent at speaking and writing, and my need for self-expression. He also reminded me of a sexually traumatic childhood experience that I had repressed, and pointed out that 1964–65 had been the year in which I had taken a wrong turn in my life spiritually. He said the face I'd seen the night before was the woman's "spirit guide" and that I had considerable psychic ability, including the ability to do magnetic healings and astral projection. Should I wish to develop my psychic gifts, he recommended contacting spiritualist churches and Eckankar, a new age religious group which emphasizes the practice of soul travel (bilocation).

Before I left, he taught me a meditation technique that involved visualizing various colors of light. He also gave me some "affirmations," which I was to repeat frequently during the day in order to develop more positive patterns of thinking. It is a basic principle of occult philosophy that thought creates reality, and that what we speak becomes reality. Thus, he said, if I could train myself in positive thinking, more positive things would happen in my life.

One affirmation, for example, was: "The infinite love of God ever enfolds me, bringing order, harmony, and peace into my mind, body, and affairs. Only good now manifests in my mind, body, and affairs."

So it was that I returned to Boston full of new hope, resolved to pursue spiritual growth and to avoid sexual entanglements. This would involve ending one relationship (which was winding down anyway) and resisting the temptation to slip into what promised to be a sexually intense, but otherwise meaningless, relationship with the man who repaired my car. As I drove, I repeated some of the affirmations: "All power is now given me in mind, body, and affairs. The power of God is now working through me to free me from every negative influence. Nothing can hold me in bondage. All power is mine to control my thoughts, to vitalize my body, to experience success, and to bless others. I am strong in the Christ consciousness. I am strong in God and in the power."[1]

The path I followed in my spiritual searching was influenced by several things. First of all I was a Christian; I belonged to Christ. I had learned the Lord's Prayer from my grandmother when I was six, gone to a Christian summer camp, and sung in the children's choir at Saint Andrew's Episcopal Church in Wellesley. But more important, I had called on Jesus when I was in great anguish at the age of twelve, and He had come. I had experienced His presence, and He brought me peace and comfort. I could never doubt Him and have always believed that Christianity was true.

On the other hand, I did not attend church or follow all of Christ's teachings. How much this was due to the failings of the Episcopal Church, and how much it was the result of my own willfulness, only God knows. In spite of a brief return to my faith my senior year in college, when I was confirmed in the Episcopal Church, I had not been willing to really let Christ in. In fact I was resisting Him so hard that I fainted one day while kneeling after Communion; I wanted to take the bit in my teeth and go my own way. About a year later, I drifted into my first sexual relationship—with a married man. These things occurred during 1964–65, the period the psychic had described as a turning point.

At the same time, I found it increasingly hard to see any difference in content between programs offered by the local Episcopal youth groups, which I continued to attend, and the prevailing secular culture. I ceased going to them and gradually went less and less to church. The year before my return to Christ was the first time I had failed to go to church on Christmas.

The idea of returning to the Episcopal Church did not occur to me at this point. I had studied Kierkegaard and Bonhoeffer, with their searing condemnations of complacent bourgeois religion and cheap grace, and perceived the Episcopal Church as a stuffy, formal, upper-class institution. The quest for God, it seemed to me, must call for daily spiritual disciplines, for passion and seriousness and not just sitting through a church service on Sundays. The Catholic Church did not occur to me either. I had never really known any Catholics, except for a few people in my high school class who were regarded as from the wrong side of the tracks. In addition, I had unconsciously adopted the anti-Catholic prejudices prevalent in the

[1]The affirmations the psychic used are from a group called the Unity Church.

circles I had moved in and thought of Catholics as generally ignorant types who believed whatever the pope told them to, and who were so benighted and irresponsible as to oppose birth control.

Eastern religions didn't appeal to me; their emphasis on nothingness and emptiness made me feel cold and cheerless. Although I had done astral projection once on my own, I decided against pursuing the study of soul travel through Eckankar upon being told by one of them that someone named Paul Twitchell would begin appearing in my dreams to give me guidance! I found this too ludicrous to consider seriously (although I do wonder what would have happened if he had a more imposing-sounding name). Finally I discovered in an occult bookstore an advertisement for a group called the Holy Order of MANS, which offered both daily Communion and training in the spiritual disciplines of prayer, meditation, and concentration.

I was favorably impressed. I heard one of their "master teachers" speak and liked the spiritual authoritativeness he projected; it appealed to my desire to attain spiritual power to fight for the good (I had always admired Joan of Arc, and rather fancied myself mounting my white horse and driving the forces of evil into the sea). I also found their local "priest" and community members to be full of life and enthusiasm, and to have a genuine personal devotion to Jesus. In my first meeting with the community leader, Rev. Jacob, he listened to me for a while and then said, "You know what Christianity is all about, I don't need to tell you. You just need to decide, do you want to change?" After some inner struggle, I said yes. He prayed with me and received the guidance that my name was now to be Rose. On the way out, I knelt to pray in their chapel and felt the Lord ask me, "Are you serious this time?" Again after some struggle, I said yes. I settled down and joined their community, sharing an apartment with another member just two blocks away from the chapel.

In spite of my (perhaps unusual) openness to things like psychics, spiritual beings, and inner guidance, a part of me continued to regard all this with great suspicion. But as William James had pointed out, if God is personal it would be most ungracious to demand that He come and prove Himself to me; at least I should go out to meet Him halfway. Many people throughout history had come to know and experience God through prayer, meditation, Bible reading, and group worship. If I opened myself to God in these ways, I would discover to what extent the spiritual realm was real. The possibility of encountering negative spiritual beings did not really occur to me; I thought that as long as I was seeking God and did not participate in any obviously occult practices, such as seances, I would be in no danger. If nothing happened, then I would have lost nothing by trying. But my experience with the order continued to confirm my belief in the reality of the spiritual.

The Holy Order of MANS (an acronym for something known only to vowed order members) was founded in 1968 in San Francisco as a result of a private revelation to a man they called Father Paul. The astrological age of Aquarius began in 1968, and the order represented Father Paul's vision of Christianity for the new age. He was extremely eclectic, and Christian doctrines were mixed with a dizzying variety of ideas taken, for example, from Eastern religions, astrology, the Kabbalah, the new age movement, and even the philosophy underlying Tarot (although they did not use cards to foretell the future). During the period that I was a community member (which was after Father Paul's death and before a new director was chosen) an excessive syncretism and a general anti-intellectualism prevented the order from trying to develop a consistent theology. Thus it was very hard to tell which elements were essential and which were merely skin deep, and depending on the religious background, interests, and temperament of the priest one was talking with, one might come away with a very different idea of their doctrines.

In many ways the Order resembled the Catholic Church, and there was a little Mary shrine in the chapel. However, they also offered a series of spiritual initiations. Of these only the first (baptism)[2] was available on request; the others (illumination, self-realization, and God realization) were given only when the priest judged the person was ready.

The structure of the order involved several levels. There were people who just came to services or the public classes, and then there were those who, like me, became community members. Members tithed 10 percent of their income and were required to do at least three hours a week of voluntary service to the broader community (I saw a child through the Big Sister program). They were permitted to attend special classes at which material not mentioned in the public classes was presented — for example, color healing or Tarot. There was also a members' brunch and business meeting on Saturday once a month. Inside this circle was a smaller circle, that of vowed members of the order, and inside that there were the priests. There were further levels within the order, culminating with the six or seven

---

[2]They baptized in the name of the Father, Son, and Holy Spirit (although I don't recall if they used water), and baptism was required of all community members, even those who had already been baptized.

"master teachers." Men and women were represented at all levels. Major decisions were made by a group called the "esoteric council."[3]

The community surrounding the order was a wonderfully warm one—my first experience of really being accepted and affirmed as part of a community. It was a small group (sixteen when I joined and seventy when I left two and a half years later) so we knew each other quite well. The community leader always prayed for unity in Christ and his prayer was answered. We were encouraged not to be cliquey, but to try to learn from one another, even those with whom we felt little natural affinity. While single members tended to live near the chapel and socialize more with one another, many of the married couples invited us to enjoy their homes and children with them on weekends.

One of the things I found most gratifying was that I felt my talents were appreciated and used. On Sundays I would wear long peasant-style skirts and dresses and prepare and serve coffee and tea, making newcomers welcome. I was sometimes asked to lead evening prayer and organized some music for the Christmas pageant. I got together a group to perform Renaissance dances at a Halloween medieval and Renaissance party, which a group of us organized to raise money to help a member who was a single mother pay her son's tuition at school. I even got cast in the lead for a hilarious skit we performed at a regional meeting of Order communities.

Probably one of my happiest moments was the Christmas party we put on for a nursing home I had worked in. I had been the one who pressed for doing it and coordinated it. One member worked at the Italian Home for Children and arranged a group of children to come and sing carols for the patients. We had the children make presents for the elderly people and went to the nursing home to help them make stockings for the children. We made corsages for the women and donated gifts left over from our Christmas bazaar. Since two of us had worked there, we knew the patients well enough to select gifts appropriate for each person. Our community comedian in residence came and played the piano, and others also sang or went around talking to patients. People caroled upstairs for those who could not come down, and someone dressed up as Santa Claus and visited rooms. I was overjoyed to see their bleak lives temporarily illuminated by warmth, humor, and love.

[3]The order has gone through major changes since that time (1975-78). It has moved more in an orthodox Christian direction, but there is disagreement within the order over how much of the original revelations to Father Paul they should keep. At last report, they have temporarily discontinued giving the higher initiations.

Another thing for which I will always be indebted to the order was the way in which they taught us to experience spiritual realities, not just to talk about them. How many times had I heard the phrase "lift up your hearts to the Lord" in the Episcopal Church, yet no one had taught me what this means or how to do it. In the community we were taught techniques of prayer and meditation; we tried to pray regularly throughout the day and to maintain a constant sense of God's presence. We also learned to be open to the Lord's guidance, exercising caution, and not trusting just any inner voice. The first time I heard an actual inner voice, it startled me dreadfully.

I continued to receive guidance from time to time—guidance that was always appropriate. For example, as I was praying something from T. S. Eliot's "Ash Wednesday," which ended "Oh, Lord, I am not worthy, but speak the word only," I heard "Take up your bed and walk" coming from within, yet with a sort of energy that I knew was not just myself. Once I felt strongly tempted to go my own way again, but made myself go in the chapel and prayed, "All things come from God, all obedience is due to God, I am God's," at which point I thought I heard angels. (They sounded more like a powerful and majestic roaring than our stereotype of angels.) Rev. Jacob saw me immediately after this and said that I looked radiant. The skepticism about the reality of the spiritual that I had absorbed through my academic training in philosophy began to give way to an unshakable belief in its reality.

I also developed a devotion to Mary during my time in the community that made it easier later for me to come into the Catholic Church. Shortly after I joined the community, the man with whom I had been about to have an affair came to supper. Afterward he leaned a little toward me and began putting out a sexual energy that almost pulled me under. I prayed to Mary for help and immediately felt uplifted and freed. This happened three times and then he left. I continued to go to Mary in prayer, seeking her help in becoming more gentle and pure of heart. Another community woman and I even went to a workshop on feminine spirituality organized by some new age groups and did a presentation on Mary.

In spite of all these good things, I began to have serious problems with the order. For one thing, their emphasis on experience as opposed to rational thought ("get out of your concepts," they would say) was very hard on me, since I am by nature an intellectual. They made me feel that this was a fault and a barrier to experiencing God. I had abandoned my thesis and had been doing nurse's aide work and temporary office work, and was becoming frustrated by the fact that my mind was not being utilized.

I was beginning to have doubts about Father Paul also. I had read a book he had written about his communications with spirits (which only order members were supposed to see) and had a strong feeling that at least some of these were decidedly evil and were playing up to his spiritual pride. I had been told that he had claimed to be a reincarnation of Saint Paul. At first I'd been willing to consider the idea, at least, but recently I had read some of his poetry, which was so dreadful that it strained my credulity to the breaking point. Father Paul had set up the entire structure of the order, including all the initiations, the words of the Communion service, and even the minutest details of the way the sanctuary was constructed. If he were in touch with evil spirits, then who knows what forces might be at work on us.

I had long had trouble with the idea that what we speak and think creates the reality we experience, since it followed logically from this that if my life was not going well it must be my fault. Either I was thinking negatively or, worse yet, rebelling against God in some way. I began to feel that I was hopelessly separated from Him. I prayed that He would show me the truth and bring me to Him, even if He had to kill me to do it. I began to feel increasingly assaulted by negative things. I went to a Catholic psychic who said she saw me held within the Sacred Heart of Jesus, but surrounded by dark spiritual forces.

Around this time, I awoke one night, sensing something overwhelmingly evil in my room between me and the red light on my prayer shrine, and the next day I felt in prayer that the Lord had delivered me. I had received the initiation of "illumination," after which I had been shivering all over for hours and felt all kinds of energy flowing through me for days. This was supposed to "seal the light of Christ" in me. Given my distrust of Father Paul, I began to wonder whether this initiation might be connected somehow with my frightening experience.

Unable to sort all these things out and unwilling to break totally with the community that had become like a family to me, I decided to go to California with the intention of staying if things worked out. The order had two communities in the Bay Area, so I could count on a community to be part of; perhaps things would be different there. Besides, my best friend from college also lived near there. As soon as I gave notice on my job, following what I thought was the Lord's guidance, a drive-away car for the Bay Area became available, and I set out at once.

I arrived at my friend Edie's house and asked if I could store my things there and pitch my tent temporarily on her lawn. Seeing that

I was in a state of near collapse, she encouraged me to stay as long as I wanted. I soon discovered that she had become a Catholic. Edie and I had often discussed theology together in college. She had gone to Union Theological Seminary, lost her faith there, and been a Marxist for many years. I knew from a letter that she'd become a Christian again and was involved with evangelicals. This I could accept, but the Catholic Church? Personal conversion was one thing, but an authoritarian, hierarchical institution was another. How could such an intelligent woman do that?

But she seemed to welcome questions and was able to provide intelligent answers. I also noticed that she had lost the judgmental tendencies she often had and was more gentle and charitable. She did not pressure me about the Order, but gave me books to clarify my beliefs—the writings of C. S. Lewis and John Stott's *Basic Christianity*. I began to realize that it was essential to have some intellectual structure to anchor one's faith—that Christianity was not merely a matter of personal devotion to Jesus.

It began to dawn on me that being a Christian and a philosopher were not inconsistent. One day I introduced myself to a Melkite rite priest, Owen Carroll, as "Rose" in Christian circles and "Celia" in philosophical circles, and he pointed out that these need not be mutually exclusive. Strange as it may seem, I had come to see it that way. A professor of mine at Smith had, it was rumored, been kicked out of the philosophy department and into religious studies because of his interest in teaching about philosophers like Kierkegaard. And my graduate training in analytic philosophy had done nothing to make me see religious beliefs as intellectually respectable.

For a while I continued to attend services at the order. But when one of my new Catholic friends began to question me about the words of their consecration and the validity of their orders, I became very uncomfortable. I felt loyal to the order and rather protective of it, and I knew Father Paul's claim that the authority of order priests derived from their membership in the "Order of Melchizedek" would be received with raised eyebrows at the very least.

A battle of world views was going on in my mind; one day the world seemed created and sustained by God, the next day it all seemed empty and meaningless. It was at this time that I had my most clearly identifiable experience with a demon. When I said, "Stand in the light of Christ," it turned its face away as though the light hurt it and vanished. Shortly after that I had an experience of being caught up and held by God for what seemed an endless time, while light and energy poured through me. Unlike the energy I had experienced during my initiation in the order, which left me feeling shaky and overwrought (as though a powerful electric current had passed through me), this time I felt whole and alive. It seemed to harmonize with my nature rather than to assault it.

My final break with the order occurred when, after a sermon embodying a seriously erroneous Christology, I felt the Lord say, "This is not how I want you to understand me. Do not take Communion." Before I'd left Boston, Rev. Jacob had encouraged me to explore other groups as well as the order; I decided that it was time for me to do this. I soon realized that the Lord wanted me to avoid all dabbling in esoteric things. One day I was at the Graduate Theological Union library and saw a book, bound in white leather with gold writing, called *Golden Moments with the Ascended Masters*. I felt an irresistible urge to take it down, but as I reached up for it, something sharp sticking out of the binding pricked my finger and made it bleed. I laughed and said, "Okay, Lord, I get the message," and left it on the shelf.

To this day, I am unable to say with any certainty to what extent (if any) the order sacraments and initiations were responsible for my experiences with negative spiritual forces. I do believe, however, that their teachings and initiations had a tendency to attract people seeking spiritual power and to encourage that desire in us. And that desire for spiritual power, in itself, is one of the main ways in which people become open to the operation of negative spirits.

The Catholic Church still seemed forbidding and somehow foreign to me. Besides, I was rather galled by some triumphalist Catholics I'd met recently who talked superciliously about the "One True Church." But I was not comfortable with the evangelicals either, because I felt the lack of a sacramental structure. On Edie's recommendation, I decided to try a High Church Anglican group (Anglican Church of North America), which had broken away from the Episcopal Church because they wanted to retain the Book of Common Prayer and did not believe in ordaining women.

I went to a noon Mass and was very moved by the beautiful prayers I had grown up with. The priest was a slight, frail, white-haired man (very English in manner) who said the Mass in a simple and humble way. He had a quiet authority about him, a confidence in the validity of the sacrament quite independent of any "spiritual power" of his own. I felt a real closeness to the Lord after Communion that day and decided this was where He wanted me to be. For the next year and a half I attended their student chapel at the University of California and sang in their Gregorian chant choir.

I began to read Catholic philosophers such as Gilson, Maritain, and Pieper and was delighted by them. I had become disillusioned with the analytic philosophy I'd been taught in graduate school; it seemed to lack any foundation and to be almost wholly destructive. I saw in retrospect that this disillusionment had been one of the factors that had made the experiential emphasis of the order so appealing; the head had failed me, so I would follow the heart. But in philosophers of the Aristotelean-Thomistic tradition I discovered for the first time a positive, systematic, and coherent view of human beings and their place in nature. The perennial debates in philosophy took on a deeper meaning for me. I met intellectual and devout Catholics, most of them converts, with whom I could discuss theology and philosophy.

I had found part-time work teaching ethics at the University of San Francisco, and as I read Catholic moralists I was struck by the incisiveness and consistency of their reasoning. When I squarely faced the abortion issue for the first time, I realized that my previous position (that it was a horrible thing, but sometimes necessary) was totally untenable. If the fetus is a human life (and I could see no way to deny that), then nothing short of threatened death to the mother could justify taking that life. I was not ready to accept the Church's teaching on contraception yet, but was troubled because I believed homosexual practices to be wrong and saw that most of the philosophical arguments against homosexuality were also arguments against contraception.

I also experienced baptism in the Holy Spirit during this time. I'd gone to a few meetings of a Catholic charismatic prayer group, and one of the Anglican priests was charismatic. So one day, as I sat alone praying in front of the sacrament at the Anglican church, I asked the Lord for the gift of tongues to praise Him. I felt a powerful welling up of praise and was soon praying in tongues and feeling such deep adoration and joy that I wanted to go on forever. I found that continuing to pray in tongues cleared away doubt, confusion, and fear and deepened both my faith and my understanding of that faith.

So why did I become a Catholic? Certainly I felt guided by the Holy Spirit. But more than that, my conversion represented the logical culmination of the development I had been going through, and I saw no reason to stop with Anglicanism.

The sacramental structure and the spiritual authority of the Catholic Church were important to me. After my experiences with the dark side, I wanted the protection of the Church. I saw the sacraments as opportunities to experience Christ, and as essential helps in Christian growth. The validity of Anglican orders was open to question, whereas that of Roman Catholic and Orthodox orders were not. I wanted to be sure I had the real thing.

I thought that the mainline Episcopal Church had surrendered to secular trendiness. But the Anglican Church of North America (ACNA) was a small, geographically localized splinter group. As far as I could see, the only things keeping the ACNA from the Roman communion were the issues of papal authority, a few of the Marian doctrines, and the papal encyclical *Humanae Vitae*.

I had no trouble with papal authority. I recognized the need for an authority to rule on disputed points of doctrine if the Church was to be saved from the schisms that have repeatedly afflicted Protestantism. Besides, I found the new Pope, John Paul II, a charismatic and appealing figure. The Marian doctrines seemed reasonable enough also. If Mary was to bear God Incarnate in her womb, it seemed appropriate that she should be without sin (could a sinful person bear to be that close to the Glory of God without going up in smoke?), and since death came into the world through sin, she should not have to pass through death in the same way we do.

That left birth control. It seemed unfair to have to abstain from sex just at the time when the desire for it is the strongest, but I also realized that pleasure is not a reliable guide to what is right. I heard a man and a woman from Couple to Couple League speak about the theory underlying Natural Family Planning and the ways in which using it had deepened their relationship, which helped me a lot.

I began taking instruction with Father Anthony Mastroeni at the University of San Francisco. It went smoothly, since I had already resolved most of my doubts about Catholic doctrines. The only thing still troubling me was contraception. I had read some attempts by Catholic philosophers to defend *Humanae Vitae*; although I did not find them wholly compelling, they at least convinced me that rational arguments could be offered in support of the Church's teaching. I also saw that the Church's position on this issue was closely connected with other teachings I accepted. Thus it did not seem unreasonable to accept *Humanae Vitae* on faith for the time being, while continuing to seek a better understanding. I discovered, to my surprise, that the emotional resistance to the Church that I had felt for so long had melted away, and I was at peace. I was received on June 24, 1980.

11

THOMAS W. CASE

The Real Thing

Thomas W. Case, a former Buddhist, majored in philosophy at San Francisco State and is currently pursuing a doctoral degree in theology and history of Christianity at the Graduate Theological Union in Berkeley, California. A published poet, Case has written numerous reviews and articles for the National Catholic Register *and the* New Oxford Review. *He is currently writing a book about the Unification Church.*

First Question:
Is Christianity the Same
as Buddhism Underneath?

All over the country (but especially in California) little groups of people have for years been invoking certain relic-deities with elaborate and exacting ritual, intense concentration, and that deep sense of awe and fear that comes from opening oneself to the unknown. Diana is invoked by a warmed-over Wicca, Isis and Horus and Hermes Trismegistus by self-styled magicians, Dionysus by bacchanalians in the May-time in Marin. The Great Mother is especially in vogue today with a broad spectrum of groups and psychologies, from radical feminist movements to those with a nostalgic reverence for the earth that has disappeared beneath the sidewalks.

I have to wonder what would happen if Jesus Christ or Mary the Mother of God were invoked so passionately and so longingly and with such authentic dread. Or more to the point, invoked experimentally and ingenuously, as if in the infancy of time. If one were to chant, "Yahweh, Yahweh, Yahweh" with the mounting intensity of a Hindu chanting, "Siva, Siva, Siva"—what would happen? If one were to sing for and worship the Holy Trinity instead of considering it a riddle fit for the deliberations of hair-splitting theologians—what would be the result? And why does the Virgin Mary appear only to children—at Lourdes, at Fatima? Because children are so uninhibited in their religion?

I think a distinction must be made between the content of a religion and "sacred techniques" per se. Sacred techniques are universal. Shamanism, which is not just altered consciousness but in its most fulsome sense is *possession by the god*, is the most direct, most radical, most dangerous, and most effective sacred technique. Though comparatively awesome and dramatic, it is in the same category as mystical contemplation: the intention of both is identification with, union with, divinity. But does it make a difference whether your union is with Quetzalcoatl or with the Sacred Heart of Jesus?

I would say so. There is a difference between a Living God "victorious and able to save" (Isa. 45:21) and a god who is in truth "no god" (Jer. 2:11).

There is a difference between a relic-deity whose power is only in the power of the ego's projections and a Deity who is previous to man and whose power is from all eternity. There is a difference between a shadow or contrivance of the soul and the I AM THAT I AM.

Kierkegaard makes much of the contrast between Truth as "Recollection"—the Socratic view that Truth is everywhere available in each human being by a process of "remembering," with its implication of timelessness—and Truth delivered by a transforming Savior, and never before available. For the Socratic view read: the timeless philosophies of Hinduism and Buddhism. Buddhism even has as an image of enlightenment the picture of a cloud clearing away to let the sun—which was always there—shine through. It is an idea equivalent to Recollection. For the Savior, of course, read: Jesus Christ, a Moment when divinity entered the world and utterly changed it. For Christianity (and to a lesser degree Judaism and Islam as well) history is crucial.

If a philosophy is timeless enough and its cosmology broad enough, it can draw a circle that includes all other philosophies within it (as Hinduism tries to do); but if the Great Father Beyond the Sky has incarnated Himself in the Person of Jesus Christ, then the world has become immediately and essentially Christianized, and for the timeless philosophies the time has run out.

Let us listen to the words of the Mexican visionary Maria Sabina:

> The Principal Ones appear . . . in the visions of the initiates.
> On their sacred table, they put out clocks, papers, books, communion wafers, stars, dew, or eagles. . . . The Principal Ones
> ask the initiates:

"What type of Wise One do you want to be? Do you want the Lords of the Mountains, the masters of the places, to guide you, or do you want God the Christ to guide you?"

Then the initiate chooses and tells the Principal Ones what he prefers. At that moment the initiate receives a Book that contains the Language he has chosen.

I decided for God the Christ. (Alvaro Estrada, *Maria Sabina: Her Life and Chants* [1981], p. 94)

Maria's pagan sacred technique and her own disposition brought her before the Principal Ones — a sort of council of elders. The question the elders put to Maria, and her answer, are unimportant, a cultural overlay, a compounding of Maria's two traditions (pagan and Christian), *only if* the vision is not a Vision but a fantasy of the mind. But it would be condescending to say that Maria Sabina's Christianity is a trivial thing, as if her choice were arbitrary.

Or one can say that the Christian spirit of Maria Sabina determined the question and answer. In either view, is not her insistence on purity and goodness, her giving of herself to others, her life of healing but never damaging, her acceptance of and valorization of poverty, even her bowing to ecclesial authority — is not this essential Christianity?

Rather than considering her Christianity an overlay atop the "real" sacred experience, would it not be truer to say that her pagan methods are a smokescreen over her beatific choice of God the Christ? Did not the God she chose make her a healer and not a witch? When she chants her identification with Jesus and Mary Magdalene and the Holy Trinity — why are certain people so ready to write off *these* names and *these* realities, as if these names and realities have no validity or power, but that the validity and power is only in the "sacred technique," the chants?

I am suggesting that if you call upon the God who has conquered — the God who lives and is able to save, who has overcome Diana and Demeter and Woden — with the intensity and ferocious heart that Maria Sabina displays, you may find yourself a healer. You may find yourself enhanced with a power so astounding and substantial and awesome that you are in for it. You may be in for something huger than life and death and sex and comfort and dismay.

We who are tired of atheism and even more tired of hang-fire agnosticism have taken our lust for reality and run to the Great Spirit of the American Plains Indians, or to peyote cults, or we have sat in lotus postures in Hindu ashrams, or raised the devil with our naive rituals, or made a god of computers or Marx or the PLO. We would perhaps do better becoming "shamans" for Jesus. Bible thumping is a sad shadow of what I mean; it is so mixed with jingoism and mean emotions and idolatry of the letter. There must not be a psychological tightening, a "self" that is "saved" simply by declaring for Jesus, but rather a very still, open, yet purposeful deliverance of the heart to the heart of things.

I suggest that the Living God may touch you then. The very subtlest of touches can become a huge thing. And this can call from us an ultimate courage—the courage of the shaman who cuts his body into a million pieces so that the god may enter. Do I mean, figuratively? Yes and no. I recall an anthropologist's account of the shamanistic ceremonies of Australian aborigines. The cutting up of the body is a dream, but a dream that is a reality to the shaman. The experience is real in feeling and in spirit. It is gruesome, painful death. And then rebirth with the voice and spirit of the god.

Why do I imply that the god who presents himself to the utterly opened up may actually be Jesus? I imagine a shaman of Siberia who lived ten thousand years ago suddenly reborn in the world of today. I imagine his childlike, naive lust for the Spirit behind what is. I imagine him saying, "What God has power for my people?" He would perhaps realize that his village has become the globe, and he would find that most of the globe counts its years from the birth of a god called Jesus the Christ. He would note that the pope is the only religious leader to have the attention of the whole world. He would learn that the unmentionable God behind all the gods and powers is said to have become a man some two thousand years ago. I doubt if he would need any more clues before he decided to cut himself in pieces to gain even the slightest touch of *this* God.

Primitive religion is both more spiritual than we can imagine and more pragmatic. Primitive religion is more spiritual because for it *everything* is spiritual. All nature is known intimately to be the abode of spirits. The world is the house of god and everything is sacred. Matter is a shadow; matter is the clothes and spirit is the body. There is no profanity and thus no need for piety. There is no distance between us and magic. Divinity is present in the babble of a stream, in the flashing eyes of a girl, in the trembling of the heart.

Primitive religion is also more pragmatic because it is moved and molded by experience. It is "scientific": it believes what is observed through the senses. I am sure that what Moses saw on Mount Horeb was a bush that burned but did not burn up. In Tibet, when people found that after a strenuous discipline of breath control they could raise a psychic heat that kept them from freezing to death in the high

Himalayas, or in a trance state could skip across the deserts at vast speeds, or by taking much thought could create half-living entities—they surely knew that something awesome lies behind the usual ways of nature, and they revered it and made it a large part of their religion, or you might say, of their science.

Tibetans who glide across the ground faster than a horse can run are Buddhists. Now we may begin to answer the question at the beginning of this chapter. The extraordinary accomplishments of Tibetan yogis are well documented. But that is just what they are—accomplishments resulting from strenuous sacred techniques. Buddhism is a mystical method, but it is not revelation. As Thomas Merton noted, it is long on insight but short on salvation. That is, it is short on salvific grace. What grace it has—help from outside—is a later accretion. The yogic wizardries noted above can be called miracles, but they are not miracles in the sense that the burning bush that spoke to Moses was a miracle.

But let us not dismiss Buddhism because it has no central miracle in anything like the way that Christianity *is* a miracle. That would be like blaming a good race horse because it was not Pegasus. What is the insight that Buddhism provides? It starts with a problem: the human condition, which is suffering. It says that suffering is caused by desire—the grasping and repelling nature of the self. It considers this self illusory. It considers the whole mental and phenomenal universe a creation of the illusory self. It says that release from suffering can come about only from a dissolution of the myth of the self. Its goal is the radical opposite of egocentricity. When this is accomplished, all actions will be precisely appropriate because there will then be no mixture of the ego's projections—its fears or hopes—in the action. In fact the ego doesn't exist—it is nothing more than the projections themselves. Up to this point we can call Buddhism a kind of radical psychotherapy. But then something else happens. The panoramic view opened up by the loss of the self-protecting self lets in another quality: a kind of unlimited generosity. And this generosity is called compassion.

There is a lot more to Buddhism than this, but this is the bones of it. You need nothing more than this to assent to Buddhism. Does it have any point of contact with Christianity? I would say that it is a prescription for carrying out the command to love your neighbor as yourself, at least in its outward result of compassionate behavior. In the "underneath" area of radical ethics, Christianity is the same as Buddhism. Is there, then, no real distinction to be made? The answer has to be an emphatic yes, there is a real distinction. By some stretch of the imagination, Buddhism can be chopped down to fit

Christianity, but Christianity cannot be chopped down to fit Buddhism.

We must make a distinction between the sacred per se, which is eternally there and correspondent to Hindu or Buddhist metaphysics, and the miraculous working out of God's plan for our salvation in the Fullness of Time. Why this emphasis on the Fullness of Time?

Every religion has in its theological insight something called the fall of man, or some equivalent to the fall of man. (Buddhism replaces the "fall of man" with "the basis of the ego.") There is an explicit or implied paradisiacal state. There is a nostalgia for a garden, when the great god was not hidden from us beyond the vacant sky — the great god mentioned by "primitives" only in whispers in caves, after the anthropologists have gone away — when the great god walked with us in the garden and we were always in love and loved. Or when the great god was so immanent He did not have to be separatively present — near or far.

In Buddhist nostalgia, it was a "time" when there was only open space; and no self to protect. Before difference and self-consciousness was invented. Before we put bars on our cages and made our walls solid and locked ourselves within the five senses. (A long time ago, it is said, we had six senses operating, or even seven; and probably then we had not yet invented Time. But I mean the place or time when we had no senses at all, when the universe was not sensed and not separate.)

If there was a falling away from this great god or this heavenly state of being, then there was a Moment unlike any other moment, a Blackout (Buddhist) or a Sin (Christian). Since that Moment we have lived in history and separation. Since we have nearly forgotten that we blacked out (or if not forgotten, then gotten ourselves so much into a box that we can find no way out), perhaps there is a recognition of our plight and a great kindness in God that has given us another Moment. Let us call this Moment redemption. Let us call it grace. Let us call this Moment something needed and wished for and prayed for and figured and foreshadowed in ritual and myth and made-up gods. Gods that had the power of our projections, but were shadows of the real thing; philosophies, paths, theologies, techniques that drove toward a realization of what we know we once had and once were. And enough of a remembrance to find ways and means resembling the real thing; always in hope and in despair; sending up trial balloons; finding vestiges of our real power and worshiping these vestiges; investigating the depths of the self or slavering over a slain bullock; throwing our children into a furnace or reaching a sublime love for a sunset; or in a Tantric sexual act increasing pleasure through inhibition until the very stars took notice. Until, in the fullness of time, a baby was born to a Virgin in Bethlehem.

The Christian Moment is the cross of eternity and history. In the timeless philosophies there is only homogeneous time stretching forward and backward forever.

You may protest that there have been many savior gods in the myths of mankind. This fact has delighted the "enlightened" debunkers of Christianity, as if it discredits both Christianity and paganism, rather than vivifying them both with the implication of great spiritual mystery foreshadowing the literal event. Oddly enough, several ancient resurrection myths were, in a sense, resurrected and made into mystery religions around the time of the historical event of Jesus Christ. The Isis-Osiris-Horus cycle was dredged up from its origins thousands of years earlier in Egypt and made into one of these mystery religions, and, incidentally, given a peculiarly salvific emphasis at this time. This is only one example. It is as if the huge despair and desire for salvation in the Near East in the last centuries B.C. had fired up not only the real thing but a number of imitations—a sort of fallout around the flower.

G. K. Chesterton makes a case for the very intolerance and intransigence of the early Christians toward all of the hodgepodge of cult and syncretism of that era as ensuring the victory of the real thing. And this intransigence is a spiritual inheritance from Judaism, so that we can have, and did have, a Jupiter-Ammon, but could never have a Yahweh-Baal or a Yahweh-Moloch. Chesterton points out that a hyphenated god bespeaks a mood of "philosophical" indifference that is signified by homogenization, and homogenization means that the real thing, if there is one, is stirred through the dross and lost. If Yahweh had allowed Himself to be amalgamated to a competitor, He would be no God today.

Second Question:
Or Do All Roads Lead to Rome?

I suppose at this point I should say where *I* fit into this contention of religions. Is Buddhism true? Is Paganism true? Is Christianity true?

I think they are all true, that one fills out some neglected area of another, but I also think that all roads lead to Rome. Let us first properly divide the issue. Paganism is the pre-Christian condition of the Mediterranean basin and Europe. In its various forms, state-

Roman, rural, or forest-wild, it held the land that Christianity conquered. Yet I think that Christianity is not a contradiction of paganism, but a cap to it. The Queen of Heaven who is Isis is a
precursor to the Queen of Heaven who is Mary—a mythological
precursor to be sure, but real enough, as the choreography is precursor to the dance. Paganism becoming Christianity is the wish becoming the fact.

This is certainly not the whole story of the relation of paganism to
Christianity; I only want to emphasize the historical relation. The
land remembers, and the old gods of the land still move in the stream
that goes to make up the Christian memory. From another perspective, a more crucial one perhaps, a Christian is first of all a Jew. God
help us if we ever lose sight of the fact that the Holy Family is a
Jewish family.

Buddhism is a horse of a different color. Buddhism comes from
the other side of the world. Its springs are in that ancient Asian
Wheel of Existence where action breeds only further action and
there is neither good nor evil in the heart of things. Buddhism is a
practice intended to remove oneself from *all* dualities. (Yet developed
Buddhism has its devils too: is this a corruption of the pure original
impulse of Buddhism or is it an irrupting acknowledgment that the
mystery of iniquity remains both a fact and a mystery?)

I can remember in 1978 and 1979 meditating in the Rocky Mountain Dharma Center twelve thousand feet up in the mountains north
of Boulder, Colorado, sitting cross-legged all day and tramping out
to a cabin at night through the snow, in a kind of ecstasy without
content. I almost became that rarefied cold scene, the stars crystal
points of clarity and the thin air becoming myself and my emotion
drying to a point, my thought losing all content, my heart and mind
becoming one thing, removed utterly from a self that wants or hates.
I think that was Buddhism, or an imagination of Buddhism.

I also remember chanting in the Dharma Center after each day's
meditation: "Cut the aorta of the distorter of the teachings."

Buddhism has its enemy too, and there is in every Buddhist meditation center a little black idol standing in the corner—a reminder of
that enemy. He is there perhaps to keep the Buddhist practitioner
from becoming too smug.

In the summer of 1980 I lived in a very small apartment in Boulder and read *The Cloud of Unknowing*, that superlative mystical work
written by an anonymous Christian savant in the late Middle Ages.
A lot of it reminded me of Buddhism—the detachment from human
desire, for example, and the feel for infinity. But there was something more: it was Christian. It was warmer. There was a Person
there. The spirit that came from those pages made me feel littler and

a little bit humble, like the kind of person who needs and can give love.

I am convinced that, despite the vastly different theological cradle, the Buddhist psychology of egolessness is akin to the Christian ideal of *caritas*. But what is meant to enlarge on the Christian dictum to love one another, to think nothing of the self, becomes instead a rarefied but for all that a more entrenched glorification of the self. It comes out in the way people treat each other in the Buddhist Sangha in Boulder: sleeping around and broken hearts, with little chance of becoming a responsible mother or father, no way to help a child grow. Not selflessness but rampant selfishness, not egolessness but giganticism of the ego.

This is not an indictment of Buddhism, but an indictment of where the Western mind takes it. The supposed correspondence of Buddhism and, say, Schopenhauer, is nonsense. Pure will is the devil of Buddhism, and German subjectivism is pure will. The Nazi swastika is the Buddhist swastika turned backward.

(That same subjectivist devil has crept into Christianity, by the way, by way of Mr. Hegel and Mr. Heidegger.)

I began to read other Christian spiritual tomes, and then Thomas Merton's *Seven Storey Mountain* (for the third time), and then his other early works, *The Sign of Jonas* and *The Waters of Siloe*. I walked down to Boulder Creek on a hot evening and felt Mary, the mother of Jesus, call to me. No, I had no "locutions." I simply began to sense that subtle uplift from earthly desires to transcendent desires: I felt her, and I began to feel Him. Now and then I would scurry into Catholic churches, where I would invariably be drawn toward the crucifix on the wall. It scared me.

It scared me, but on the far edge of consciousness there was the glimmer of a notion or a feeling that in Jesus Christ was a special kind of joy.

I read more Merton and then Graham Greene and G. K. Chesterton, and Xavier Rynne's books on Vatican II, and Hans Küng. I read Sir Frederick Kenyon's books on the ancient manuscripts. (I recommend Kenyon's "lower criticism" to anyone who wants to know how our Bible was made.) I picked up a book (non-Christian) about the Virgin Mary and found in it the first half of the rosary. I began to say that prayer at night, half asleep or half awake. I thought it was the whole rosary.

You might think from all this that I was alone, reading and feeling and thinking my way to Catholicism. In a sense this is true. But a lot of other things were happening, like certain women, and friends, and parties that seemed to call up the devil. Boulder is a very sophisticated town.

Perhaps my conversion had more to do with the way people were acting, clever and sad and crazy, than with what I was reading. Perhaps I was drawn to those crucifixes on the wall because of what I was experiencing in what seemed like an increasingly disordered society.

There was a scene in the Boulderado—the downtown watering place for sophisticates—that I remember. A table in a side room near the balcony. A clutch of Buddhists debunking Christians and Christianity, all the time fingering their Buddhist rosaries. My remark that they were counting their beads with the same unconscious fervor that a certain kind of Catholic counts his beads elicited an immediate contemptuous denial.

It's the same damn thing, I thought, only we all need a group to be in and another group to hate.

If Boulder Buddhists sing "Om Mani Padme Hum" to a string of black beads, aren't they in the same category of religious practice as the (contemptuous?) old-guard Catholics who sing the Ave Maria on a string of black beads?

I saw that correspondence and then began to see a superiority in the Catholic way—the practice is the same, but the God is different. There is no God in Buddhism, but rather a state of mind supposedly freed from the self. The God of Catholicism is at least outside myself and so can keep me from becoming an utter egomaniac. Or solipsist. Able, at least, to make me consider the pure fact of another human being.

I read seven or eight books on Vatican II, and four or five books on biblical criticism, and then I began to read about Lourdes and Fatima and Garabandal and Pontain and all the other visitations of Mary. I was in search of miracle and I found it. No latter-day Buddhists ever saw the cosmos ripped apart like it was ripped apart at Fatima. No uncorrupted bodies lay in Buddhist tombs for centuries, nor in Protestant tombs.

Plain empirical facts lead me on. Miraculous facts. Liquefied blood. The sun dancing for seventy thousand people in Fatima in 1917. Uncorrupted bodies of saints in European Cathedrals . . . What is this sign? It is a sign of the spirit overcoming matter—and matter is finally fictional. Or put it this way: bodies are a dream of spirit.

Miraculous facts, wise words of faith, spiritual experiences of Christian saints led me on.

K.K., a woman I loved, loved another man, a crazy man. Another friend of mine went crazy. He thought his roommate was the devil. I helped as best I could, and hurt, and joked around with good friends, and messed around with Tarot cards and mytho-poetic cele-brations and surrealistic poetry, and felt more and more drawn to that man hanging from a cross. He scared me so much I finally had to go to Him.

Let me say that from my perspective—Eastern religious experi-ence corrupted by Western minds; correspondent practices East and West; a deep feel for tradition, for I valued the purity of real Bud-dhism as I did the purity of real Christianity (all true religion has the mark of spiritual life)—I knew that if I was going to be a Christian I must be a Catholic. The Protestant churches (from that perspective) appeared to be nothing more than a kind of teen-age rebellion—a rebellion by and large *against* the mystical life.

This is no indictment of the truly religious people within the various Protestant communions; I am just saying that from a per-spective totally outside of Christianity there is no fully Christian church but the one that was there from the beginning, and has the mark of miracles, and the mark of contemplative life.

And it has the mark of Authority, which is to say, the Vicar of Christ.

I prayed nightly in the summer of 1980 to Mary, thinking that my half prayer was the whole Ave Maria. I also experimented with the Jesus Prayer, which seemed to be more mystically oriented since you are supposed to say it in tune with your breath and your heartbeat. But when you do that, strange things begin to happen. I realized that *that* practice could be dangerous without a spiritual guide or mentor, so I discontinued it.

I dreamed one night that the Pope had been shot and killed. Six months later he was shot—but not killed. Another time I had a vivid dream of Joan of Arc. She said to me, "I never expected you to be here." And one morning I wrote in my notebook, "All roads lead to Rome or all roads lead to myself."

But though large sections of the Church have fallen into the temp-tation of moving with the spirit of the times, its supernatural struc-ture is in place as always: the Vicar of Christ and the Successors to the Apostles. It is this supernal authority—guaranteed by the Holy Spirit to be kept free from apostasy—that has over and over again in history brought the Church back from the edge of ruin. And this same Authority is today engaged in that sacred work—much to the chagrin of the fashion mongers.

In the fall of 1983 I ran into a priest who looked at me with fierce, loving eyes and said, "The gates of hell shall not prevail against Rome." I entered the Church under his auspices and have been in his parish ever since.

12

SHELDON VANAUKEN

The English Channel
Between Canterbury
and Rome

Sheldon Vanauken, a Virginian, considers himself at home also in England. Formerly a professor of English and history, his first book, A Severe Mercy, (1977) won seven major awards and international acclaim. Mr. Vanauken is also the author of Under the Mercy *(Thomas Nelson: Nashville, 1985), from which the following testimony is excerpted with his permission;* Gateway to Heaven *(1980);* The Glittering Illusion *(1986); as well as numerous magazine articles, editorials, and poems. His life has been greatly influenced by his friend and mentor C. S. Lewis.*

1. The White Cliffs

The spires of Oxford, long ago, directed my thoughts successively to two great questions. Although nominally an Anglican, a 'highchair Anglican' (as one says 'Cradle Catholic'), I was, in fact, a vaguely theistic agnostic. It had never occurred to me, not since childhood, to *believe* in fairies at the bottom of the garden or all that old stuff about Jesus's being the Son of God. But now I suddenly saw that the towers and spires of Oxford had been raised in heart-lifting beauty by men who *had* believed: and I perceived that the question—the Question of Jesus—that I had never asked had got to be answered: *Was* Jesus, in fact, God? God incarnate crying forsaken upon the Cross? I saw that the world might hinge upon this Question. Thus I became 'an Anglican with leanings towards Christianity' by setting myself, as I have told in my book, *A Severe Mercy,* to finding the answer. Here I need say only that, after much writhing about, I finally answered: Yea, my Lord and my God.

Not long after this life-&-death affirmation, being now astonishingly a Christian, I realized that if the towers and spires of Oxford spoke in stone of deep Christian faith, it was the *Catholic* faith they spoke of. And I perceived that logically a further question followed the Question of Jesus, followed it so logically indeed that I marvel that all converts to the Faith do not at once ask it: If Jesus is God the Son, a fact that very naturally (or very supernaturally) casts a new light upon His words, then what of His words about His Church, founded so clearly upon the Rock that was Peter? What of the mere existence of the Catholic—the Universal—Church, twice as large as all the splinters of Protestantism put together? Twice as large, too, as the faithful Eastern Orthodox, which for centuries had accepted the primacy of the successors of Peter in Rome before the unhappy separation. Rome was the centre of the ancient unity, the centre of Christendom. Logically (and C. S. Lewis had taught me to be logical) the claims of Rome came *first*, that is, before I as a new Christian could decide whether Anglicanism's *Via Media* or any other separated church was a legitimate offspring and a valid way, I had to decide whether the *Mother* Church—as unmistakably the Mother Church as England is the mother country of English-speaking North America—was exclusively what she has always, whilst empires rose and fell, claimed to be: the *visible* One, Holy, Catholic, & Apostolic Church that Christ founded. Logically that was where one *began*. First things first. I was already an Anglican, loving the Book of Common Prayer; if *any* separated church was legitimate, then I would remain an Anglican. But first, logically, there was the Question of Rome.

In a booklet, *Encounter with Light* (1961), written about my conversion to the Christian faith, I put the Question of Rome as it had presented itself to me at Oxford.

> I began to think seriously of the mother church and to ask myself the question that every Christian must sometime ask: Is that enormous church, so full of faith and learning, so full of variety except in the strong, unchanging faith, is it, after all, *The* Church? The True Vine? The question, essentially, seems to be: *What is the Church?* . . . [Thus,] once the earlier question—is Christ God?—has been answered in the affirmative, one must face up to the further question posed by the existence in history and the undeviating assertion of the Catholic Church.

I looked at the glorious spire of St. Mary the Virgin there in Oxford, conscious of the missing spire of Osney Abbey, destroyed by the reformers; and I looked at the melancholy ruins of Godstow

Nunnery and Tintern Abbey and Great Glastonbury with thoughts about the less-than-inspiring origin of the semi-detached Church of England [hereafter: C of E]. I knew of course that we—we Anglicans—asserted daily in the creeds that we believed in (and, hence, were in) that One, Holy, Catholic, & Apostolic Church; and we handsomely admitted that Rome was, too. And we asserted that our church—the "Bridge Church" or the *Via Media*—had valid apostolic orders and the Catholic Faith, even though we had cleverly seen through the pretensions of the Papacy, which previously, for a thousand years, we had accepted; and we cut off the heads of Sir Thomas More and Bishop Fisher and others who were willing to die for the ancient loyalty. But the fact that our moment of keen insight into the governance of the Catholic Church had come about through a pope's refusing the self-willed Henry VIII, not perhaps a *good* man, a divorce to marry his doxy (a not-uncommon cause of others leaving Christ's Church ever since) didn't suggest a *holy* insight. And I was not persuaded by those who claimed, pointing to Wycliffe and the Sarum Rite, that the C of E had 'really' had an earlier, nobler origin. Not only Sir Thomas More, Saint, but the Pilgrimage of Grace argued against it.

Once in Southern France in Oxford years, I slipped into the rank kneeling for communion at the altar rail of a Catholic church. God in the hands of a wrinkled French priest. As I received the Host, I thought: Whatever may be the validity of Anglican orders, now at least I have truly eaten Christ's body.

One might suppose from the foregoing that I was near to answering Yea to the Mother Church also. Perhaps I was, but *near* is not *there*. Both Newman's *Apologia* and *Brideshead Revisited* (which one read at Oxford) haunted my mind; and my wise mentor, C. S. Lewis, had instilled in me an essentially Catholic vision of the Church, incidentally making that "Romish Doctrine concerning Purgatory" (Article XXII of the Thirty-Nine Articles) not only believable in *Great Divorce* but necessary. But, at the same time, Lewis, who had, I presumed, thought deeply on the Question of Rome, remained C of E. And I myself wished the Question of Rome would go away. I loved the C of E: it was at once beautiful and homely: and there was holiness in it. Besides, I was having enough trouble just *being* a Christian without venturing into 'foreign' RC (Roman Catholic) country. I continued, therefore, to follow the beloved Anglican way with one eye upon C. S. Lewis and with occasional bouts of uneasiness.

So the years passed—I was caught up in various kinds of crisis that made deep thought on the matter impossible—but the Question of Rome did not go away. In reading of theological and ecclesiastical disputes I found myself invariably on the Catholic side. The real question for me (as for Newman) was not whether Catholicism was right but whether I as an Anglican *was* a Catholic. In the mid-'70s, I was impelled (by, I believe, Our Lord the Spirit) to write *A Severe Mercy*, which brought the Oxford years and later spiritual developments into focus. In it I spoke of the "unswerving faith of Rome: the place of last resort." And a journey to Ireland and Ulster made me aware as never before of what C. S. Lewis, who grew up in Ulster, would have had to overcome to convert to Catholicism: his remaining C of E became less significant.* These events turned my thoughts anew to the Question of Rome.

Today in the last quarter of the twentieth century the vital issue in Christendom is not Catholic v. Protestant but the orthodox Christian Faith (Catholic, Eastern, and Evangelical) v. secularizing heterodox Neo-Modernism — both ecumenical. Or Supernaturalism v. Naturalism. The very essence of Modernism, whether paleo (early twentieth century) or neo (the '70s & '80s), is *the denial of the Supernatural* — hence the Incarnation and the Resurrection: *the Faith*. C. S. Lewis, penetrating as usual to the heart of the matter, described

---

*I once proposed to write an essay on "C. S. Lewis as Moses". A Moses who led people *towards* the 'promised land' — the Mother Church — that he himself could not enter (and to which he had no intention of leading them). The ones thus led might be, in particular, Anglicans, like me, and others, again like me, without ingrained Protestant prejudices, brought to the Faith by him. They might see, as Lewis presumably did not, that the Question of Rome had *got* to be answered. And, indeed, a great many devoted readers of Lewis have become Catholic.

With "C. S. Lewis as Moses" in mind, I wrote to a lot of them — all I could find — and got some fascinating replies that tended to support my idea. One woman wrote: "C. S. Lewis dispelled most of the prejudices that I, as a very Protestant Episcopalian, had against the Catholic Church." A Virginian who later became a Catholic lay brother wrote: "What Lewis did for me was to make me willing to take a second look at Rome." A young man who hopes to become a monk said: "He influenced the Catholicity of my mind . . . and gave me the capacity to think in terms of Universals and Wholeness." A woman wrote: "By incorporating in his books distinctly RC doctrines, he led me to consider them on their merits and not dismiss them as concerning only RCs." A man wrote: "He showed me how utterly coherent and cogent were the claims and teachings of the Catholic Church; and, like the man in Molière who was astonished to find that he had spoken prose all his life without realising it, Lewis, I'm convinced, was a Catholic apologist all his life without realising it." And a clever woman said: "After reading deeply in Lewis, I had the sudden shock one day of finding that the Catholic Church agreed with *me*."

So there in a paragraph is my unwritten essay on "C. S. Lewis as Moses".

himself as a Supernaturalist: one who believes that a transcendent God is able to reach into His creation with miracles. But indeed Incarnational Orthodoxy needs no clarification: it is, quite simply, the *Faith*; and those who hold it may be called, quite simply, *Christians*. The sort the lions ate. The Secularizing Modernists, many of them, are, in fact, *not* Christians (though they may be priests or even bishops) because they have abandoned the faith in Incarnation and Resurrection without, of course, openly admitting it. They represent treason in the Church, a secular Fifth Column; and a lion with a taste for genuine raw Christian would not care for them.

Modernism (condemned by St. Pius X in 1907 as "the synthesis of all heresies") is often spoken of as a past phenomenon only; but what we have today, best called Neo-Modernism or Secularizing Modernism, has become more respectable but is, all the same, the final poisonous fruit of Modernism (short of leaving the Church altogether): an empty husk, form without faith, except an exaggeratedly humanistic faith in Man as the creator of 'god' as well as the builder of heaven on earth (so far not very heavenly). Neo-Modernism is secularizing in that it seeks earnestly to conform the Church to its own disbelief as well as to every with-it worldly trend; its biblical critics interpret the New Testament, not only by means of honest scholarship but on the basis of unadmitted secular assumptions or presuppositions, especially that the miraculous cannot be accepted. It is perhaps the deadliest heresy of the centuries because of its intellectual dishonesty: the lying pretence of faith even as it undermines the faith of others. The secularists are this-world-ers, serving the Prince of this World, though they no longer believe in the master they so truly serve.

Yet this very danger, threatening Protestant and Catholic alike, caused the Question of Rome to re-present itself to my mind with a fresh vigour. If all of Evangelical and Eastern Orthodox faith were united once again to the tremendous power of the Catholic Magisterium, what a force for Christ! Not a Church, as Chesterton said, that will move *with* the world but "a Church that will move the world." Unity that would make the Faith more credible to non-Christians. Unity, I was beginning to see, that could *only* be brought about in and through the primacy of the Successor of Peter and the teaching authority (Magisterium) of Holy Church.

Even as I was seeing the Magisterium in this new light, not as an obstacle to becoming Catholic but as the true center of the defence of the Faith, my deep love for Anglicanism was being jolted as I saw that it was falling helplessly into the hands of the Secularizing Neo-Modernists. It used to be said that whatever might happen in the

Anglican Communion, two things would always remain to bind it together: the beloved Book of Common Prayer and the Apostolic Orders. But now the Prayerbook, which Chesterton (again in *The Well and the Shallows*) called holy and powerful "not in so far as it is the first Protestant book, but in so far as it was the last Catholic book", was not merely revised but virtually rewritten. That tie was weakened: the people wanted the old book; the clergy, the new; the old book perished.* Then the Episcopal Church, not waiting for the rest of the Anglican Communion and without even a consensus vote, hearing only the voice of the Spirit of the Age, recklessly and with almost indecent haste compromised its claim to valid orders and Catholicity by 'ordaining' women as priestesses. And the tie of the orders was weakened. Thousands left the church. Approval of divorce and of homo*sex* — shown vividly by the 'ordination' of a known, practicing lesbian as a priestess — further proved that Anglicanism, at least in America, was controlled by men who subscribed to the values of the trendy secular world, not those of Christianity. Whether I was to leave the Anglican Church or not, I began to see it as leaving me.

I am not — fortunately perhaps for my faith — one of those would-be shepherds of the flock, the academic theologians who (some of them) present themselves, not at all modestly, as the new 'magisterium'; but, like C. S. Lewis, I am educated in other ways (history and literature, including the classical), which allows me, as a scholar myself — hence aware of the limitations of scholarship — to keep the relationship between theological scholarship and faith in perspective. Neither a shepherd nor a would-be shepherd, I am merely one of the sheep. But it is, after all, the sheep that, inadequately fed, may nerve themselves to bolt away into other pastures. This sheep, as a result both of the Question of Rome re-presenting itself and of the melancholy decline of Anglicanism, read deeply in the works of those great Anglican Catholics, J. H. Newman, G. K. Chesterton, and Ronald Knox, whose road to Rome I was treading. And I entered into discussions with other thoughtful sheep, including a French Catholic philosopher in Québec, a Lutheran convert to Catholicism in Australia, and a sturdy Anglican in England, all undermining my irresolution from different directions. Whilst all this was going on, it was given a certain impetus by the joyful radiance of John Paul II's

---

*There were some old clerks who said, "Oh!
    The Prayerbook's a bore and must go:
        For the spirit of prayer
        As to fun can't compare
    With our NEW 'Church Variety Show'."

appearance among us, giving this sheep intimations, however faint, of what the Second Coming might be like.

More months passed. Suddenly I found myself on the brink of the precipice, the very edge of the white cliffs of Anglicanism. The wide, dark Channel lay below: the English Channel that lies between the Canterbury of Anglicanism and the Rome of Holy Mother Church. One more step and I'd be gone. Paling slightly, I drew back a trifle and sat down, one leg dangling over the edge, staring across the Narrow Seas towards Peter's dome. Impulses—were they suicidal?— to leap off and start swimming clashed with desires to turn away and go home. It seemed impossible either to take the plunge or to turn firmly away. I continued, therefore, to sit there, not very cheerfully.

Some examination of what, by courtesy, may be called my think-ing at this point—and my feelings—may be of interest to other sheep. I saw no doctrinal obstacle to becoming Catholic, least of all, as I've said, the Magisterium or the infallibility of the pope in his rare *ex cathedra* pronouncements. It was altogether clear that, just as Christianity itself stood or fell upon whether Jesus was all God as well as all man, so the Catholic Church—defined as the Successor of Peter and all those in communion with him—stood or fell upon whether it was *The* Church, the visible Church that Christ founded. The Question of Rome. What did Christ, doing the will of the Father, *mean* by 'Church' when He said, "I will build my Church"? Did He mean the Church in the singular or in the ten-thousand-sect plural? He *spoke* of His Church in the singular (and those who believe in an inerrant Bible may well contemplate that singular).

Protestants, to be sure, have an answer: *The* Church, they say, is the invisible church of the faithful: this is appealing (though it may be confusing the Church and the Kingdom), but the fact that the invisible church was never heard of until after the Protestants broke away, fifteen hundred years after Christ, does rather suggest ration-alizing after the fact. I, at all events, could not escape the impression that He did *not* intend the incredible splintering of Protestantism. Moreover, that very splintering showed the inadequacy of the major Protestant doctrine of *Sola Scriptura* and the necessity of the teaching *authority*—the Magisterium—of the Church Catholic. Even a rela-tively simple document like the U. S. Constitution requires a 'Teach-ing authority', the Supreme Court, to interpret it: How infinitely more does the Bible and the Tradition need it! How *obviously* neces-sary, if we, many of us, were not blinded by old hostilities! Just as the Apostles under Peter—long before there was a New Testament— interpreted Christ's truth, so their successors, the Bishops under the

Successor of Peter, have ever since interpreted that truth. Protestant-ism (probably the first known instance of throwing out the *mother* with the bath water) has no 'Supreme Court'—hence the continual splintering. The Catholic Church has the Magisterium.

Moreover, although Protestants will not squarely face the fact, we must, if we are to rely upon the New Testament, accept that the Church, which guided by the Holy Spirit defined (chose the canon of) the New Testament, was *then* infallible. The question, therefore, is *not* whether the Church can be infallibly guided by the Spirit in matters of Faith (as she has always claimed to be) but, rather, when did the Spirit leave off the infallible guidance—if it did? When men, when popes, became sinful? But when were they not, even Peter? Their fallenness is, precisely, why the guidance is needed.

Three arguments in particular convince me that the Holy Spirit did *not* leave off His guidance of the Church of Peter in matters of the Faith. The first of these concerns that very period that Protestants rightly point to as having the most corrupt of popes: the hardly-Spirit-filled popes of the Avignon 'Captivity' and the Great Schism as well as the not-noticeably-religious popes of the Renaissance who triggered the Protestant revolt. Lots of sin. No question about that—the sin—but the Protestant critics fail to notice the really significant fact: not one of those wicked popes altered doctrine. To this histori-cally-minded sheep, that fact is quite the most remarkable proof that the Holy Spirit was on the job, guiding His Church away from error. In the very year that Henry VIII's obedient Parliament named him head of the English church, Pope Paul III went through the streets of Rome in sackcloth and ashes for the sins of his predecessors—but not for their errors in doctrine. That is the significant fact: not what the good popes did, but what the bad ones *didn't* do.

The second argument for the continued guidance of the Holy Spirit is the *timing* of the pronouncement of the long-believed-in doctrine of papal infallibility (the infallible Church saying infallibly that the pope is infallible). Springing from the Tradition, it was formally defined as dogma by Pope and Council a little over a centu-ry ago. Newman, though not disagreeing with it, thought the defini-tion "premature". That it was not. It was just *before* the unforeseeable inroads of Secularizing Modernism. Imagine the howls from the likes of Hans Küng if it were defined today! As it is the Catholic faithful (and all the faithful everywhere) know that, if need be, out of the depths of Parnassus the oracle will return into the world: the *ex cathedra* utterance of the Magisterium. The Church has the bomb.

The third indication to me of a Spirit-led Church guided beyond the vision of men is the series of events that made possible the pontificate of John Paul II, the pope we need at this moment of history, the white knight of Christendom. First, following the beloved John, a reserved, seemingly timid and cold pope, Paul VI. Then the cardinals met, determined, it is reported, to choose an elderly pope who wouldn't live too long but would project an image of warmth. Cardinal Wojtyla had no chance—too young and vigorous, as well as non-Italian. The cardinals had their way. John Paul I: warmth indeed, captivating the world; and dead in a month. Now the weary cardinals re-assembling wanted a younger man, and now perhaps a non-Italian. So John Paul II strode forth from behind the Iron Curtain, where, like the early Christians, he had dwelt under the shadow of martyrdom (which wonderfully concentrates the mind upon the *Faith*), to become the intellectually powerful Defender of the Faith. No mortal—no cardinal—could have foreseen this chain of events that alone could have led to John Paul II: but the Holy Spirit could.

But doesn't the Holy Spirit dwell within us all, guiding us if we permit? Of course. But does anyone really see the *Holy* Spirit, as opposed to the Spirit of the Age, guiding, say, the Episcopal Church—*as a church*—away from all error? Come on!

God's revealing Himself in the Incarnation for man's redemption is often called the Revelation. But it was not hidden from God—who knows what we call past and future in His eternal Now—that fallen man, *because* he is fallen, will corrupt any truth. How was that once-given Revelation to be kept from corruption? By the Spirit-led Church interpreting the Bible in the light of Tradition, say the Catholics. By the Bible alone—*Sola Scriptura*—with individual enlightenment from the Spirit, say the Protestants. Moreover, say the Protestants, Rome itself has corrupted doctrine: the Assumption (of Mary), for instance. Here a study of Newman's *Development of Doctrine* would be enlightening. Analogically, the Supreme Court (the guidance of the Holy Spirit is not suggested) has developed constitutional doctrine, and the Constitution might not have survived if it hadn't. Similarly, the Magisterium has functioned like a strict-constructionist court for twenty centuries. The question, then—one must ask the right questions—is *not* the validity of the doctrine of the Assumption; the question is the *Church*: Is it Christ's Church, prevented by the Holy Spirit from doctrinal error? If so, one simply accepts the Assumption. One does not argue with the Holy Spirit. And the Faith has remained whole, if in some ways developed, in the Catholic Church.

On the other hand, the Protestant dependence on the Bible alone—*Sola Scriptura*—with individual enlightenment from the Spirit: How has that worked since the Reformation? The truth is, the Bible, divine though it is, is simply *not* enough to guard the truth. The three great Reformation churches—Lutheran, Calvinist, Anglican—have splintered into thousands, yet they all, even the Mormons and the Christian Scientists, have the Bible—and they can't all be right. The Bible, in the absence of the teaching authority of the Magisterium and the Tradition of the visible Church, is being asked to do what a book, however holy, cannot do. Hence the countless sects.

Even as the Reformation Protestants rejected the teaching authority of Holy Mother Church—a rejection that led to *their* authority being rejected and the splintering of Protestantism ever since—so today in the Catholic Church, notably the American and Dutch branches, there are men in the universities who, in their pride of intellect and enfeebled faith, hold that *they*, not the shepherd-bishops and the Holy Father, ought to be the modern 'shepherds': an intellectual 'magisterium', not the old spiritual one. These men are, whether they know it or not, on the road to ever-more-secular Protestantism. Contemplating that intellectual pride that not only destroys their own faith but that of others, I think of a man who was at once an intellectual giant and a spiritual giant and withal humble.

John Henry Newman of Oxford, one of the finest, most powerful minds of the last century, wrote some words in his *Apologia Pro Vita Sua* that have haunted me since my own Oxford days. Describing his own conversion from high Anglicanism to Holy Church, he says that there is a "fitness" to the idea that it might be the Will of God to provide for "retaining in the world a knowledge of Himself, so definite and distinct as to be proof against the energy of human skepticism." And then he says that "when I find that this is the very claim of the Catholic Church . . . I find no difficulty in admitting the idea."

Neither do I. I cannot believe that God's Revelation was for the first century only. There *is* a "fitness" to the idea that the truth of it should be guarded. I cannot imagine the state of Christendom today if all the early heresies, springing from that "energy of human skepticism", had not been extinguished by the *visible* Catholic Church. But if that Revelation was for all time, its truth must still be guarded by the Magisterium of the Church against the ferocious "energy of human skepticism", manifested in this century by Modernism and Neo-Modernism, which is precisely "human skepticism" or the failure of faith: *the very essence of Modernism is the denial of the Supernatural.* The *Faith* is supernatural or it is nothing. Literally nothing. Nothing that needs faith.

The fact that we (most of us, anyway) have never even seen a miracle in this materialistic age (would we believe it if we saw one?) may make us doubtful of stories about healings or of Sister Marie finding her second-best thimble by the aid of the Blessed Virgin. It is possible to be too credulous— or, today especially, too incredulous. But one truth should be kept in mind: however rare miracles may be today, it is not proof that at the supreme occasion of man's history by *any* reckoning there were not miracles. As St. Paul said (1 Cor. 15:14): "If Christ was not raised, then our gospel is null and void, and so is your faith."

But there are men in the Church, many of them theologians (or, more precisely, *a*theologians), and their intellectual fellow travellers (especially the social scientists) in the university, who, in fact, disbelieve in the Bodily Resurrection, yet, concealing their loss of faith, they still presume to speak for the Church. They speak in learned and often opaque language, and they are a particular danger to the faith of the less learned (Christ's "little ones") who suppose that men so learned must have authority and wisdom as well as some hidden source of knowledge. But, in fact, in great matters like the Bodily Resurrection of Jesus they do *not* have a scrap of secret knowledge (evidence) hidden from the rest of us.

I would not be thought to oppose legitimate biblical scholarship or the faithful theologians; but I know that the Catholic theologian's job is to inquire into and clarify the mind of the Church; and if he goes beyond that to 'explain away' the miraculous that both Scripture and the mind of the Church attest to, he is as dishonest in doing his job as a chemist who falsifies an experiment or an historian who suppresses a document. If, to be sure, there is valid, ancient, documentary evidence against a particular miracle, it should be brought to our attention; and if there were evidence against a miracle that is an article of faith, it should be quietly presented to the Magisterium for decision, not rushed into print. The burden of *proof* rests upon those who would *disprove* a prophecy (prediction) or a miracle. The truth of Revelation—God Incarnate and the Bodily Resurrection—is for the Christian theologian a given. But what these Neo-Modernist theologians are, in fact, doing—but never honestly admitting—is bringing *to* the New Testament, not faith but assumptions or presuppositions from secular thought: *unverified and unverifiable assumptions*. They *assume*, merely assume, that the miraculous—the intervention of transcendent Supernature into nature—cannot occur, an assumption for which there is not an atom of proof in all science (since science is exclusively concerned with nature). Christianity is a *supernatural* faith, or it is not faith at all.

If a biblical critic says that a prophecy by Jesus of the destruction of Jerusalem or the Temple (which, in fact, happened in 70 A.D.) was inserted by the gospel writers after the event, that is, 'proving' that Jesus never said it and further 'proving' that the Gospel was written after the event, he is merely exhibiting his assumption that prophecy cannot happen. What a refreshment it would be if biblical critics stated all their secular assumptions on page 1! But then of course Christians wouldn't buy the book if the assumptions denied the Faith. But the assumptions are usually not stated, though they are easy enough to spot.

Many of the Neo-Modernists assert belief, especially in preaching, but then speak of New Testament events in a way calculated to shake their listeners' belief. The preacher may say he has deep faith in the Resurrection (in a Pickwickian sense no doubt), but then speak of it as a "faith-happening", a code-word meaning that what *he* believes is that those naïve apostles *really* believed that they had seen the Risen Lord, but of course we know they didn't. How we know that they didn't is not made clear.

The Christian reader and churchgoer needs to train himself to look for the unstated assumptions behind what he reads and hears. Otherwise his faith can be undermined and destroyed by men who, too secularized to believe the Faith themselves, are yet unwilling to do the honest thing of throwing up their jobs as priest or theologian and leaving the Church. Instead, they try to reduce the faith of others — if they could destroy everybody else's faith that would prove that they were right and comfort them. There are of course splendid Catholic scholars who see with the eye of faith, but it is the secularized intellectuals and theologians who have lost their faith that I am concerned with; often they are the very ones who hold that *they* should be the shepherds of the flock. My poem is about them.

The Shepherds' Reformation

The new apostates' breath
Shrivels divinity up.
Unproved assumptions gauge
Their scholarship: their lord's
The Spirit of the Age.
They stab with secular swords
   The wounded side
   Of the Crucified,
And holding the holy cup
They urge the ultimate death.

As suavely they speak the Creed,
With every word forsworn,
From His Father's Side
And His fainting Bride
The Son of God is torn.
The flung´stone´shat´ters
The blue´stained´glass´:
The Light of Heaven scatters
Upon the pitying grass.
— But what if He's risen indeed?

I saw, then, the real war within the churches, the war of Supernaturalism (the Faith) v. Naturalism (the World); and I saw that the best hope of all the churches was the Successor to Peter and the Magisterium of the Catholic Church. There was no doctrinal obstacle to my becoming a Catholic: intellectually I already was a Catholic. And I saw more clearly than many confused members of that Church the vital necessity of the Magisterium in confronting the terrible "energy of human skepticism". But seeing the way clear to becoming Catholic is not quite the same thing as being willing to follow that way.

Indeed the reader, especially the Anglican reader, may be asking when I shall be coming to the case for Anglicanism. It can be argued that it is more Catholic than other Protestant churches and more Protestant than the Catholic Church and so deserves its nickname of the "Bridge Church." But bridges are usually to be *crossed*, by people going one way or the other.

I myself clung to the fond delusion of many Anglicans, especially the high-church ('Anglo-Catholic') ones, that we were somehow *in* the Catholic Church, even if we were not in communion with the pope and even though our own church was becoming less and less 'catholic'. Nevertheless, this unrealistic assumption or delusion that we, unlike other Protestants, are somehow *in* the Universal Church because we retain the Apostolic Succession in the Orders (at least until a bishopess queers it) gives rise to the peculiar difficulty of Anglicans in contemplating Holy Mother Church. The difficulty that I call the *English* Channel that lies between Canterbury and Rome. As a result of it, the Question of the Church, the precise question itself, becomes for us rather elusive; and we tend to live in a somewhat unreal world, shutting our eyes on the one hand to the heresies of the Episcopal Church and shuddering on the other hand at the commonness of the Catholic Church; and comforting ourselves with the beauty of liturgy and incense.

But my love for Anglicanism was not exclusively high-church but was based on the Book of Common Prayer and on Englishness, and I found it ever more difficult to keep my eyes shut and to sustain the delusion that I was, somehow, a Catholic. The number of Anglican priests queued up to become Catholic priests as well as other Anglicans going the same way indicated that others were having the same difficulty and that the 'Bridge Church' was indeed a bridge. Newman, in the end, had decided that the *Via Media* of the Oxford Movement (later to be called 'Anglo-Catholic') that he had done so much to create was simply not valid, and he had become a real Catholic. As did Chesterton and Knox (and more recently Malcolm Muggeridge). Ronald Knox, an Anglican priest like Newman, was steeped in Anglicanism, being the son and grandson of Anglican bishops. Yet in his book, *A Spiritual Aeneid*, about his journey to the Mother Church, he wrote that Anglicanism itself

> is not a system of religion nor a body of truth but a feeling, a tradition, its roots intertwined with associations of national history and of family life; you do not learn it, you grow into it; you do not forget it, you grow out of it.

Yes. Precisely. I had been an Anglican long before I was a Christian, and that feeling he speaks of and that tradition can be very strong indeed. Moreover, when I became a Christian, my faith was nurtured in the Church of England. I hadn't yet quite grown out of it. I wanted to be a Catholic, but I wanted the whole Church of England (and its American branch) to come with me and remain Anglican. I did see, though, that it wasn't a question of opposing arguments, RC v. C of E: it was a question of whether one accepted or rejected the arguments for Rome. One of the arguments is implicit in defining a Catholic as one in communion with the Successor of Peter.

One familiar argument against the Catholic Church troubled me for awhile in a vague way until I realized how intellectually disreputable and *ad hominem* it is. An argument by innuendo. In a veiled way it will be hinted that anyone even considering submitting to Rome (born RCs are exempt because they can't help it) is, if not quite fascist, at least yearning for authoritarian answers and intellectual chains, not brave enough to accept uncertainty and wanting in the valiant questing spirit of man. Needless to say, the suggestion could only come from an essentially-secular humanist, though possibly a secular humanist in sheep's clothing. But, surely (one may reply), the questing spirit of man seeks in order to *find*? Otherwise, dear friend, would there not be something genuinely absurd — something a bit *silly*, in fact — about a valiant seeker determined *not* to find lest he should lose his 'Seeker's Status'? Or lest the finding impose an uncomfortable awareness of his creaturely position?

Indeed, apart from these 'professional seekers' who value their Seeker's Status more than truth, most of us would be only too glad to have some certain answers straight from the ultimate authority, God. We should welcome an angel very warmly indeed should one stop by. "Ask me anything you like," he would say kindly, folding his wings. "Oh, thank you, sir!" we would reply. "Do you mind if I put on my sunglasses — the, er, brightness, you know? Ahhh, that's better! Now, please sir, just what *is* the Church? And would you say a few words about — well, birth control, you know? And divorce. Oh, and homo*sex*. Just for starters. — Oh, some whisky? No, I suppose not. You don't mind if I do?" — "Not at all," the angel would say. "Now, first of all, about the Church . . ."

However unlikely an angelic visitant, the question about the Church, though seldom asked with an open mind by Protestants, is *there*. It is implicit in the very existence of the two-thousand-year-old Catholic Church. Logically it *must* be asked. I asked it — and so arrived on the edge of the white cliffs.

Why have I stopped on the brink? [I shall leave the rest of part one, "The White Cliffs", in the present tense as originally written.] I have not stopped because of intellectual difficulties ahead but because I am being pulled in opposite directions. There's no question but that it would be right to go on to Rome, but would it be *wrong* to stay? *Must* I go?

In my faith and worship I am a child of the Church of England. C. S. Lewis, who shaped that faith and was my counsellor and friend, was Church of England. My wife's ashes lie in two Anglican churchyards, one in England and one in Virginia. When I nerve myself to leap off the white cliffs, I hear voices in my ears — gentle, courteous Anglican voices — saying: "Stay! Stay with us. We are your people. We are *your people*, and you speak our language. Do not leave us. You don't want to be a — Catholic!"

I — a *Catholic*! Loving the English thing in Prayerbook and history, I feel it to be almost like treachery — and real pain, too. The English ships stood out under Howard and Drake, Hawke and Nelson, to sink the fleets of their several Catholic Majesties who were minded to conquer England. Anglican Cavaliers fought the Puritan Roundheads; and in the return match Virginian Anglican 'Cavaliers' fought the Puritan Yankees. Anglican poets — Vaughan and Herbert—touched the robe of Divinity. The deep graves in the English earth and the Virginian earth. How does one tear the past away? "If I forget Jerusalem . . ."

And the present. A country parish, St Stephen's, a century and a half in this place under the blue Virginian mountains. People who are dear to me, living about the county in old country houses, full of old and beautiful things, and with an old tradition of courtesy. Houses with names like Elk Hill and Trivium, Bellevue and Lochwood Hall, where I go to dine. These folk are troubled about the new Prayerbook and other things the secularizers are doing, but they would never leave St Stephen's where their people are buried. How can I?

They would never understand if I converted to popery. I can hear them now, saying—not to me, they'd be too polite, but to each other—saying: "Something damned unsound about a feller who'd do a thing like that!" At the same time, of course, they would remember their second-cousin Randolph's great-great-uncle Charles who stole a horse or fought for the Yankees or some such thing.

Past voices, present voices, saying: "Stay! We are your people."

In England there is an *English* RC tradition. Sir Thomas More, Saint, who died for Holy Church with the words: "I die the King's good servant, but God's first." The old Catholic houses that kept the Catholic faith at the risk—often at the cost—of their lives. The English martyrs like the heroic Campion. The English abbeys that have risen again, and all the stream of conversions stemming from the Oxford Movement. The parish churches themselves built when the Church was one. In England there wouldn't be quite that feeling of treachery perhaps, of abandoning one's roots.

But in America, the Catholic Church looks—well, foreign. Probably collections for the IRA. Maybe the Mafia. Of course I'm exaggerating—I think. And a liturgy that makes even the new Episcopal Book of Varietal Prayer sound good. Still, choosing a church is not like choosing a suit or a house, a matter of taste and comfort. A little matter of truth.

The Episcopal Church, if the secularizers retain control, may be on its way to some sort of national pan-protestant church with no claim to catholicity—and perhaps not much to Christianity either. But whatever the prospects, including priestesses or even a bishopess, that future doesn't affect St Stephen's now.

In the greatest play of our times, *A Man for All Seasons*, the Duke of Norfolk, speaking of the men who have gone along with the King in the break with Rome, says with dignity and pain to Sir Thomas More: "But damn it, Thomas, . . . You know those men! Can't you

do what I did, and come with us, for fellowship?" The most moving
of appeals. It is the appeal to me of the courteous Anglican voices in
my ears: "Stay! Stay with us, for fellowship." And, indeed, staying —
inaction — is a bit easier than going, if it's not a matter of your neck.
Still, I must not conceal More's reply to Norfolk's appeal: "And when
we stand before God, and you are sent to Paradise for doing according to your conscience, and I am damned for not doing according to
mine, will you come with me, for fellowship?" Not a comfortable
remark.

But the truth is — and this is the point of real pain — I do not know
what my conscience or the Holy Spirit is saying. I am not unaware
that my love of Anglicanism is an earthly love or that the Devil may
use our legitimate loves for his purposes, I have not neglected pon-
dering Our Lord's words about leaving father and mother to follow
Him. But — which way *is* following Him? Even believing that the
Catholic Church is the only possible way of unification, should I do
more towards unification by 'poping' or by speaking for it, in an
'Anglican voice', within Anglicanism? But even if I knew the answer,
which I don't, it is the wrong question, for it is substituting human
reason for God's.

The right question is, what is God's will? But I do not know that,
either. Nor how to find out.

Uncannily, at just this point in the essay, not knowing how to end
and pausing for coffee and thought, the post arrives with a letter
forwarded by my (Catholic) confessor, from a monk of Ampleforth
Abbey in England who knows of my 'point of pain'. He advises me to
leave off floundering about in the which-is-God's-will dilemma, but,
instead, *step over the dilemma to God alone.* "Anything less than Him is an
idol — even the Catholic Church." Yet, by seeking God alone, I shall,
nevertheless, discover His will, for "I will reveal myself to him who
loves me." It seems that God is speaking to me through this monk of
Ampleforth.

I ought, though, to make clear the dilemma. It appears to me to
be God's will that the Church be One, in union with the Chair of
Peter. And at the same time it appears to me to be His will that we
should love the people He gives us to love, with a love as much like
Christ's as possible. It follows from the first proposition that I should
submit to Holy Mother Church; and it follows from the second that I
should stay in St Stephen's, loving the people God has given me to
love. And it's no good saying that I could go on loving them even if I
did leave — people drift apart. This is the dilemma I turn over to
God. My mind says *go*, but my heart says *stay*.

Thus I remain on the very edge of the white cliffs, and the wide, dark Channel lies below. A fine intellectual gallop—or, more appropriately, canter—to the dangerous edge of the cliffs is refreshing; but then one wants to go *home*. Sitting here on the brink, I hear across the English Channel from the distant dome of Peter's Church the trumpets of Rome; but behind me, across the green fields, homely and dear, the change-ringing bells singing from the towers of Canterbury.

2. Crossing the Channel

The foregoing essay, under the title "The English Channel" (and subsequently somewhat revised) was published, nearly a year after it was written, in an Anglican journal and produced a storm of letters, praising it and damning it and me. And personal letters, all kindly, both from Anglicans saying, "Do not leave us," and from Catholics saying, "Come on, start swimming!" One Catholic correspondent pointed out that the bark of Peter had sprung some leaks since Vatican II but "Come along and help bail!" Though I was still perched on the white cliffs, that letter appealed to me—the idea of being of some help. And I thought: Yes, leaking a little—but a superb helmsman and straight on course to the East. But that luxurious liner that passed, everybody waving but nobody on the bridge and going in circles—was that Anglicanism? Or perhaps *Titanic*?

I had been on the cliffs, now, for about a year and a half and was growing a little tired of being there. There was some consolation, though, in the fact that Newman and Chesterton and Knox had all, it seemed, come to the very edge of the cliffs of Anglicanism and hung about there for a long time before taking the plunge. And C. S. Lewis, despite a truly Catholic mind, had never come near to leaping. So I said my prayers and waited, for something.

In the May of 1981, a couple of months after the "Channel" was published, I went up to Portsmouth Abbey on Rhode Island, a monastery of the English Congregation of the Benedictines, to see my old friend and Confessor, Dom Julian. Apart from visiting him, my purpose was to help him with a forthcoming book of his deep-Christian poetry, *There Shines Forth Christ*, for which I had written an introduction. At the same time, I was wondering, as perhaps he was, whether some special grace would move me to submit to Holy Mother Church. Just in case, I asked him to examine me in the Faith. But nothing happened. After a week I drove north to the French village of La Pocatière in Québec to talk with another friend, Georges Allaire, a Christian philosopher who had given me many insights into the case for Catholicism—and into G. K. Chesterton as well. But Georges who had sharpened my reason could not assist me in determining my will, or God's. Then I came home to Virginia.

On the fridge a fragment of a yellow poster proclaimed: "Not to decide *is* to decide." A kindly old Austin friar (Augustinian), Father Robert Regan, had pointed out that in choosing Christ Himself long ago I was in a sense refusing to *reject* the Lord—without any special compelling grace. I had said then, "I *choose* to believe." And yet, I now thought, I had chosen Christ with *enough* (sufficient) grace; and it had been only *after* I chose that I had *felt* myself sustained by grace. It was, or it seemed to be, *my* choice. So now it occurred to me that to expect a special grace in this matter of the Church was perhaps a kind of Anglican hauteur: "Anglicans will receive engraved invitations and enter by the main door." This thought, along with Father Bob's observation, supported by the yellow poster, gave me an uneasy feeling that Someone might be expecting me to make up my mind.

At the Abbey in late May, Dom Julian and I had been visited by Peter Kreeft (the man who'd suggested I come along and help bail the bark of Peter) and Tom Howard. We were all four writers, two Catholics and Tom and me, Anglicans: indeed, Tom read us his then-unpublished essay, "Lead, Kindly Light", on his own approach to Rome. And there was talk of it as well as of the published part of "The English Channel". It was a pleasant afternoon of the "Junior Inklings", as someone suggested we call ourselves. In the course of the discussion Peter suddenly said: "I have a question for Tom and Van. If you knew you were going to die tomorrow, what would you do about the Church?" Tom hesitated; but I said instantly: "I should ask Julian to receive me into the Catholic Church." I was faintly surprised at my own certainty, but then I added: "Because, you know, if I were going to die, I should be leaving St Stephen's anyway."

Now at home that question and my reply came back to me. I hadn't thought much about it at the time, but now it occurred to me that I had, in fact, suggested to God a way to bring me to decision: perhaps I had best decided on my own first. "Not to decide *is* to decide." To decide by drift. Then it came to me that perhaps I could go on drifting, but, if I faced up to decision, I could not *reject* Holy Mother Church—just as, long years before, I had realized that I could not reject Jesus. But if I cannot *reject* the Church, that means that only one way is now possible, for I couldn't finally choose Anglicanism without rejecting the Catholic Church. (I, at least, cannot go on drifting unless I can persuade myself that either way is possible.)

Therefore, if I *cannot* reject the Church — if only one way is possible —
I *have* decided, haven't I?

So I came to decision. I mentioned this to God in prayer.

It was August now, about the first. I telephoned Dom Julian. He,
who for years patiently answered my questions about the Church, as
well as being my Confessor, must be the one to receive me. We set
August 15th, the Assumption, for the Reception. Julian had never
urged me to become Catholic and had indeed seemed almost indifferent (not that I believed he was). Now he wrote me that he had
prayed for me to come into the Church every day for thirty years.
Eleven thousand prayers!

A fortnight to wait between the Decision and the Act. A fortnight
of feeling — what? Joyful? Elated? Peaceful? None of these. Gloom,
rather. Pain and sadness about St Stephen's and its dear people.
Forebodings about what the Catholic Church would actually be like
at the parish level. Feelings of treachery towards all that Canterbury
represented: old churches in England, my first vicar there, Anglican
friends, the very history of England. I buried myself in studying
Rome, not papal Rome but classical and pagan Rome — gloomily. I
went to St Stephen's a last time — nobody knew — and it almost undid
me. The lovely ancient words of the Book of Common Prayer. The
people. Three days later the Rector dropped in, and I told him. It
almost undid us both. We hugged each other. And my decision
remained firm.

The next morning I flew north.

Portsmouth Abbey and Julian. His welcoming smile and our talks
helped, as did the loving-kindness of some of the monks. And Peter
Kreeft coming in from Boston to be my sponsor or godfather, bringing me an old Russian cross. It was appropriate that he should be the
one, for his question at the Junior Inklings meeting had unlocked
my indecision. In a deeper sense of course Dom Julian had fathered
my Catholicism, beginning at Oxford thirty years before: his prayers
and his friendship and his always being there to answer my questions.

The ceremony itself: Father Julian received me into Holy Church.
I chose not to waive the conditional baptism. An old and beautiful
monk who was also a bishop, Ansgar Nelson, OSB, anointed me in
Confirmation. A few Catholic friends looked on. It was done.

As if to show that I wasn't cut off from all things English, the first
man I was introduced to as a Catholic was Cardinal Hume, OSB, of
England, paying a brief surprise visit to the abbey, the abbey that
had begun as a priory of English abbeys. But I was pretty well past

feeling anything. Numb to all I thought I should feel—a resolute numbness. The only feeling I can remember was gratitude for the loving-kindness of everybody.

By the time I left two days later, a sort of chuckle was welling up in me, breaking through the numbness. A small parcel Julian gave me—a book I thought—proved to be, when I opened it at home, his carved-wood, mediaeval crucifix that was with my wife when she died. It is beside me as I write.

A papist now, I went the following Saturday evening to my first Mass in Virginia. Julian had written to the pastor, Father Warner; and he and I had had a talk. At the Mass I was startled—almost believing for one amazed instant that it had been 'fixed'—when the Gospel turned out to be Matthew 16: "and upon this Peter/Rock I will build my Church . . . and give unto you the Keys . . ." In his homily, Father Warner spoke of the Faith with his own firm, loving faith in every word; and then he celebrated the Eucharist with moving power. There are two Catholic churches in Lynchburg, Holy Cross where Father Warner is, and St Thomas More, which of course drew me by its name. I had meant to check them both out; but after that first Mass at Holy Cross, I looked no further. I felt then, and have not since changed my mind, that I was blessed in my priest.

That Mass was on Saturday evening because I had decided to go to St Stephen's one more time and tell people in person what I had done. I still didn't feel elated or joyful, but I did, now, feel a sort of peace and rightness. And that inner chuckle—at myself, I think—persisted. I thought *God* to be rather amused.

I knew that the service at St Stephen's was Matins (morning prayer, not communion) as it is every other Sunday. Then, between the evening Mass and next morning's Matins, it came to me: There wasn't a reason in the world or in Heaven above why (without neglecting Mass) I shouldn't *always* go to Matins at St Stephen's *as a Catholic*—a graduate Anglican, as it were. Unless they stoned me. This sudden plan might seem a bit like having one's cake and eating it, too; but the motive is love. Moreover, it seemed to me *real* ecumenism, not the muddled sort that says that all varieties of religion are equally true as long as people's hearts are in the right place. Suddenly I had a sense of mission—if only to show that becoming papist doesn't lead to growing horns. (Not so far.)

So, with a sort of astonished happiness added to the peace and the chuckle, I drove out into the country to St Stephen's with Nelly, my border collie, beside me and my pocket bulging with copies of the "Channel" (part one), which explained not only why Rome but why

St Stephen's still. And I told people, some before Matins, some after, offering the "Channel", which everybody wanted. When I said I'd become RC, they responded with kindness but looked sad. But when I added that I'd continue to be part of St Stephen's at least for Matins, their faces brightened. The Rector gave me a faint, possibly wry, smile at that Petrine Gospel. And in the months [now years] since, I have continued to go to St Stephen's as well as Holy Cross.

What is, to me, so amazing about this whole thing is that in all the years since perceiving my dilemma of doing God's will—either by becoming Catholic *or* by loving the people He gave me to love in St Stephen's—and in all the talks and letters about it, *nobody* saw that I could go to St Stephen's *as a Catholic.* Not even I with my sometimes ingenious (not to say tricky) mind—not even in that fortnight of gloom. No wonder God seemed amused! Now Dom Julian wrote that he thought my going to St Stephen's was "exquisite charity." That shocked me: I was doing it because I wanted to. —But why did I want to?

It seems to me that I had to be willing to leave—actually, in fact, *leave*—'father and mother' *before* they could be given back to me in a new way. An Irish nun, Sister Hilary, who knew of the dilemma said, in response to my note about the Reception, "You will find that you will not lose your friends, for God is not to be outdone in generosity." The words leapt out at me. In pain and sadness I had bidden farewell to St Stephen's and all the Anglican things in my heart, but— "God is not to be outdone in generosity." I could not—I cannot—but believe that this resolution of my anguished dilemma was a gift of grace, the grace of a most loving Lord. A merry gift. It was a deep confirmation of my decision to submit to Holy Mother Church.

Remembering, now with laughter, my gloom on the eve of reception, I thought of that beautiful Catholic poem, "The Hound of Heaven" by Francis Thompson:

> *Is my gloom, after all,*
> *Shade of His hand, outstretched caressingly?*

13

FLOYD I. NEWMAN, JR.

The Search for a Shepherd
(Jeremiah 23:4)

Floyd I. Newman, Jr., is a 1980 graduate of Asbury College, Wilmore, Kentucky. His graduate studies are in information systems and, most recently, English literature at Virginia Commonwealth University, Richmond, Virginia. Newman currently works as a systems analyst for Best Products Company, Inc. Floyd and Angel Newman have one child, Jessica.

This is the story of a sheep's search for a shepherd. The story has a happy ending. For the sheep finds what he is seeking and is now safely in the fold of Rome, under the care of the faithful shepherd John Paul II. I am the sheep, and the story is the chronicle of my conversion to Roman Catholicism. Since I am only a sheep, and not a theologian, I do not intend my story to prove the validity of the Church of Rome. I intend to relate only how I came to believe in her.

It is said that all true faith begins with doubt. In my life, spiritual growth has quite often been preceded by a crisis of faith. One such crisis occurred shortly after I graduated from college. After marrying my college sweetheart and settling into our life together, the faith-rotting skepticism of the secular world began to infect me. I had been a Christian since childhood. Four years in a Christian college further affirmed my faith. But although it was easy to believe in God when all around me encouraged that belief, I was unprepared to meet the challenge of a post-Christian society. My faith began to crumble like a castle of sand before the rising tide. I was not in danger of flatly rejecting Christianity, but worse: of simply drifting away from it. As Georges Bernanos wrote, "Faith is not a thing one 'loses,' we merely cease to shape our lives by it."

But God does not willingly surrender His children to the world. My rescue came in the form of a book, *A Severe Mercy*, by Sheldon

Vanauken. Never before had I read a book that tapped so deeply into the truth and beauty of Christianity. *A Severe Mercy* explores the awesome paradox of God's mercy, a mercy so perfect that it sometimes seems cruelty to mortals. But the book is far more than a theological treatise. It is the true story of a powerful faith and a steadfast love, and the vision of Christianity it portrays was so appealing that it tore my heart with longing. Not only did the book point the way back to God, it forever altered my perception of Christian faith. For the first time I fully understood the experience C. S. Lewis called Joy, because I found it in every page; clear, piercing Joy that melted my uncertainty and doubt like dirty snow in the spring thaw. Pulled from the mire, I found my feet on a higher path than before.

When I finished the book, I was so moved that I wrote to Mr. Vanauken, telling him how much his book had meant to me. When he replied right away with a friendly acknowledgment, I resolved to meet this remarkable man. A few weeks later found me knocking on the door of a tiny house in Lynchburg, Virginia.

I was a bit nervous about meeting this Oxford scholar and friend of C. S. Lewis, but Vanauken quickly put me at ease. There was not a trace or smugness or elitism about him. His voice bore traces of his English alma mater, but his manner was Virginia gentleman. We talked for an hour or so about his book, his memories of Lewis, and the nature of prayer. It was a pleasant visit until, unexpectedly, Vanauken told me he was close to becoming a Catholic.

A Catholic! I could scarcely have been more surprised if Vanauken had confessed an attraction for Mormonism, or perhaps Transcendental Meditation. At the time, I regarded the Catholic Church to be little better than a cult. My feelings were the result of a lifetime of solid Protestant training. The fundamentalist church I attended as a teen-ager taught that the terms "Catholic" and "Christian" were almost incompatible. Later, at a Protestant college, I learned to be more tolerant. Catholics could be Christians too. Nevertheless, we studied the Bible, theology, and history from a thoroughly Protestant standpoint and never heard the other side of the story. Thus, the possible validity of the Catholic Church had never occurred to me. Perhaps it never would have, given my assumptions. But God had other plans.

During my visit, Vanauken gave me a copy of an essay he had written, titled "The English Channel," about his journey to the Catholic Church. The essay outlined the reasoning that had brought him to the "white cliffs of Anglicanism," ready to plunge into the English Channel in a swim to Rome. I read it out of curiosity, surprised by

the puissant arguments. One point in the essay impressed me greatly: if the Holy Spirit had once been leading the Catholic Church (as
even Protestants must admit, if they accept the canonization of the
New Testament), when had He stopped leading? "When men, when
popes, became sinful? But when were they NOT sinful? Their fallenness is, quite precisely, why the guidance (of the Holy Spirit) is
required." The essay put a slight chill in my Protestant bones.

"The English Channel" did, however, help me overcome a major
obstacle in my thinking. I began to think of the Catholic Church as a
"legitimate" church, a force to be reckoned with. There were strong
arguments for her validity, and a man I greatly respected believed in
her firmly. I realized that I had been wrong to dismiss her so casually.
Perhaps I also felt, ever so gently, the beginning of the longings for
Catholicism that were to become so forceful later. But I had a long
way to go before I could follow, or even acknowledge, those longings.
The Catholic Church, and Vanauken's conversion (he was received
into the Church later that summer), remained a curious riddle.

I was content to leave the riddle unanswered for quite a while. For
the time being I was busy reading all the books by C. S. Lewis that I
could find. But the Catholic Church never entirely left my mind, for
at least two reasons. First, I continued to write to Mr. Vanauken,
and often his replies contained a reference to the Catholic Church.
In fact, he remarked on several occasions that he couldn't escape the
impression that I was a Catholic, since my name — Newman — reminded him of the great Oxford Catholic, Cardinal John Henry
Newman.

The second thing that kept the Catholic Church in my mind were
the writings of C. S. Lewis. I had discovered Lewis in college and
was heavily influenced by his rational approach to Christianity. The
foundation of Lewis's thought is the belief that faith and reason are
complementary, not antithetical. He therefore maintained that the
worship of God must be an intellectual act, as well as an emotional
experience. When I applied this reasoning to Catholicism, I began
to see the appropriateness of liturgical worship, with its ceremony
and ritual. The Catholic Church became more attractive.

But attraction alone is not sufficient grounds for belief. Lewis also
maintained that the only reason for believing something is that it is
true. The Catholic Church claimed to be the Church Jesus told Peter
to found, and to occupy a place unique among all the churches that
bear the name of Christ. I could not flatly dismiss those claims as
false, but I couldn't affirm them as true either. Anglicans like Vanauken and Lewis were no doubt attracted to Roman Catholicism
because they were in closer proximity to the Roman Church. But

though the English Channel separates Canterbury and Rome, the entire Atlantic lies between American evangelical Protestantism and either. I might stand on the shore and admire the view, but I had no desire to attempt the swim. Not yet.

In the two years following my first visit with Vanauken, however, a resolve to find an answer to the riddle of the Catholic Church began to solidify. Though I felt no compelling desire to have the matter settled, my indecision haunted me. My friends were surprised to find me defending the Catholic Church in discussions with them. One such discussion became a heated argument when I tried to get a friend to admit even the possible validity of the Catholic Church. And all this time, Pope John Paul II was in the news almost weekly. I felt growing admiration for this holy man, fearlessly proclaiming the gospel of Christ to the world.

Then something happened that forced me to confront my unresolved questions about the Catholic Church. Sheldon Vanauken sent me an article he had written titled "The Knight's Move." It was partly about a young man named Tracy who became a Catholic through Vanauken's example. The theme of the story was how God moves us to accomplish His ends like a chess player moves his pieces. But I was most forcefully struck by Tracy's conversion, since his background was similar to my own. My identification with him was so complete that I realized for the first time that I, too, might become a Catholic. A door stood open. The prospect excited and terrified me. Before that moment, I had not realized I could even *want* to be Catholic. Caught up in conflicting emotions, I unexpectedly blurted to my wife, "I think I might become a Catholic." She was only slightly more surprised than I was.

That winter began my education in Holy Church. I was possessed by a feverish desire to settle the Catholic riddle, and to answer it truthfully, not ignorantly or emotionally. My feelings couldn't be trusted anyway, since they were constantly shifting. At times the Catholic Church appeared glorious and appealing, at other times cold and repulsive. Fortunately, I realized from the first that any Catholic doctrine would appear false to a Protestant taught from childhood that Catholicism was untrue. I would have to put aside my presuppositions and consider Catholicism objectively. Most important, I must learn as much as possible about the Catholic Church, for a rational choice can only be made between known alternatives.

Just as I decided to learn more about the Catholic Church, I found a book of excerpts from the writing of John Henry Newman at a secondhand book shop. Since Vanauken mentioned Newman frequently, I thought a collection of his work might be a good place to begin my investigation. The hand of God was in that choice as my first reading in Catholic thought.

Newman was a convert to Catholicism from the Church of England. He had a formidable mind and wrote with power and conviction. One by one my objections to Catholicism were answered. I was finally hearing the other side of the story, and I couldn't have had a better teacher. The Catholic Church Newman revealed to me was a logical extension of the teaching of Christ, an instrument of His continuing revelation in the world, and the army of God, marching triumphantly through the ages with Christ as its head.

Along with my reading, I began to investigate the Catholics of Richmond. I arranged several meetings with a local priest, who patiently answered my numerous questions. I also began to attend Mass. At first, unaccustomed to the order of the liturgy, I was unbearably self-conscious, convinced that the whole congregation knew of the Protestant "spy" in their midst. When the strangeness finally wore off, the beauty and reverence of the Catholic service was quite appealing, with the kneeling, genuflecting, and sign of the cross. Soon I was looking forward to Sunday Mass, though I always slipped out the door when Communion began.

I cannot pinpoint when I began to love the Catholic Church. The feeling grew on me gradually, as I studied and observed. There was a "rightness" about Catholic belief that struck a responsive note in my soul. The dry and lifeless Church my Protestant education told me to expect was instead a living body of exquisite beauty. Even the Catholic veneration of Mary seemed fitting once the reasons for the devotion were understood. I began to wonder if perhaps my earlier instruction had not been seriously flawed. But as I started to move closer to Rome, I was faced with an unexpected obstacle.

Angel, my wife, was alarmed by my growing interest in Catholicism. She had undergone no challenge to her beliefs, as I had when I met Vanauken, and saw no reason to reexamine her choice of churches. Now I seemed to be moving in a direction she could not follow, unless she denounced the church she knew and loved. Though she believed in me and trusted my poorly articulated reasons, she couldn't resist a plaintive appeal not to leave her behind by becoming a Catholic.

A powerful appeal indeed. I had not realized the strength of Angel's objections to Catholicism. Her determination faced me like a wall, impervious to both arguments and reassurances. Was I right to endanger our love for my new convictions? The stakes were too high to make careless assumptions. If I continued on the road to Rome, I risked a breach with the most important person in my life. But turning back seemed unthinkable. Torn by indecision, I would have welcomed a sign from God to point the way. But no angelic visitors appeared to give me guidance, and no voices spoke in thunder as I writhed in prayer. There were times when the impossibility of my position almost drove me to despair.

Facing this bewildering maze of conflicting emotions, I realized that reason alone was not sufficient to show me the right path. I had never practiced a daily program of Bible reading and prayer. Now, aware of the limitations of the mortal mind and will, I was driven to seek God's guidance. Each morning I would read a few chapters of the Bible and pray in that peaceful time just before dawn. I was surprised how much I enjoyed those morning meetings with the Father. As I consumed chapter after chapter of the New Testament, I noticed things I had never seen before, such as the primacy of Peter among the Apostles. I was not seeking confirmations of Catholic doctrine, but I noted them when I found them, and they played a part in my decision. But the most important benefit of my devotions was a continual awareness of God and seeking of His will. The quest itself was certainly reforming my spiritual life.

Of course, I wrote to Sheldon Vanauken about my desire to settle the Catholic riddle. Excerpts from that letter will provide an insight into my thoughts and feelings at the time.

To Sheldon Vanauken, January, 1984:

Since I met you, I have been unlearning all my Protestant misconceptions about Catholics. Reading your article ("The Knight's Move") I was struck by all the similarities between Tracy and myself, and came to recognize my own attraction for the Catholic Church. I began to read a collection of excerpts from the works of J. H. Newman; cautiously at first, and then with enthusiasm. Now I am forced to admit the possible legitimacy of the attraction the RCC holds for me, but the excitement I feel at the prospect of becoming a Catholic is mixed with uncertainty and fear.

My problem is simple: I don't trust myself. I'm afraid that the impetus behind my attraction is not zeal for the will of God but the desire to win your approval. Certainly, there are times when I WANT to become a Catholic. But I can not, MUST not, convert until I am satisfied that I serve God by converting. Before I take one more step toward Rome, I must be absolutely sure that it is Christ's favor I hope to win, and not yours.

Not long ago I had a telephone conversation with a dear friend and devout Christian. He was in complete sympathy with my quest, and confessed his own attraction to the Church of Rome. Yet he urged me to be sure of my path, for my decision would affect Angel as well. While she vowed with all her heart to support me she is opposed to the idea of becoming a Catholic herself. James foresaw that my conversion might become a source of disunity for us. A disunity I must risk IF my leadings toward Catholicism are of God.

I hope this letter has conveyed to you my confusion. I do feel the attraction of the RCC. Is it the image of Christ that attracts me? I've heard the best "arguments" from both sides of the issue, and I have not found any RC doctrine I could not accept. But I would never forgive myself if I suspected my decision was made for selfish motives, especially given the possibility of disunity with Angel.

Would you please pray for me, Mr. Vanauken? That I will not only find the solution to my dilemma, but also that I will KNOW that I have found the right answer (whatever it might be). All my friends are praying too, and I believe J. H. Newman is as well (I asked him). Whatever my decision, I thank you for introducing me to the question. I have gained a great deal spiritually from my quest, meditating on God and reading scripture (and the incomparable Newman). I'll be ahead whatever the outcome. Perhaps that's all I should expect.

Confused but trusting,
Floyd Newman

From Sheldon Vanauken, January, 1984:

I shouldn't think any Catholic convert—including Newman, Chesterton, Ronald Knox, Muggeridge, me, & my godson Tracy—has ever not begun by saying, "The Catholic Church is not for me." I don't therefore find myself impressed when it is said. The only safety is not to think of it ever. True of Christianity, too. As C. S. Lewis says "A good atheist can't be too careful of his friends." (something like that) Although I haven't pressed you to become Catholic, there is the fact that I did—and Tracy did—and now James Hege (my godgrandson) has been received into the Church with Tracy as godfather.

I got from the publishers, at the authors's request, Christopher Derrick's new book: *That Strange Divine Sea: Reflections on Being a Catholic*. His father was converted by G. K. Chesterton. This book is by no means an argument for the Catholic

Church . . . just reflections. Nonetheless, I urge you to have your bookseller order it for you right away. The title is something a brilliant Englishwoman, Helen Waddell (NOT RC), said of the Catholic Church. Can you imagine anyone calling the Anglican or Methodist or Baptist Church "That Strange Divine Sea"?

About Angel — she must acknowledge, if she's honest, that she doesn't KNOW . . . that the Catholic Church MAY be the Church that Christ told Peter to found. Ask her only to go with you in familiarizing yourself with it, learning what it teaches, getting past the strangeness, and being as open minded as she can be.

All this is on the assumption that you want to go deeper & further in to reach certainty. At the same time, you probably have impulses to turn your back on the whole business. Perhaps you will — for awhile. But unanswered questions always come back.

I do understand your "confusion of mind," partly because I've felt it and seen it in others. You rightly see that you must not become a papist in order to please me; at the same time, even as CSL was an influence on me, so am I bound to be (*A Severe Mercy* and after) on you, since I have put my thought, feelings, and actions cogently in essays. You must wait until you are sure, whether that be a month, or a year, or. . . . At the same time, recognize that absolute certainty is seldom granted to us, and motives are never pure.

It appears to me that, since John Paul II mounted the chair of Peter, the tide is setting strongly toward Rome. I hear of conversions on every hand. The editor of the NEW OXFORD REVIEW, Dale Vree, has just converted along with his wife. I just had a letter from a young wife who, like you, is drawn to Rome, who said that during Christmas she suddenly "saw" Mary as the Church sees her — and that ceased to be a difficulty.

You could hardly have a better guide than Newman. In my own decision, both Newman & Sir Thomas More ("A Man For All Seasons") were much in my mind, along with G. K. Chesterton and that other great Oxonian, Ronald Knox.

I shall of course pray, as I have been since your letter, for you — and Angel . . .

Write if you think I can help in any way.

Yours,
Under the Mercy
Sheldon Vanauken

Reading Vanauken's letter, I knew that a moment of decision was approaching. The points of my dilemma had been formalized and clarified. My choices were either full acceptance and submission to Holy Mother Church, or final rejection. There was no honest compromise. I saw the gulf ahead that I must cross before embracing the Catholic Church, as well as the chasm behind, which I could not cross back to Protestantism without rejection of Catholicism. The ground on which I stood was not a destination, but a way station. My only course of action was to continue the quest. If Catholicism was true, then I must submit to Rome regardless of the risk, but the importance of making the right decision was critical.

Books played an important role as my quest intensified. Along with my Catholic catechism, a gift from a sympathetic priest, I read a wide range of works by Catholic writers, from theology to fiction. J. H. Newman's brilliant defense of his own conversion, *Apologia Pro Vita Sua*, was especially meaningful to me. Newman, my first Catholic tutor, seemed an old friend now. Thomas Merton's *Seven Storey Mountain* offered another conversion story, as well as a glimpse of the strange world of the monastery. *The Everlasting Man* and *Orthodoxy* introduced me to G. K. Chesterton, undoubtedly one of the greatest Christian minds of the past century. Graham Green's novels *The Heart of the Matter, The End of the Affair*, and *The Power and the Glory* taught me more about the Catholic mind than any book of theology, and the deep Catholic undercurrents in Evelyn Waugh's *Brideshead Revisited* were compellingly beautiful.

Two books were extraordinarily helpful. Tom Howard's *Evangelical Is Not Enough* helped me understand my own evangelical presuppositions and explained the order and purpose of liturgical worship. Howard wrote from a religious background nearly identical to mine, and his thoughts and observations were indispensable in my understanding of the Mass. The other book, recommended by Vanauken, was *That Strange Divine Sea: Reflections on Being a Catholic*, by Christopher Derrick. In a series of thoughtful reflections on the Roman Church and the state of "being a Catholic," this English Roman Catholic captures the essence of Catholicism simply and powerfully. *That Strange Divine Sea* remains the best introduction to the Catholic faith that I have read.

As a result of my reading, I became convinced that Catholic dogma was indeed consistent with the teaching of Christ and the tradition of the Early Church. The sacraments, ritual, liturgical symbolism, even adoration of the Blessed Virgin — all served to focus the mind on Jesus and His Good News. Protestantism seemed stark and minimal by comparison. The validity of Catholic elaborations on primitive Christian doctrine rested on the question of authority. If the Church spoke with the authority of Christ's continuing presence in the world, then she had every right to formulate doctrine and compel the obedience of all Christians. Moreover, only a church like the Roman Church, with its centralized authority, was capable of withstanding the assault of heresy through the ages. Christ promised that the gates of hell would not prevail against His Church. The fact that the Roman Catholic Church had faithfully preserved Christianity for nearly two thousand years argued strongly that she was that Church.

Just when my quest was most intense, Angel and I spent a weekend in the hills of West Virginia with James and Penny, dear Christian friends we had met in college. In the beauty of the awakening spring we hiked mountain trails, catching up on our friendship. At night, sipping Dutch beer around a blazing fireplace, Angel and I poured out our hearts to our friends. James and Penny listened intently, offering moral support and encouragement when necessary, but mostly just lending us the strength of their love. As the embers of the fire died to a ruddy glow, the catharsis was complete. The rift that had been developing between Angel and me began to be healed. God had touched our lives with mercy through the love of friends.

That weekend was an important milestone in the quest. James and Penny, by helping us to face our fears, helped us begin to conquer them. And I discovered that Angel was on a quest of her own. As I sought signposts on the road to Rome, Angel sought the meaning and bounds of her love for me against forces that seemed destined to tear us apart. We fully understood each other's position for the first time. There were still barriers to overcome, but the worst was over. Whatever my decision about the Catholic Church, we knew our love would survive.

A few weeks later I made my choice. While writing a letter to Vanauken, the Holy Spirit moved me to action, and I surrendered to Holy Mother Church without further deliberation. I had expected a cataclysmic release of emotion following my decision, but there was only the warm glow of blessed peace, as if God were smiling. Excerpts from that letter reveal my thoughts and feelings upon submitting to Rome:

> I am convinced! The Catholic Church, regal and beautiful, is all she claims to be. I acknowledge her claim to orthodoxy as well as her claim upon my heart—for I have come to love her.

For the first time in my life I have found in a church, home. . . . Your last letter, full of concern and gentle advice, touched me deeply. Your statement that "absolute certainty is seldom granted us, and motives are never pure" struck straight to the heart of my dilemma. I remembered Newman's assertion that religious certainty may be based on an aggregate of proba- bilities . . . and I surrendered my demand for "scientific" cer- tainty. Even if I admit that the Roman Church is a valid church, the implications of that admission irreparably weaken the claims of Protestantism. And if the Catholic Church is the infal- lible church founded by Christ, then the Protestant Reforma- tion (despite good intentions) was a hideous mistake.

Vanauken warmly welcomed me into the "Bark of Peter." He had been praying for me and my quest, along with many others, includ- ing a Benedictine monk. Those prayers were undoubtedly a channel for the grace that enabled me to make the leap. I chuckled as I read how the (ironical) Martin Luther commemorative stamp on my letter had caused Vanauken to fear that I'd "rejected Holy Church." Finally, I was invited to travel to Lynchburg to meet Tracy Simmons (the young man in "The Knight's Move") and his godson James Hege, who were visiting Vanauken that week.

Tracy and James welcomed me into the Catholic Church with smiles and handshakes. I soon felt as if we were old friends. Tracy was a quiet, confident fellow with a reputation for attracting appre- ciative glances from young ladies. His sagacious friend, James, was a nimble-minded intellectual. We spent a couple of hours recounting our individual journeys to Rome (all were converts) and how they were all linked by the remarkable man who was our host. Vanauken regarded us with pleasure. I believe he thought of us as his adopted sons, as indeed we were in a spiritual sense. After an exhilarating ride to dinner packed into Vanauken's tiny Morgan, it was time to leave. I drove back to Richmond with a full heart, watching an unusual spring lightning flicker across the night sky like celestial laughter.

Once I had made my decision God blessed me with a greater portion of affirmation. The Catholic Church was the Church found- ed by Christ. I never doubted that again. Angel, however, did not share my certitude. Though she supported my decision, I could tell she was still a bit fearful of its consequences.

Those lingering fears were dealt a mortal blow in late summer. Angel and I spent a week alone in a cottage on the beach, where we could concentrate on our relationship without distraction. There was much to discuss, including, of course, my conversion. We strolled along the breaking waves holding hands and rediscovering our love for each other. During that week, the healing process begun with James and Penny was completed. The distance that had grown between us melted away. We laughed a lot that week. Deep, genuine, soul-cleansing laughter. I had found my church home, Angel had found an end to her fears, and we had found each other again.

I was received into the Roman Catholic Church the following spring, during the Easter Vigil Mass, with Sheldon Vanauken as my godfather. It seemed fitting that the man who had started me on the road to Rome should be with me as I completed the journey. The following is a description of that evening as written in a letter to a Catholic friend:

I volunteered to do the driving, since Van's old Morgan was not to be relied upon for long trips. When I arrived at Vanauken's house, he presented me with a copy of *Under the Mercy* (his new book, made personal with an inscription and colored illustrations) and the old Russian cross (given to Vanauken by his Godfather, Peter Kreeft, and passed in turn to Tracy and James at their confirmations). I was deeply touched by both gifts, though I had expected the cross. It was in my jacket pocket, near my heart, along with the little wooden rosary Angel gave me as a reception gift, when I was received.

I greatly enjoyed the talks Van and I had during the long drive. We talked of everything, from our mutual distaste for modernist nuns to the War between the States and sailing.

When we finally arrived at the church, after dinner and a stop by the babysitter's, I was quite worn out, and felt distant and cold. The enormity of what was happening didn't sink in until I began the renewal of my baptismal vows. Never will I forget the upwelling of the confirmation surety of the Spirit, as Father Brian received me into Christ's Church, with Van's sturdy hand on my shoulder. When I went forward for my first Eucharist it was as if in a dream. Looking down into the cup of His Blood I thought "this is the holiest moment of my life." I will always treasure those vivid memories, and Van's welcoming smile and murmured "Now you're a papist!"

The drive back to Lynchburg was filled with peace and gladness. When we finally arrived at Vancot I hugged Van and tried to tell him how much his being there had meant to me. The words failed me, but I think he understood. As I walked out to the car, I shouted back over my shoulder "I can't believe I'm really a CATHOLIC!"

The restless sheep had found his fold.

Epilogue

In retrospect, the seemingly haphazard road I followed to Rome was filled with purpose. For a Christian who believes in a providential God there are, strictly speaking, no accidents. My conversion to Roman Catholicism is a part of the "Great Dance," that infinite and ever-joyful drama of salvation. I follow a longing that Lewis and Vanauken helped me articulate; a longing buried deep within all of us, but often smothered by the trivial concerns with which we fill our lives. Lewis called that longing Joy, and described it as those moments when the curtain is drawn aside, and we catch a glimpse, as through a dark glass, of the consummation of all our legitimate earthly loves. It is a little taste of heaven, the place we were made for, and the One we were created to love. My path to Him lies squarely within the Catholic Church, and I must follow it as faithfully as I can, by grace, and with the prayers of the Blessed Mother of God and the saints. Here I stand, on the hope of the severe mercy of God's love, that calls this sheep of Peter's fold to dreams of death, and life.

14

JEAN M. L. ROSSNER

Further Up and Further In

Jean M. L. Rossner was born in New York City to a secularized Jewish family and has lived since then in the New York suburbs and in New Hampshire, Pennsylvania, and California. She became first a "mere Christian" and then a Roman Catholic after reading a great deal of C. S. Lewis's work, while studying medieval history, literature, and religious thought at the University of Pennsylvania. Miss Rossner lives in Berkeley, California, where she is a student at the Dominican School of Philosophy and Theology of the Graduate Theological Union.

I used to say that I became a Christian because I was a romantic, and a Roman Catholic because I had turned into a cynic. Fortunately, I have learned that the Catholic Church is much more than an escape from the alternatives.

My parents were atheists; we called ourselves Jewish but nothing about our lives except a few scraps of culture and the occasional use of a Yiddish word or two would have so identified us to others. A friend of mine has described my parents' belief system as Orthodox Reformed Freudianism, with a touch of Marxism.

My parents were both writers, and my father taught high-school English; books set the pattern of our lives. Having learned to read early, by first grade I was acquiring the basis for my own view of the world from the local library's shelves. I read everything, mysteries and sports stories and juvenile biographies; but J. R. R. Tolkien's Hobbit stories and C. S. Lewis's Narnian chronicles were particular favorites, and then the adventures of E. Nesbit's and Lloyd Alexander's and Joan Aiken's and Edward Eager's characters. Laura Ingalls Wilder's "Little House" books, too; and Madeleine L'Engle's novels, one of which gave me the verse of "Two Tramps in Mud Time" that I took for a motto. These were the stories that spoke of *real* things (truth and courage and survival, good and evil, where the librarian's recommended books were about school and dates and clothes and cars); they were about adventures that brought together the seen world and the unseen, the side of life my parents acknowledged and the further dimension of which they seemed utterly unaware.

I learned to pray the "Our Father" and "Hail Mary" from one of my two friends, Jeanne, when I was about eight. She was probably trying to shut me up: I kept asking questions, attempting to learn what this mysterious thing with which she was so much occupied, the preparation for First Communion, was. All the admirable characters of my favorite books said prayers at bedtime, and I tried to imitate them.

We had moved from Manhattan to the New York suburbs just after my fifth birthday, in April 1965; my brother Daniel was born the same year. In August 1970, the family moved to a small town in New Hampshire, where Daniel and I were to go to an "alternative," counter-cultural community school. We were excited about the idea of living in the country, gardening and raising chickens and making our own clothes; my father, in his beard and jeans and tie-dyed T-shirts, spoke of the wonders of a school where students were to be given perfect freedom to be themselves.

The New Hampshire experiment failed, and in November, 1971 we moved back to New York City — separately: my mother, Daniel, and I moved into an apartment on the Upper West Side and my father to a different apartment sixteen blocks away. I was sent to the local public school, which was at that time rather a rough place for anyone, let alone a child accustomed to country schools. Soon I was refusing to go, feeling that I could learn more, and more safely, reading at home. My mother sent me away to school in the suburbs where I spent two wretched years, burying myself in books again to get through the time — science fiction, *Catch-22*, *The Once and Future King* (re-read about once a month).

The school was run by a Jewish organization, and for the first time in my life I attended services and received some "religious education." Very much Reform and modern Jewish, it was still better than nothing. For the first time I tried to be actively a Jew, even having a bat-mitzvah. But all that was less than satisfying, and after leaving the school I stopped trying to be "religiously Jewish."

In June 1974, I came home and in the fall I began ninth grade at the Bronx High School of Science. The previous school had been a miserable place, but the beatings and threats from the other kids, and the terrible solitariness, had all led me to more constant prayer, and thence to the knowledge that I was alive only by God's mercy. And that is a great experience of grace. In Bronx Science's competitive atmosphere I began to wonder: what would happen when people learned what I was really like? I made a number of suicide attempts at first, but mostly tried to hide.

By junior year I had made a few friends and earned some respectable grades — feeling all the while that this appearance as a "real person" was mere facade, worrying constantly what would happen when people found out my secret. I had to fit in with the others; I had to show them that I was odd, weird, alien. And I had to have the right views; so, though continuing to pray privately and even reading the King James Bible through ("necessary background to studying English literature"), I denounced "organized religion" as a tool whose only purpose was to enable some people to control others, to prevent them from worshipping God in a way personally appropriate.

Around then, my mother's fourth novel became her first bestseller. *Looking for Mr. Goodbar* gave me a niche: it was easiest to prove my folly and difference in the way that (I thought) people expected of my mother's daughter. So I slept with my first serious boyfriend. When the next boy I dated saw me home and refused to leave without sex, I had no reason except lack of desire to say no. And that time, I got pregnant. My mother "took care of things" — arranging for what we both knew was "the only possible solution."

I had felt myself to be going downhill before; the abortion was the push that sent me rolling down an incline suddenly much steeper, with no way to stop. I felt guilty, depressed, more constantly suicidal than ever. It was a devastating experience with no context, no way to make sense of things.

I punished myself by becoming further involved with the boy who had gotten me pregnant. By the summer between high school and college, I was also sleeping with his best friend and several other people, while smoking enough marijuana (and occasionally dabbling in other drugs) to be unconscious as much of the time as possible. I even accompanied him to Plato's Retreat, a notorious "swingers' club" in the city — where I stood in the corner and played pinball while he prowled — and wore a Plato's Retreat T-shirt to school. (At that point Mr. Rifkin, an English teacher and adored mentor, called me into his office for a lecture — "I know you're not worried now, but later in life you'll regret it if you don't straighten out.")

But how *could* I straighten out? I don't think I went a week, that year, without attempting suicide, and there wasn't a day I didn't consider it. There was the old feeling of unworthiness, and now the implications of the abortion added to that. I wrote in my diary that summer that, however deserving of death, I was lacking the actual courage for suicide; but perhaps the weight of one degradation piled on another would break me, make me stop holding on to life, push me over the edge to the relief of death. I was skidding downhill without brakes; only the crash that would kill me could stop the descent.

My boyfriend and I broke up after I left for the University of Pennsylvania, and during my freshman year I was able to mend my ways somewhat. At the beginning of what would have been my sophomore year, I fell in with a bad crowd again. Everyone seemed to be sleeping with everybody else. One man, however, was less comfortable with the situation. T.G. (as I shall refer to him) was a minister's son, generally more conservative than the rest of us, who nevertheless joined us for a while. I found him a brilliant and fascinating man, and after we spent a night together, my fascination became thorough infatuation; it was only then that I learned of the girl from college to whom he was "practically engaged," and soon we agreed to be "just friends," though I continued to hope for more even when he broke away from the group.

Meanwhile, I had taken a year's leave of absence from school starting in November, when I found myself unable to go to class or talk to anybody outside my small clique but stayed in my room and cried. By February I was seeing a therapist several days a week, and it was largely Kyra's help that brought me through the next few years. After my own conversion I learned that Kyra was an Orthodox Christian, whose prayers no doubt helped me greatly in ways I would have scorned at the time.

When T.G. said our relationship would never be a romantic one, I still didn't lose hope. For some months we remained, it seemed, close friends, and he came over almost daily to sit and talk and listen to music. My depression grew blacker and blacker, however, and the yearning for death again more persistent. In August he told me that he was now officially engaged to the other girl and did not want to hear from me again—even as a friend, considering my circle of friends and my own behavior. Rather than attempt suicide yet again, I went backpacking with a friend, feeling closer to God in the mountains among all the greenery than I had in years, and returned convinced that my only hope was to become the sort of person T.G. would want to be friends with—even, perhaps, the sort of woman he could consider falling in love with.

By the time I returned to school in September 1980, I had made plans. T.G. would be interested in a serious academic program; so I planned my new major in medieval studies. He had disapproved of the promiscuous behavior; so, though I found myself yet another boyfriend, I dropped out of my old crowd. And perhaps, with enough change, T.G. would want to talk to me; so I tried to learn about the things that interested him—of which Christian thought was the most obvious. Pleased that I had read the Narnian chronicles, shocked that I didn't know C. S. Lewis's other writings, T.G. had lent me *The Great Divorce* and *The Screwtape Letters* the previous winter and, at another time, had recommended *Mere Christianity*.

I picked up *Mere Christianity* to please T.G.; I put it down again knowing that it would have a major impact on my own life. I was amazed by Lewis: was *this* Christianity? But it made so much sense! Organized religion was supposed to be irrationality, superstition based on avoidance of reality. Why, then, did Lewis's Christian explanation of the world suddenly make my life seem a coherent whole with a purpose, while the philosophy implicit in everything with which I had grown up only succeeded in reducing it all to hopeless chaos? Surely, if any view glorified irrationality, it was the familiar one!

Yet I could not accept it, for a time. Christianity's outline made sense, philosophically; but how could I believe this central absurdity? That God, the Inconceivable Absolute, had lived the most common of lives — and died the most vulgar of deaths — on *our* earth — this seemed incompatible with my knowledge of God. So I continued reading medieval history and philosophy and literature and all the Lewis I could find. I had never stopped praying, but now I asked for something specific besides a way to go on living: "God, show me whether this be true or false, whether it is just another path that I can take or leave — or the Truth and the Way."

There remained another difficulty: there was obviously a reasonable case for Christian morality, but while the extremes of my own behavior had lessened, I was still on that downhill path. *I* had not changed, and had no power to change myself. As I found myself explaining to God in March 1981 as I walked to class (for by this time I was engaged in almost constant argument with God), "This is all very well, it explains a great deal — but here I am, *this* is what I am, this is how people know me. How can I suddenly stop, turn around, and start back up the hill? become a completely new person?"

And it seemed that I heard God say in exasperation, "Well, what do you think it's all about, then? *What do you think this is about, and what do you think I came down there for?*"

And I stopped short, feeling very foolish, and said, "Oh. Yes. I see. All right — uh, well, I guess I'm yours, then."

Though afraid to write anything like that last in my journal, and in fact stopping all writing for nearly six months, I started calling myself a Christian from that day. But though I knew that (in Lewis's terms) I had entered the house and had to find the room in which there was light and fire and food, I did not yet know what sort of Christian I was. (Christopher Derrick writes that, just as nobody was ever converted to liberal Christianity, so nobody was ever converted to Lewis's "mere Christianity" — but I must disagree with him. Of course, reading Lewis had made me expect a conversion at first simply to Christianity-in-general, though emphatically not to Christianity-and-water; it may be the peculiar mistake of a "Lewis convert.") So I read, and reacted, and wrote, and asked for advice.

Some aspects of evangelical Protestantism were attractive, but its somehow *flat* world could not be "my room." Roman Catholicism was much more fascinating — dangerously so; wasn't the Church terrifically anti-women, what with the bans on contraception and abortion and the women's ordination, didn't the Church teach that women were good for nothing but child-bearing? So I had always been told, and Catholic friends refused to argue — wisely; I wouldn't have listened. Barbara, a staunch Catholic who nonetheless stood sponsor at my baptism, refused to discuss our differences at any great length, saying she'd already seen one friend hardened in his arguments by such debate. Lewis's church sounded very Catholic in theology but no longer held the "unreasonable" doctrines. In June I went to speak to the rector of Penn's Episcopal church about baptism. He listened, amused, and suggested waiting — "to make sure it's what you want." I thought that silly, having waited three months before speaking to anybody and now wanting only to be washed clean immediately, but what argument could I make? So I spent the time reading Scripture, and Lewis again, and now George MacDonald's sermons, and G. K. Chesterton, and Dorothy L. Sayers.

In August, reading one of Lewis's epigrams (it ends, "The price was cheap. The price was all I had."), I realized that God required *everything* I had to give. Even my idolatrous love was not to be spared, but transmuted: T.G. could no longer be any part of my reason for doing this. (And even my self-pity! No more suicide attempts permitted.) I was baptized on November 22 — "Lewis's feast day," I called it, and never learned whether the pastor had given me the day intentionally or by chance.

And at that point it seemed necessary to tell my parents. My mother tried not to express any negative feelings about the matter other than refusal of the invitation to attend the ceremony. (I had not meant it sarcastically; rather, in my new-found flush of Christian love, I was attempting at least half-heartedly to carry out the Commandments.) My father, on a business trip to Philadelphia, took me to lunch one day early in November and explained that, it was just, well, that he felt I was rejecting everything he believed, the world-view with which he had tried to bring me up. . . . I interrupted, "Wait a minute; [the pastor] told me you might feel that way, that I'm rejecting being Jewish by becoming a Christian—but you never brought me up to be Jewish!" My father looked stunned: No, no, no, he said; it wasn't as a Jew that he felt rejected, but as an *atheist*.

"You know," he continued, "when you were about two years old, your mother and I had a conversation one day about how kids always do what will upset their parents most. The Republicans' kids become hippies; the beatnik's kids become Whartonites—We tried to figure out what you could do that would really kill us, so we'd be prepared, and we decided you'd become an Orthodox Jew." He paused. "But you double-jumped us!"

I was, however, already beginning to wonder about the Episcopal Church. It wasn't quite what I had expected; it *wasn't* the church of C. S. Lewis, and my parish, "high" in liturgy, was extremely "broad" in faith and morals. But what alternative had I? Catholicism? A Catholic friend had said, "Look, the Catholic Church is all right for me; I grew up in it. But you're a convert, and you came to Christianity by intellectual questioning—you would never be satisfied." I went ahead with the baptism, even writing in my journal the night before that something was wrong. How could I be a real medievalist, loving my subjects—and an Episcopalian? Was it irrelevant that the professors I admired were all Catholics? And—more and more as time went on—how to resist the pull of "Romanism," when I constantly felt the need to explain *not* being a Catholic?

But I had certain ideas of how the world ought to be, with which "being a Catholic" was incompatible. I had found some part of the truth (*and can anyone* [I argued] *hope for more? How dare that one church claim to be the One Universal Church, to contain the One Truth?*) Desperately justifying, I said that there must be good reasons to prefer remaining outside the Church of such arrogant claims. *Lewis* had been satisfied with remaining an Anglican, hadn't he? Those preposterous claims to exclusivity and catholicity, not to mention infallibility!

So I spent two years trying to ignore the evidence of head and heart. I wrote to my old mentor Mr. Rifkin—who was not (to the best of my knowledge) ever a Christian, but I never stopped respecting his advice—of my conversion to Christianity. He replied that the conversion sounded like the natural result of a process of "serious study and careful consideration."

And I bet that Catholicism will become more attractive to you as you ripen: it's where you want to be . . . Have you built in

yet another torturing device for yourself? Once you have made a
commitment, can you hedge successfully?

If Anglicanism was a hedge, it was also the *via media*, was it not?
But as I ran after the Anglican compromise of the *via media* to study it
at close range, it receded into the distance. I asked for moral guidance, and heard only the relativism that had made my life such
chaos before. I wrote a paper on the Eucharist and came to the
conclusion that if the Eucharist were not the Body and Blood of
Christ it was nothing at all. I read Augustine, and fell in love — and
how could anyone pretend that Augustine would have favored splitting the Body of Christ in order to pursue individual enlightenment?

In Religious Studies and Medieval Literature and History, I studied the Catholic Church. What was this mystery? Where was the
anti-rational emotionalism for which one department at school
might blame Catholic Christianity, when I was reading St. Thomas
and St. Anselm? But on the other hand, how could I see the arid
intellectualism which other departments condemned, in this road
upon which St. Augustine's restless heart (whose language spoke to
my own heart) was travelling homeward? This very Body which
appealed to every human sense and satisfied intellect, psyche, emotions — all at once, apparently with no awareness of the separation
within the person taken for granted by everything in my upbringing?
But I was still split, still under the influence of that upbringing; to
keep my world from *really* changing, I had to fight the Church's
integration of the person.

In March 1982, I met Geoffrey Deacon, who had recently returned to Episcopalianism after thinking of making a formal conversion (he told me) to just about every major religion: Hinduism,
Buddhism, Judaism, Islam — as well as to the Quakerism of the
school he had attended. We spent a great deal of time discussing our
lack of satisfaction with both the Episcopal Church and any visible
alternatives; in June we were married at City Hall so as to be able to
spend all our time talking together. Over the next school year, we
explored local alternatives: a charismatic fundamentalist fellowship,
a Messianic Jewish congregation, a conservative Presbyterian
church. Geoffrey was very interested in community, politics, and
"radical evangelicalism"; I had never been interested in politics at all
but was convinced that I ought to be, and so we applied to the
Sojourners community (who, quite wisely, rejected us).

We tried everything without ever finding a home. And we both
needed a home: not a place where neither best manners nor self-

improvement are required, but a source of food and fire that neither poison nor burn. All our alternatives felt *wrong*, but at least they had a certain seriousness I found lacking among Episcopalians. It wasn't just our parish church; the rot apparently went much deeper. I wanted to study formal theology and was told that I must seek ordination (and, though the arguments against women's ordination made no sense to me, I never felt that the priesthood was my vocation). Was the priesthood to be reduced to a means for displaying one's own liberation? Then it appeared that even at seminary I would be unable to study the theology that interested me (for modern seminarians read Barth and Bultmann, not "irrelevant" people like Augustine and Aquinas). What of Lewis's "the reading of old books?" How could we claim that all important truth had only been discovered in our age? And, if novelty and progress were the important things, where would our brave new truths be a few years hence?

In July, 1983, I went to a discussion of C. S. Lewis at my church. The consensus was that Lewis was a fundamentalist, because he believed that such Scriptures as the Gospels and Acts were to be taken as historical records rather than mythic statements (but, I wondered, didn't all Christians believe that?); he was a Manichee, because he believed that there was both a natural and a supernatural world (but weren't Christians required to believe that?); worst of all, perhaps, he was a bigot, because he believed that Christianity had something more and better to say to the world than could be found in any other faith or philosophy (but how could you — and why would you — be a Christian if you didn't believe that?) Lewis's views, I was told, were irrelevant to our modern pursuit of — well, not truth exactly. Progress, maybe. But I wanted to find an eternal truth open to all, not simply the latest fad with which to prove one's membership in the knowledgeable elite. And surely the desire for the Inner Ring was a temptation, not the goal of Christian perfection?

What was said within the Episcopal Church seemed to bear greater resemblance to the Religious Studies department's official stance of "methodological atheism" than either did to what I found in God, in prayer, in all the spiritual writers whose work rang true. The last straw was a sort of Episcopal seminary/night school course, "Education for Ministry," with denatured, modernistic textbooks. I discussed it with an official of the program when he spoke to my class in October 1983; that failing, I tried to make the point clearer in a letter: one did not have to be a fundamentalist, I argued, to find the Bible a more reliable guide than demythologizing critics who dismissed out of hand what the Biblical authors thought they were saying. The official had said that it would be a good thing if we found new challenges in the books. Certainly, but the problem was that they were insufficently challenging to a contemporary secular-materialist world view. Did we really need scholarship that simply told us there was nothing new and difficult that our faith might require us to believe in and live up to?

The letter was never finished, for the only conclusion I could find was, "And so I will be leaving the Episcopal Church, for one where one's words and heart are expected to correspond, where this dishonesty is not taken for granted." I was still not ready to take such a step. Where could I go, except Rome? But — all the old objections — Rome was authoritarian, stifling, male-oriented. . .

Well, was it? A few months before, I had come unwittingly to accept the Church's basic ideas on contraception: not for the Manichaean reasons that I assumed were the Church's, but because it seemed evident that using contraception itself involved acceptance of dualism, splitting oneself in half and committing only one part or the other. One brick in the wall, my bulwark against the Church's force, had fallen out. And the resulting hole, rather than a break to be mended, had proven a window to Truth. What next?

I started to notice that opposing ideologies criticized Catholicism for mutually exclusive reasons. The disagreement as to whether the Church was intellectual, excluding emotion, or emotional, excluding reason, was one example. Another: The feminists claimed that the Roman Catholic Church was male-oriented, excluding women. Very well; but then why did men leave the Church, claiming it to be weak, feminine, excluding virile spirituality? I saw that the Church was masculine, in structure and authority, in some forms of its asceticism; no less was it feminine in its appeal to our mutual connections, in the understanding of surrender to God. (And how, I began to wonder, was a sexual morality rejecting the suppression of female functions "anti-woman?") The Church provided for differences among individuals, and therefore for different vocations in life, while its critics provided only for individual freedom and rejection of authority — and ended up with the totalitarianism of enforced identicality.

What of this offensive authority? Had I simply accepted, uncritically (for once!), one of the unquestioned tenets of my childhood? And if not, what was inherently evil about authority? Had it not, in fact, proved to be precisely what was missing elsewhere? The Church, as it now appeared, was indeed a Body; and a body's skeleton by itself may be cold and rigid, but nobody can walk without that skeletal structure. Would I really rather be a jellyfish than a human being?

That was perhaps the strongest argument; somehow, still, the simple distaste for "being a Catholic" remained. Geoffrey was equally dissatisfied with the Episcopal Church, but whenever the topic came up he seemed to be heading towards Protestantism, alternating between fundamentalism and radical-evangelical views.

Then, that autumn, I read Christopher Derrick's *C. S. Lewis and the Church of Rome*—with distress, as the author showed that Lewis's reasons for remaining an Anglican were not *reasonable* excuses. And at the beginning of November a friend's involvement in civil-disobedience activities inspired me to write some comments on loving one's neighbors: whether the enemies be politicians promoting oppression, or workers at a G.E. plant building nuclear weapons, or parents virulently opposed to one's faith and practice—still, it seemed, only by loving one's enemies could one avoid the trap of defining oneself according to what the enemies are *not*. Fearful, I waited two weeks before reading the essay to Geoffrey, saying shakily at the conclusion, "And that . . . uh, well, I don't know how you're going to feel about this, but . . . that's why I have to become a Roman Catholic." I had spent too long (I explained) justifying *not* being a Catholic; struggle though I might, feeling dragged through the doors by my hair, I could no longer avoid the Church. Geoffrey, having come to a similar conclusion through quite a different approach, was amused and relieved to learn of my decision.

But then we had to find a way in—a greater difficulty than we, brought up on the spectre of a bogey-Church converting people by force when guile failed, could have expected. "Why would you want to do that?" Catholic friends asked. A priest who finally agreed to talk to us gave us Richard McBrien's *Catholicism* to take home and read. (It sounded enough like what we were trying to escape that we almost gave up the idea right there!) But there was hope. We began taking instruction at our local parish, and after some conversation the ·pastor decided that we didn't need to spend a full year in preparation but could be received at Easter. We still weren't sure what we were getting ourselves into, and when we were sure we certainly didn't like the idea much, but we were coming in.

Remembering their reactions to my baptism, I did not want to tell my parents. One day my mother mentioned having met some close friends of a favorite professor of mine; "did you know he was a Catholic?" I said there had been rumors to that effect; what of it? She said, "Well, I know what strong feelings you have against the Catholic Church . . . Don't you?" Then I had to say that in a few months I expected to become a Catholic; the Church taught the *truth*, and that was what mattered. Oddly, my parents suddenly began to take my conversion to Christianity seriously in a way they hadn't when it was simply a matter of joining the Episcopal Church. What was this Church, that unbelievers so acknowledged its power?

Not long thereafter, I was visiting my mother at the same time as a friend of hers, a recent Catholic convert, who said with affectionate irony, "All right, so why are you joining the One True Church?" The only possible answer was, "Yes, exactly." And that was another part of the answer, for there was a recognition of truth even in the joking. What was this Church, that could be so described?

As Geoffrey one day put it: we had concluded that the Catholic Church was in fact what it claimed to be. And so we were received at Easter, 1984. I don't mean to imply that the way has always been easy since, that becoming a Catholic makes life easy; sometimes it has been as hard as anything before the conversion! (It was after we had become Catholics—the relevant points not having been discussed earlier—that Geoffrey and I were told that our marriage was in fact invalid; we were instructed to separate and as of this writing are awaiting the tribunal's decision.)

The most interesting discovery, in this Church I have come to love, is its provision of the antidote to the poisonous desire for the Inner Ring. As on the mountain path to "true Narnia," one keeps climbing for the sake of the Good on each level and for what is above, and then sees that each level holds more than the previous one which appeared so much larger—while the things on each level are more truly themselves than before. Further up and further in! The road may grow harder and steeper, and rockier, as one climbs; but there are shelters, and water, and a map to guide me. And there are companions along the way (no more solitary wallowing in self-pity!), for, with the sinners and saints who have gone before, the Catholic is part of the Body of Christ, incorporated into that Body by the sacraments, in which the whole nature and supernature of creation are joined to praise God. What more, on earth, can one ask?

15

THE REVEREND JAMES PARKER

A Married Catholic Priest?

Father James Parker was ordained a Roman Catholic priest on June 29, 1982. He became the first married Latin rite priest in the United States and currently serves as assistant to Bernard Cardinal Law, Archbishop of Boston, who is the Holy See's ecclesiastical delegate in matters pertaining to married former Episcopal priests seeking Roman Catholic priestly ministry. Father Parker also serves as diocesan director of Catholic Charities in Charleston, South Carolina, and shares in the ministry of the Cathedral of Saint John the Baptist.

On Pentecost in 1981 I stood at an altar before the people of Saint Mark's Parish in Albany, Georgia, whom I had served for almost ten years. I celebrated my last Mass as an Episcopal priest. It was, of course, a memorable moment. On the following Friday evening, my wife and I made a profession of faith at Pulaskifield, Missouri, in a church dedicated to the Apostles Saints Peter and Paul and were received into full communion with the Roman Catholic Church by the then Bishop of Springfield–Cape Girardeau, the Most Reverend Bernard F. Law. On the feast day of the same Saints Peter and Paul, in 1982 in Holy Trinity Church, Springfield, Missouri, the same Bishop Law ordained me to the priesthood with my wife and two daughters present. I became the first married priest in the United States under the guidelines of a pastoral provision requested by the bishops of this country and granted by the Holy See.

This unique circumstance finds its roots deep in history. Four centuries ago political causes brought about a schismatic division between the Roman Catholic Church and the Church in England. For dynastic reasons King Henry VIII took advantage of the influences of the continental Protestant Reformation to renounce allegiance to Peter's successor and to place himself in administrative leadership of the Church of England. Mind you, he tolerated no Protestant novelties, but he cut the tie to the magisterium. This

Ecclesia Anglicana considered itself the inheritor of the past glories of English Catholicism and continuous with the Church of Saint Augustine of Canterbury, the Venerable Saint Bede, Saint Anselm, Saint Richard of Chichester, and Saint Hugh of Lincoln. But Henry himself martyred John Fisher and Thomas More, whose perseverance in faith was formed by the same ancient Church in the British Isles.

The reigns of Edward VI and Elizabeth I, the Puritan movement, and other less grave influences brought to the Church of England a kind of national spirit that introduced a need for survival based on a spirit of compromise. Its state connection molded Anglicanism into a national religion intended to encompass every Englishman's private search for God. The schism from Rome set the Church of England adrift from the gospel's magisterial truth and opened her to the prevailing attitudes of many who had tasted the flavor of the Reformation of Calvin and Luther.

The Oxford movement of the early nineteenth century revived a sense of the English church's Catholic heritage. With great courage the Oxford fathers began to teach anew the faith that they saw as England's true heritage, and with this great revival came a deeper understanding that the separation from Rome was no boast but the real tragedy of the Anglican Church. Far from freeing English churchmen from spiritual bonds, it had, in fact wrenched them from the guarantor of the Catholic truth the Church was heir to. There had always been a faithful remnant who held that the Church of England had no faith but Catholic faith and no guide but Rome. The Oxford movement at its very core took up that cause and taught a need for corporate reunion with the See of Peter. The argument held that the Church of England was not a Protestant denomination sprung anew from the Reformation like the Lutheran and Presbyterian bodies, she was a schism from the rest of the Catholic Church that needed to be brought back to communion with Rome, where she would again be loyal to the universal pastor of Christ's flock. The so-called Anglo-papalists who held and taught this faith found in the Book of Common Prayer only Catholic religion and Catholic sacraments, believing that the faith of an Anglican was Roman Catholic. They earnestly and devoutly prayed and worked toward a day when Canterbury and Rome would join in full communion, a day not to be expected in the twentieth century any more than the nineteenth but a goal that seemed real to them. As long as the *official* teachings of Anglicanism were compatible with a Catholic understanding, the Anglo-papalist felt justified in remaining outside full communion because he saw himself as a means toward union.

In recent years, actually since the 1970s, the Canadian Church, the Episcopal Church in the United States, and a few other Anglican bodies began to deal with theological matters as though they were sociological issues. For the first time in Anglican history many of us began to feel that the integrity of Catholic faith in the Episcopal Church was being formally violated. Certain decisions were taken that led us to believe that the corporate union so deeply desired was no longer a viable goal. We were no longer morally justified in being out of communion with the successor of Peter. What were we to do?

As provincial vicar of an Anglican-wide secular institute for clergy, I convened a synod of the province that deliberated over the gloomy prospects of our cause for almost three days. A unanimous resolution directed me to seek a meeting with the apostolic delegate in Washington, D.C. In 1977, with another Episcopal priest from our society, I was received by Archbishop Jean Jadot, who listened carefully to our request for married Anglican priests who were formed in Catholic faith and spiritually to be considered for priestly ministry in the Roman Catholic Church and for the possibility of some means of preserving the spiritual heritage of Anglican parishes seeking full communion. His response was not discouraging. He would be traveling to Rome within days and would present the subject to the appropriate dicastery. He asked if I had a name in mind should the Holy See wish to appoint a Catholic bishop to preside over further conversations. I asked for Bishop Law, who was indeed selected to head a small committee to continue the question posed by our group.

From 1977 until 1980 a number of conferences were held to deal with the details of the request, the possibilities to be considered and the canonical ramifications. Time seemed to move slowly. The Catholic authorities asked for confidentiality, the numbers of interested Episcopalians increased, and I was unable even to disclose my intentions to my Episcopal parish, though my bishop was told and was entirely sympathetic. Would the discussions ever end? There was every reason for us to despair and to give up the goal of priesthood in favor of a much easier goal — communion as lay people.

Early in 1980 the Sacred Congregation for the Doctrine of the Faith made the public announcement of its pastoral provision in response to a sincere, conscience-based request made by us Episcopalians. Bishop Law was appointed ecclesiastical delegate to implement the provision. Our dreams and prayers were fulfilled. With great joy I accepted Bishop Law's offer to me to become his assistant in this work. I resigned the Albany, Georgia, parish where I had spent my happiest years of ministry, and my wife and I prepared for the move to Springfield, Missouri.

After my ordination by Bishop Law, I remained in Missouri until the bishop became Archbishop (later Cardinal) of Boston, which required a move to that city, where the work continued.

After attending the 1985 consistory in Rome, where Bernard Cardinal Law received his "Red Hat," my wife and I once again moved. This time my own bishop, Bishop Ernest L. Unterkoefler, requested that I return to my birthplace to accept an assignment in Charleston, South Carolina. By agreement with Cardinal Law, the bishop has allowed me to continue assisting the cardinal with the provision that I handle the task of diocesan director of Catholic Charities and share in the ministry of the Cathedral of Saint John the Baptist.

As I look back over my life and ministry, I do not regret my years as an Episcopal priest, in fact, I treasure the formation in Catholic truth that I received in that church. I am grateful to an all-merciful God for my communion with Rome and the joy I know as a Catholic priest. I can see the many ways in which Divine Providence prepared me and urged me in my spiritual pilgrimage. God has been very good to me and to my family.

16

DAN O'NEILL

The Pearl of Great Price
My Search for the Church

Dan O'Neill is a cofounder and chairman of the board of Mercy Corps International, an ecumenical relief and development agency assisting the world's poor. He is also the president of Messenger Communications and the author of numerous books, including Mother Angelica: Her Life Story *(1986),* Marrying for Life *with Raymond E. Vath, M.D. (1982), and* Troubadour for the Lord *(1983), the award-winning biography of John Michael Talbot.*

Sunlight flooded my upper-story brick apartment in the spring of 1972 as I sat at my drafting table staring at the travel documents before me: a passport, air tickets, and visas. What a precipitous turn of events indeed! A sixth-year student about to graduate from the University of Washington with a degree in visual communications, I had many promising leads in the advertising industry. Already a syndicated political cartoonist, I was moving deeper into photography and illustration, loving every minute of the challenging pace. Yet there I was, about to skip the country for two years—as a missionary! Obviously, I had experienced a change of heart.

As I considered the work I would soon be doing in Africa, I reflected on the path that had brought me to this point in time and to this interdenominational, evangelical missions organization, Youth with a Mission. Born into an Assemblies of God family, I was "dedicated" as an infant in 1948 by the Reverend Ed Scratch, my great uncle, a man of God who to this day is an inspiration to me and to many. Missionaries, preachers, and Bible professors filled my family tree. After moving to another town, our family attended a conservative Baptist church where I "received Jesus into my heart" at seven and was baptized at eleven. In high school I attended a nondenominational Bible church with my family and later went to a Free

Methodist university. By 1967 I was attending Saint Luke's Episcopal Church near Seattle, the center of an explosion of charismatic renewal under the leadership of Father Dennis Bennett. The vibrant excitement of the baptism of the Holy Spirit filled me with zeal and wonderment—I had found what I thought was the end-all of Christian faith experiences. I was on a high, a spiritual mountaintop. The only direction to go from there, of course, was down. The fall was long and hard.

I had no foundation on which to stand. When my emotional exhilaration inevitably cooled, there was no consistent, authentic church teaching to undergird my spiritual convictions and I became easy prey for well-informed critics. My twenty-year smorgasbord of denominational affiliations, which I had always regarded a rich blessing in plurality, became a millstone around my neck when it came to theological consistency. Each denomination preached its own unique doctrines, many of which were diametrically opposed.

The Baptists told me that once one has accepted Christ as "personal Lord and Savior" (a phrase I could never find in the Bible), salvation was guaranteed forever. "Once saved always saved," they asserted. My Assemblies of God brethren, on the other hand, assured me with equal conviction that serious sin could send me straight to hell, which meant frequent trips to the altar to constantly secure salvation. The Baptists whispered to me that speaking in tongues was "of the devil," while my dear Assemblies of God friends and fellow charismatics claimed it to be a miraculous gift of the Holy Spirit. I became confused and then disillusioned by this doctrinal tower of Babel.

To hell with it, I finally concluded. It was hopeless. Each one of hundreds of Protestant denominations claim a right to interpret the Bible. It was, they all agreed, their "final authority." And I shall always be indebted to my Protestant background for encouraging in-depth study and knowledge of the Scriptures. It has been a wonderful inheritance. But there was no consensus on its interpretation. It seemed a bit like handing a technical 747 flight manual to a roomful of schoolteachers and expecting agreement on how to fly the jumbo jet. Without the authors present to interpret the data, a plane flight would be out of the question. This competing jumble of voices, which claimed as their ultimate authority a book that commanded Christian unity, seemed to me a scandal of divisiveness.

Between 1968 and 1971 I was a skeptic—I think I even called myself an agnostic. In any case, I thoroughly lost my religious bearings.

Dropping out of church attendance, I tasted the worldly life of

1960s America, dabbling in dope and in the prodigal pursuits of self-indulgence. If there was no God, there could be no absolute moral values—a very liberating thought at first, until the consequent despair of self-destructive nihilism became apparent: spiritual, and occasionally, physical death. And to put it in the words of a rock hit, "Dyin' don't seem to me like all that much fun." There had to be something more. I began my search. I became hungry for the truth if, indeed, it could be attained in the cacophonous din of the world's many faiths, philosophies, and ideologies.

Something happened when I entered that search mode. My heart softened ever so slightly. Suddenly, one day in August of 1971, I simply fell to my knees as though throttled by an unseen hand. I wept and prayed and repented of every sin that came to mind. I felt cleansed, renewed, and a little embarrassed. I felt as though I had been jolted out of the blue by a loving God seeking my undivided attention. It was most certainly unmerited. It was grace. I was turning for home.

"C'mon, O'Neill," one pothead friend scoffed when I refused a joint, "religion just got socialized into you from your youth. You couldn't outrun it. It's a fairy tale, man!" Initially disturbed, I came to see this criticism as irrelevant. So what? It would be just as easy to speculate that my infant dedication and subsequent baptism had pursued me with the indelible mark of miraculous grace. In either case, my metanoia experience was no less efficacious.

But where was God? Who are his people today? Is he a she? Is he a Baptist, Buddhist, Jew, or Moslem? I prayed with an open mind, reading everything I could get my hands on while daily studying the Scriptures. Early one morning I read about the pearl of great price in Matthew 13: " . . . the kingdom of Heaven is like a merchant looking for fine pearls; when he finds one of great value he goes and sells everything he owns and buys it." This parable of Jesus inspired yet sobered me, launching me on what I have come to call my "search for the church."

In the midst of my final year of university studies, I began to question my professional ambitions. Could I really spend the rest of my life designing ad campaigns for consumer goods? Do I want to live life pursuing dollars and the American Dream? I became depressed at the prospect. It was then that I joined Youth with a Mission, volunteering for an assignment in Africa. Indeed, I had experienced a change of heart. While sharing in nondenominational ministry, I would continue to seek that expression of Christian faith that is most in harmony with the teaching of Jesus and the Apostles.

It was a wonderful two-year odyssey. At the age of twenty-four, after selling and giving away most all of my earthly possessions, I traveled and lived in Africa, Europe, and, finally, in the Middle East. In Africa I was confronted with shocking poverty, famine conditions, disease, and political upheaval. Our simple "Jesus loves you" message paled next to the harsh realities of human suffering, which we were obviously unprepared to address. My heart broke with a sense of inadequacy and helplessness. Our gospel message often fell on deaf ears. Hunger hurts and all the preaching and teaching in the world will not touch a starving family. What church, I wondered, is most effectively propagating an integrated gospel of love that physically and spiritually feeds the hungry? In my experience, there were precious few Protestant missions engaging such a mission theology.

In Europe, I worked temporarily as an artist with a Christian newspaper at the Munich Olympics. There international terrorism resulted in the infamous slaughter of Israeli athletes. How do we deal with violence as Christians? Again, there were many opinions among my peers.

Following three months of biblical studies in Switzerland in the winter of 1973, I drove a Land Rover from Germany to Jerusalem, retracing the mission journeys of Saint Paul before settling into a kibbutz on the shore of the Sea of Galilee. Between exhausting six-day work shifts in fruit orchards, I studied Judaism, the Hebrew language, and church history, attempting to take the measure of the entire historical span of Judeo-Christian faith development. Taking the long view, and attempting to remotely analyze Christianity, I became increasingly fascinated — and fearful — of my findings. I found the historical, liturgical churches to be the most intriguing and I grew ever more uneasy about historically recent and diverse Western Christian spinoffs. When viewed from the perspective of two millennia, most American Protestant churches are mere blips on the time line of history and quite alien to the theological development of the ancient Christian faith. Troubling indeed.

To complicate matters, I began to encounter Catholics in Jerusalem who broadened my understanding of Catholic faith. I was spellbound yet skeptical. My old Baptist prejudices were more persistent than I cared to admit. In the middle of a deep conversation with Ed Durst, a new friend and himself a Catholic convert, he asked, "Dan, what are you protesting against?"

"What do you mean?" I said.

"You're a Protestant — that means you are protesting against something, namely the Catholic Church."

Ed was gentle with me. A linguist, theologian, and university professor, he knew I had not a clue as to the finer points of the Protestant Reformation and he could have overwhelmed me with historical facts and persuasive arguments. But his approach was loving. His motive was simple: to inspire deep, honest inquiry. He succeeded wonderfully. I studied in a mild panic to discern the issues at stake in Luther's rebellion and the subsequent schism that rent Christianity. A most startling realization for me was the fact that it was the Catholic Church, through its councils and canonical process, that authenticated and compiled the Scriptures. The Bible, that supreme authority for Protestants, is essentially a Judeo-Catholic document.

I found that the objects of typical Protestant challenges to Catholicism—the role of Mary (Protestants frequently state that Catholics *worship* Mary), the pope, the sacraments, and prayers to the saints, among others—were easily understood when studied from Catholic teachings instead of secondhand Protestant propaganda. I came to see that I was terribly uninformed about what the Catholic Church actually teaches, as, unfortunately, are a significant number of Catholics.

"But, Ed," I protested self-righteously, "what about all the Catholics who live seemingly godless, worldly lives?"

"God looks upon the heart, upon our faith," he said simply. "Who are we to judge? Besides," he countered enigmatically, "consider the Roman centurians of biblical times."

Of course I was puzzled and, taking the bait, begged for clarification.

"Well, there are documented cases of Roman occupiers who, in the face of a shattered and beaten Jewish society, nevertheless recognized that, indeed, these were the people of God. Salvation was of the Jews. In spite of a history of wicked, faithless kings, temple harlots, arrogant and manipulative priests, and competing religious views—in spite of all these formidable stumbling blocks—they endured circumcision and humiliation among their peers to convert. They recognized in the Law and Prophets that God was speaking through this people."

The message was quite clear. If the Jews continued to be the people of God before the advent of Christ in spite of their many human failings, the Roman Catholic Church could be the people of God today even though the sin and failure of its members may be quite apparent. It was back to the books and back on my knees. My protests were wearing thin and sounding weaker by the hour.

Slowly, but very surely, I was becoming convinced that the Catholic Church was indeed that Christian entity with authentic, apostolic credentials. The teaching authority of the Church, I discovered, interpreted the Scriptures in much the same way as Jewish written and oral traditions ratified each other. At last—an objective Church authority to teach and interpret a consistent, integrated, and enduring theology!

Unlike many Catholics I had previously met (some of whom I had convinced to leave their "dead church" for evangelical Protestant Christianity), the Catholic Christians I had come to know in Jerusalem were highly informed, patient, and loving. Most important, their lives bore the fruit of real Christian faith.

My pilgrimage was sidetracked temporarily when, in October of 1973, the Yom Kippur war burst upon us with a wild flurry of shelling, air raids, and desperate combat. Syrians and Israelis dueled in clear view of our kibbutz and death seemed a real possibility. I photographed the war and wrote for stateside periodicals, including the *Seattle Times*. This turn of events further enhanced my desire to resolve the ecclesial questions at hand, if for no other reason than a growing awareness of my own mortality.

After a brief visit to the States in November and December, I returned to the Holy Land to resume my studies in a kind of self-exile to the desert. The words of a wonderful Youth with a Mission Bible teacher in Switzerland rang repeatedly in my ears: "God is not the rewarder of casual inquirers but, rather, the rewarder of those who diligently seek."

I spent another eight months on a second kibbutz situated on the beautiful Mediterranean Sea. Increasingly, I came into contact with the indigenous Church of the Middle East, the ancient cradle of Christianity that had gifted the world with Christian faith. I became extremely interested in Arab culture, both Christian and Islamic. I also began attending Mass with Ed in Jerusalem, as an observer. Afterward, I would subject the poor man to an unending and merciless line of questioning: why genuflect? What about the candles and the incense? What do the priest's vestments represent? And those garish-looking statues? The holy water and the ritual crossing of oneself? Why is there always a dead Jesus on the cross? What about salvation, purgatory, and . . .

As I attempted to lay my Protestant prejudices aside, I came to see at first a vague image of the Church, emerging like a gradually developing photographic image, increasing in clarity and detail. When asked what attracted me most to Catholicism, I cannot say, for it wasn't *something*: it was *everything*. The art, the architecture, its antiquity, the beauty of the liturgy (which had come to make perfect sense to me), the social conscience of the Church, its prophetic role in our modern world, the lives of the saints, the mystery, the presence of Christ, the sheer universality—I was falling in love—and perfect love casts out fear, if not all apprehension.

When pressed to share a single thing that attracted me more than others, I will point to the sacrament of the Eucharist. In all the churches I had encountered in my life, Communion was a monthly (at most) appendage, hurriedly tacked on at the end of a service. Grape juice (never, God forbid, real wine) and crackers represented *symbolically* Christ's presence. In Catholicism, Communion was central, Christ's presence real—a sacrifice and a celebration. In the same way ancient Jewish sacrifices were real sacrifices that atoned for sin and looked toward Christ's sacrificial death as the unblemished lamb, the sacrifice of the Eucharist was a real sacrifice, looking back at, and celebrating, Christ's atoning death. In the same way humankind fell from grace through eating the forbidden fruit, we are redeemed through eating in the Eucharist. I longed to enter in.

My Protestant heritage, emphasizing literal scriptural interpretation, suddenly and unexplainably became symbolic and weak in the face of John 6, a most significant Eucharistic teaching of Christ: "I am the living bread that came down out of heaven; if anyone eats this bread he shall live forever . . . truly I say to you, unless you eat the flesh of the Son of Man and drink his blood, you have no life in yourselves. He who eats my flesh and drinks my blood has eternal life; and I will raise him up on the last day. For my flesh is true food and my blood is true drink. He who eats my flesh and drinks my blood abides in me, and I in him."

Now, how much more literal can a passage of Scripture be? Jesus forcefully states and restates his case with unambiguous, shattering clarity, yet Communion was dispatched as symbolic or parabolic in Protestant teaching. Not that this passage of Scripture was frequently the subject of discussion in Protestant churches. In fact, I cannot recall ever hearing a Protestant sermon preached on these particular verses.

I was hungry for Jesus; I was in a desert and he was the manna, the Bread of Life! I was beginning to find the pearl of great price—in the Catholic Church. As I continued to study, pray, and converse with friends, priests, and other faithful Catholics, my objections, while fewer in number, became more strenuous in nature. I was resisting—grasping for any excuse to slow my plunge into the waters of Catholic baptism. I searched for a fatal flaw. G. K. Chesterton pinned me to the wall, saying in his book *The Catholic Church and Conversion*, "For the convert's sake, it should also be remembered that one foolish word from inside does more harm than a hundred thousand foolish words from outside." Only the words of a Catholic could now keep me from Catholicism!

My search seemed to undergo three phases. At first, in learning more about Catholicism, I began out of fairness to defend it as a legitimate expression of Christian faith (I'm O.K., you're O.K.).

This quickly led, however, to further exploration and a process of discovery rather like, as Chesterton says, "discovering a new continent full of strange flowers and fantastic animals, which is at once wild and hospitable." Finally, the most terrible phase was that of trying not to be converted. I had come to hear the truth, as Chesterton points out, and truth is a magnet with the powers of attraction and repulsion. The moment I ceased pulling against it, I was drawn into it.

Like a drowning man whose desperate struggle gives way to exhausted acceptance of the inevitable, I yielded to, and embraced, the Catholic Church.

I remember the moment as if it were yesterday. In the summer of 1974, on a sunny Saturday afternoon, I bobbed in the clear blue waters of the Mediterranean with my mentor, Ed. Floating on my back and looking up at a cloudless sky, I choked forth the words, "Ed, I guess I'll have to become a Catholic." The search had ended. The weight of the world was lifted from my shoulders, and we laughed together uproariously.

I returned to the United States in August, fully intending to enter the Church—and preparing myself for the inevitable onslaught of disapproval that I was certain to encounter on the home front. But I was sidetracked once again when I met Cherry Boone, daughter of entertainer Pat Boone, in their Beverly Hills home. Mutual friends brought us together because of our similar interests in the Holy Land. She had been studying Hebrew and looking into Jewish history. There were many other mutual interests, including the arts and writing.

As our relationship deepened from friendship to the prospect of something more enduring, I shared my journey and was pleasantly surprised to find acceptance and strong areas of affirmation. Together we agreed that we would develop our relationship, look toward marriage, and delay our Catholic pilgrimage until circumstances seemed more conducive.

Nothing could have prepared us for the challenges that were to follow. Our mutual faith journey, at first delayed, seemed hopelessly derailed by events that would overtake us like a horrible nightmare in the form of a major and protracted health crisis.

But that's Cherry's story.

On Easter Sunday, 1981, we were received into full communion with the Catholic Church by Father Mike Schmitt at Saint Brendan's parish near Seattle. We were home at last.

17

CHERRY BOONE O'NEILL

The Family Reunion

Cherry Boone O'Neill, oldest daughter of entertainer Pat Boone, is the author of
Starving for Attention *(1982), the internationally best-selling book on her
recovery from anorexia nervosa and bulimia. She subsequently wrote* Dear Cherry: Questions and Answers on Eating Disorders *(1985). Cherry is the
mother of three children and has been twice nominated for a Grammy Award for her
songwriting.*

" " . . . and please bless Mommy and Daddy and Lindy and
Debby and Laury and Frosty. God bless all my friends.
God bless Lassie and . . . " A moment of silent anticipation interrupted the simple prayer pouring forth from my four-year-old heart.
With a furrowed brow and one ear cocked heavenward, I asked,
" . . . and could you please talk a little louder, God? I can't quite
hear you."

This childhood tale not only produces parental chuckles but
evokes nostalgic memories of innocent and uncomplicated faith — the
kind of faith we long for in later years when age, experience, and
worldly realities interfere with our lines of spiritual communication
with God. For as far back as I can remember, I always had some kind
of interaction with God. Likewise, I have always had an understanding, however primitive, that Jesus was God's Son and our Savior.
And as the preceding account clearly demonstrates, I have always
expected prayer to be a dialogue.

Christianity has, from my earliest recollections, been more than a
moral code or a specific spiritual path. It has been a *relationship*. As in
every long-term partnership, there must be growth and change, not
only because relationships are dynamic, but because we as individuals are transformed over a period of time. Without development,
there is stagnation. We seem to resist change, but it is essential to
growth — physically, emotionally, and spiritually.

Needless to say, I have certainly changed from the four-year-old pigtailed sprite I was when my prayers consisted of long lists of "God blesses." In many ways the changes have been for the better, yet at times I wonder if certain changes have pulled me from the simple faith I had as a child. Sometimes, frankly, I wish it was that easy again. But then, my faith as an adult would hardly be realistic in light of the world we live in and the person I have become. However, in order to understand just who I am now, I must review the road I have traveled thus far. The lessons learned, the mistakes made, the pain suffered, the joy experienced, the growth accomplished — all lead me to this moment.

As the oldest of Pat Boone's four daughters, I was thrust into a unique position from the very beginning. I have often referred to my situation as having been a preacher's kid and an entertainer's kid at the same time. Obviously, this had its own special challenges, but even before my father's career took off like a rocket (with all of us along as passengers unprepared for the rarefied atmosphere of celebrity life), there was an environment full of Christian values and influences. My parents took great care to instill in us a deep faith in the things of God and to establish a pattern of prayer, worship, Bible study, and church attendance. This carried us through the tempestuous times we confronted. There were seductive influences (which seem an integral part of the Hollywood life-style), financial crises, marital storms, moral and ethical compromises, and even spiritual doubt. But through it all, a mere thread of faith remained. In order to survive the challenges and turbulence of those hard times, my parents had to be willing to undergo a fairly dramatic transformation in the form of spiritual renewal and rededication. Without those changes — without this new spiritual development — our family might have fallen by the wayside as one more Hollywood divorce statistic.

I was raised in a particular Protestant denomination that had been that of my parents, my grandparents, and probably their parents as well. It was a very fundamental and narrow expression of faith. The Bible was our ultimate authority in all matters. Although I had certain questions, such as who could claim to interpret the Scriptures and how this authority of interpretation was passed down from generation to generation, I generally accepted the legalistic bearing the church had on our lives. I also wondered why we were never taught the history of Christianity from the time of the Apostles. It seemed there had been a great historical leap — we were simply to take our current denominational status on faith. I knew there had to be more to the story — a bigger picture of Jesus as seen through His people.

Early in 1968 my parents recognized their need for a spiritual renewal in their lives. Not only were they surprised to find that this renewal would take the form of charismatic gifts, but they were stunned to discover that this renewal would be condemned by our denomination. In spite of the amazing turnaround experienced in our lives for the better, we were publicly disfellowshiped from a church that refused to accept both the essence and the evidence of our renewed Christian lives.

Our faith became the single most important aspect of our existence as a family and as individuals. The fire of the Holy Spirit had entered our hearts in a new way and had become all-consuming. Our problems were manageable once again—some were even resolved in miraculous ways. I observed with fascination as my parents began to truly love one another again. I saw them change and grow before my eyes like flowers unfolding with the first rays of the sun following a stormy night. My own spirit was encouraged to see that even when life looks its blackest, there is always hope.

Our family's expulsion from our previous spiritual home was the end of one chapter but the beginning of another. We embarked on a journey—a pilgrimage of faith that would continue as we sought God. We became members of a small Four Square church in the San Fernando Valley, a dynamic charismatic assembly. It was the church where, seven years later, I would be married and it is the church my father still serves as an elder. The Church on the Way, as it is called, has grown into one of the largest in Southern California.

When I met Dan O'Neill in the late summer of 1974, his heart was set on its inevitable course toward Catholicism. As Dan and I shared our spiritual convictions with each other, we were amazed to find how similarly we had evolved, bringing us to comparable conclusions on issues that have been the source of denominational debate for Christians. Whereas Dan's journey had been greatly intellectual in nature, mine had been more emotional and intuitive. As a songwriter, my artistic sensibilities had enabled me to experience God through symbols, images, and analogies—like the parables of the Bible. As I discovered the wealth of the sacraments and the liturgy of Catholicism, my spirit eagerly embraced an expression of Christianity that spoke in the language of my heart, while simultaneously satisfying the needs of an expanding intellect. I had already begun to feel a bit awkward in my evangelical Protestant church setting—not that the Four Square church had ever failed me, it was simply that I could no longer fit comfortably with my new awareness. In retrospect, I have found that the first church our family attended and later the Four Square church have been extremely valuable experiences in my process of spiritual development. As I continued to grow, I felt an increasingly stronger urge to find my own place within the body of Christ—a place where I could freely express myself spiritually and worship God in a way consistent with the convictions of both heart and mind.

Although Dan was ahead of me on the road toward Rome, he never pressured me to accept things I had not worked through. His own strong faith and my questions were motivating enough. Our journey, however, was interrupted by illness. When Dan and I met, I shared with him my battle with anorexia nervosa, a severe eating disorder. As our relationship deepened, we determined that together we could conquer this disease.

We were married on October 4, 1975 (the feast day of Saint Francis of Assisi). In our first year of marriage I suffered a devastating relapse, which landed me in the hospital, an eighty-pound victim of self-starvation. In 1976 and 1977 we desperately struggled for my survival, and thanks to Dan's support and the help of Dr. Ray Vath, a Christian psychiatrist, I gradually pulled through to total recovery.

In 1977 we moved to Hawaii, where we lived for two years doing volunteer work in a Christian community. It was a refreshing time of recovering my health, sharing fellowship in an interdenominational Christian environment, and continuing our path toward Catholicism. We began attending Mass regularly in Kailua-Kona.

In the fall of 1979 we returned to the mainland to found Mercy Corps International, a humanitarian response to the Cambodian refugee crisis, which had captured the world's attention at that time. The organization literally began in my parents' Beverly Hills living room as Christian leaders gathered from around the country. It was November 19. Several nationally known television evangelists, numerous ministers, and a number of emergency relief experts gathered for a rice-and-water dinner to discuss the tragedy unfolding on the border of Thailand. We were successful in forging a nationwide Christian response to this disaster, a response that continues to this day in other parts of the world.

Although Dan was elated with the tremendous outpouring of support from well-known Protestant Christian leaders, he insisted that a Catholic Bishop be present, and at the urging of Doug Wead, a minister and well-known author, Bishop Bernard Law of Springfield–Cape Girardeau (now Cardinal Law, Archbishop of Boston) flew in to participate in the meeting.

At the end of the evening, as guests were leaving or doing interviews with network camera crews, I found Dan in a dark corner of the house in animated discussion with Bishop Law. I knew exactly what was happening.

"Well," said Bishop Law after listening to Dan's story of discovering the Catholic Church during his international travels, "what's holding you back? Why don't you take instruction?" Dan was elated, yet mortified—he explained that we both felt a significant amount of anxiety over how our families and friends would react to our conversion. "Come out to Springfield and spend a couple of days with me," Bishop Law responded. "We'll talk."

After Dan's two-day visit to the bishop's residence, I knew there could be no turning back. We were deeply moved that, in spite of a heavy schedule of many church responsibilities, Bishop Law had taken us under his wing and personally assisted us in dealing with the many questions and conditions that we would encounter as we moved closer to full communion with the Catholic Church. I was admittedly more hesitant than Dan, but I was determined to join him in the fall of 1980 as he attended catechumenate classes at Saint Brendan's parish near our home in Bothell, Washington.

The more I learned of Catholicism the more I was able to readily accept and adapt it to my own belief system. It was not so much a matter of discarding the old in favor of something new as it was a feeling of coming home. It felt right. It was where I knew I belonged. My Protestant upbringing had been like that of a child reared by a kind and loving stepmother, but upon entering the Catholic Church, I felt I had discovered my true mother—the Mother Church—at long last. I found a richness of history, tradition, and symbolism in the liturgy, along with the realities of the sacraments and apostolic authority that I had never before known. To deny myself access to this storehouse of treasures would have been to deny my own nature, my own mode of spiritual expression, my own growth process.

We entered the Church in the spring of 1981. Shortly thereafter I composed a song that, as a parable, relates my feelings of having united with the Catholic Church:

The Family Reunion

There once was a man—both gentle and wise,
A judge of the wicked—a hope to the poor.
The hearts that he touched saw that love danced in his eyes,
He offered them life if they'd knock at his door.

Out from among all the people who heard him
He chose up a woman to be his young bride.
As one man alone, with him would the word end
But with children to help, it would spread far and wide.

The man taught his children with love and with kindness,
The woman was wondrously mother and bride,
But still there were those who clung to their blindness
And so at their hands the great love-teacher died.

The woman was crushed at the death of her lover
But somehow down deep she believed him alive.
And so he appeared one night to say "Mother,
My life is in you; live on — you are mine!"

Then she sang: Come, celebrate family communion
                Your father is sharing his life with us all
                Come share in our family union
                The feast is prepared for those
                    heeding his call.

The family grew larger, in love with their living
The woman, she taught, and the children obeyed,
But many around them maintained their misgivings
They'd killed once already and she was afraid.

The power of their hatred could injure her children
And so she reacted as all mothers would,
She built up a wall to protect and secure them
But in hiding from wrong, she was blocking the good.

She drew up some rules and some strict regulations
That they were to follow as proof of their blood.
Her attractiveness withered in close correlation
To the rising of law and the falling of love,

The children remembered the words of their father
Some were confused and many rebelled
Saying, "Better to live in the home of another —
Our mother's forgotten the joy our love held."

They sang: Come let's start our own family union
            To the word of our father we'll ever be true.
            We will celebrate family communion
            We'll teach our children to love his words,
              too.

Some of the children began their own households
They had their own children and lives of their own.
Stories of father and his words were oft-told
But little was said of their mother and home.

The family expanded with each generation,
Tales of their history were twisted with time.
Self-preservation outweighed close relations
And stories emerged from absurd to sublime.

One of the children discovered the woman
Quietly lost in tradition of old.
Struck by mysterious beauty he saw then
He knew that beneath the old rituals lay gold.

He encouraged the woman to share her deep treasures,
That night in a dream her dear husband concurred:
"My love is for all who'll receive without measure —
My family is one! Share your heart — spread the word!"

They sang: Come, come to the family reunion
There'll be a great feast like the ones long
ago.
Come, come to the family reunion
For love we were born and His love we will
show
— In love we must grow . . .
— His life we will know . . .
— For life we must go . . .

In the same way I had observed my parents' pilgrimage, leading them from one denominational affiliation to another, I also had come to the point of transition. There were those who could not understand, or even tolerate, the changes my parents experienced. Likewise, there were some who expressed shock and anger in the choice Dan and I made. But the fact remains that our first priority is to love and serve God and to obey His leading. If we are unwilling to change or to accept change in others, we threaten the most natural and necessary function of life: growth. Life is change and if we belong to the Source of all life, we must follow wherever He leads.